DAY TRIPS®

FROM COLUMBUS

Help Us Keep This Guide Up to Date

Every effort has been made by the author and editors to make this guide as accurate and useful as possible. However, many things can change after a guide is published—establishments close, phone numbers change, facilities come under new management, and so on.

We would love to hear from you concerning your experiences with this guide and how you feel it could be improved and kept up to date. Although we may not be able to respond to all comments and suggestions, we'll take them to heart and we'll also make certain to share them with the author. Please send your comments and suggestions to the following address:

The Globe Pequot Press
Reader Response/Editorial Department
P.O. Box 480
Guilford, CT 06437

Or you may e-mail us at:

editorial@GlobePequot.com

Thanks for your input, and happy travels!

Day Trips® Series

GETAWAYS ABOUT TWO HOURS AWAY

DAY TRIPS®
FROM COLUMBUS

Second Edition

Sandra Gurvis

The Globe Pequot Press

GUILFORD, CONNECTICUT

The prices and rates listed in this guidebook were confirmed at press time. We recommend, however, that you call establishments before traveling to obtain current information.

To buy books in quantity for corporate use
or incentives, call **(800) 962–0973**
or e-mail **premiums@GlobePequot.com.**

Text design: M. A. Dubé

ISSN 1536-3589
ISBN 978-0-7627-2973-9

Manufactured in the United States of America
Second Edition/Third Printing

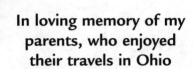

In loving memory of my
parents, who enjoyed
their travels in Ohio

Contents

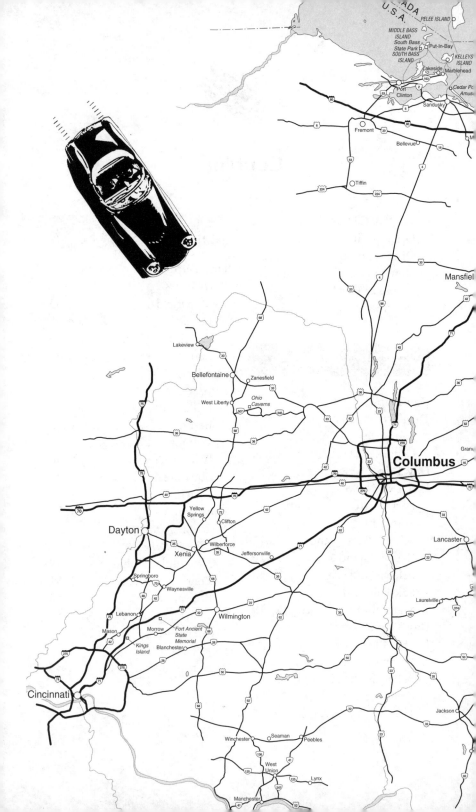

Introduction

I have lived in Ohio all my life, but I also have journeyed throughout the United States and overseas. Whenever I return, I am again reminded how much can be found within the borders of my home state. Not only are many cultures represented here, from Amish country to the Underground Railroad to the ethnic neighborhoods of Cleveland, but you can also experience a vast array of cuisines, learn about the manufacturing of baskets or glass, romp on the shores of Lake Erie, and encounter one of the largest concentrations of amusement parks in the Midwest. Museums and cultural entities abound, making science, rock and roll, dead presidents (not the green kind), and pioneer exploration fun and relevant for both children and adults.

Along with a rich history of elegant and quaint homes, farms, covered bridges, and unique communities, there are wonderful shopping and recreational opportunities. Clusters of outlet stores can be found in Ohio and in nearby Kentucky, while small towns such as Yellow Springs and Dresden offer an eclectic array of goods. Columbus, Cincinnati, and Cleveland have malls galore, from upscale to discount. You can go horseback riding, ranching, learn how to care for animals, and explore Native American heritage by visiting their ancient burial places and witnessing live reenactments of their lives and times. Ohio's state park system has a wonderful assortment of lodging as well as camping, fishing, hiking, boating, and other sports opportunities. And most things are reasonably priced, making tourism here a bargain compared to more heavily trodden areas.

Ohio is a state for all seasons. The clement spring and summer provide an abundance of outdoor options, while winter offers skiing and ice fishing. The fall foliage, particularly in spots such as the Hocking Hills, is magnificent. The color lasts several weeks, providing quite a window of time to visit during this moderate and generally sunny period.

But perhaps Ohio's greatest appeal can be found in the people. Most are pleasant and genuinely willing to help but mind their own business if that's what you want. They'll say, "How are you?" and mean it, without ulterior motive or desire to impress. So if you ever need anything, ask. You'll generally get more assistance than you originally bargained for. People who come from out of state are amazed at how quickly they feel comfortable and accepted.

In the middle of this "old shoe" is Columbus, which is about two hours away from the farthest points north, south, east, and west. Because of its central location, Columbus offers rich access to the state's many and varied pleasures. Therefore, most of the entries in this book are within Ohio's borders.

So if you like to relax, enjoy, and explore new and old cultures and pastimes, this is the place for you. You needn't spend a fortune on gasoline or deal with the hassle of flying on an airplane. Good food, nice people, lots of things to see and do inexpensively—what more could one ask?

Driving Tips

Ohio state troopers and local police are notorious for cracking down on speeders and reckless motorists. They also strictly enforce seat belt and drunk driving laws. So although drivers from other states might find it frustrating to be surrounded by seemingly pokey vehicles that go no more than 5 miles per hour over the posted limit, they may quickly learn the reason when they receive additional points on their licenses and hefty fines. The good news is that many of Ohio's major interstates and highways have a 65 miles per hour speed limit.

Law enforcement is also quick to help those in distress. If you're lost or having car trouble, call the State Highway Patrol at (877) 772-8765, and they'll dispatch someone to provide assistance.

Also be on the lookout for the dreaded orange barrels; those mean road construction and possible delays. It's especially wise to stay within posted speed restrictions, as fines may be more than doubled for offenders. Signs often designate alternate routes. Although these detours may require more actual driving, they save aggravation and, in some cases, travel time.

Ohio Quirks

This state has its idiosyncrasies. For instance, the term "deli" is very loosely interpreted here. In Ohio a deli is generally one cut above a fast-food eatery and serves mostly sandwiches, soups, and prepackaged salads. It's nothing like what you'd expect in New York, Los Angeles, and other big cities. One exception is Corky & Lenny's in Cleveland (see Northeast Day Trip 6); Columbus, Cincinnati, Dayton, and even Athens have their versions.

Ohioans have a sense of humor (some might say an inferiority complex) about their lack of mountains and ocean. If you hear someone refer to Mt. Parnassus, it's a very steep slope at Denison University in Granville. Mt. Campbell (actually Campbell Hill according to the map) near Bellefontaine, a mere 1,550 feet above sea level, is the highest elevation around. "Buckeye Ocean" is a pond-turned-lake, while "Surf Ohio" generally refers to waterskiing or other wet 'n' wild activities on Lake Erie or one of the artificial bodies of water.

How to Use This Guide

In the interest of accuracy and because they are subject to change, hours of operation, attraction prices, and credit card designations have been omitted. Most places take credit cards, although some may accept certain types and not others. If you have questions, contact the destination for specifics. Whenever possible, Web addresses have been included so you can obtain more information on the Internet.

Pricing key

Accommodations:
   $—inexpensive, less than $65 for a room
   $$—moderate, between $65 and $100
   $$$—expensive, $100 and up

Most rooms are for two people, but if you want to be certain of whether the pricing applies to a single or a double room, you will want to call the establishment. Many of the properties listed are bed-and-breakfasts. When making reservations, always check to see if accommodations include a private bath and what type of breakfast is included, particularly if you have food allergies. Also let proprietors know if you're bringing children or pets, and find out if they have animals themselves.

Restaurants:

$—inexpensive, $7.50 and less for entrees

$$—moderate, between $7.50 and $20.00

$$$—expensive, $20.00 and up

Highway designations

Interstates are prefaced by "I" (for example, I–270) and are generally multilane divided highways.

U.S. highways are two- and three-lane undivided roads and prefaced by "U.S." (for instance, U.S. 68).

State highways are paved and divided and prefaced by "SR" (for example, SR 256).

County roads can be paved or even gravel and are prefaced by "CR" (e.g., CR 10).

Where to Get More Information

This book attempts to cover all bases and interests, but those looking for additional material can contact the following agencies by phone, mail, or the Internet. Many of the areas have chain hotels and restaurants, which are generally not included in the listings in each chapter. Along with a roundup of festivals and celebrations, the back of the book provides the addresses and phone numbers of chambers of commerce and/or convention and visitor bureaus. Here are some additional resources:

General Information

Ohio Department of Development, Division of Travel and Tourism
77 South High Street
Columbus, OH 43216
(800) 282–5393
www.ohiotourism.com

Bed-and-Breakfasts

Ohio Bed and Breakfast Association
5310 East Main Street, Suite 104

Columbus, OH 43213
(614) 868–5567
www.ohiobba.com

Ohio State Parks

Division of Parks and Recreation
1952 Belcher Drive, C-3
Columbus, OH 43224
(614) 265–6561
www.ohiostateparks.org

Historic Sites

Ohio Historical Society
1982 Velma Avenue
Columbus, OH 43211
(614) 297–2300
www.ohiohistory.org

If you want to go around in circles, the Sandusky–Cedar Point area is the place, what with all the merry-go-rounds and roller coasters. Several of the few remaining hand-carved antique carousels in the United States can be found here, along with Top Thrill Dragster, which Cedar Point claims is the world's tallest and fastest roller coaster. The Point, as it's known, has plenty of other gut-wrenching scream machines in addition to lots of milder stuff.

SANDUSKY

Sandusky is about 110 miles from Columbus, a straight shot north from I–270 to U.S. 23 to SR 98, which turns into SR 4 about halfway at Bucyrus. With its small-town charm, late 1800s limestone architecture, and easy accessibility, Sandusky is a great place to get your feet wet in the vast and varied tourist attraction that is Lake Erie.

WHERE TO GO

The Merry-Go-Round Museum. West Washington and Jackson Streets, Sandusky, OH 44870. Talk about life imitating art: The museum is housed in a former post office shaped like a horseshoe (carousel horses, get it?). The city of Sandusky also issued four commemorative carousel stamps in 1988. There's a real working 1936 merry-go-round inside, a colorful medley of animals and chariots from various manufacturers and eras. You'll also find the tools, work-benches, and other implements of master artisan Gustav Dentzel, in addition to his partially chiseled steeds. Other acquisitions include works by well-known carousel crafters such as Daniel Muller, M. C. Illions, and Charles Loof; a primitive horse that was part of the first merry-go-round in the United States; and a stained-glass replica of one of the stamps. Hours vary according to season. Admission is charged. (419) 626–6111.

Underground Railroad Tour. Various sites, Sandusky. Those willing to take the time to follow this self-guided tour will reap great rewards in terms of learning about a little-known chapter of history. By visiting the places on the instructional brochure, you will get a sense of the extraordinary courage and inventiveness of "conductors"—black and white citizens and leaders—moving the "cargo" (escaped slaves) from one "station" (safe place) to the next. Sites of interest in Sandusky include Marsh Tavern, Sandusky Docks, Second Baptist Church, and Follett House (see below), along with several private "safe houses." Free. For a copy of the brochure, call (800) 255–3743.

Sandusky Area Maritime Museum. 125 Meigs Street, Sandusky, OH 44870. This nautical but nice collection boasts arti-facts, photos, and maps, providing a rich sense of the area's maritime history, including fishing and ice-harvesting activities. Displays include locally constructed vessels from different eras, and there's even a boat-building class. The gift shop offers books, prints, and clothing relating to the Sandusky area. Hours vary according to season. Admission may be charged. (419) 624–0274; www.sanduskymaritime.org.

Eleutheros Cooke House. 1415 Columbus Avenue, Sandusky, OH 44870. This Greek Revival jewel boasts an ornate collection of glassware, porcelain, and antique furnishings from several eras and an elaborate garden with a working greenhouse. Built in 1843–44, it was moved to its present location in the 1870s and reconstructed, then completely redecorated in the early 1950s. Open Tuesday through Sunday, April through December; other times by appoint-ment. Admission is charged. (800) 940–9478.

Follett House Museum. 404 Wayne Street, Sandusky, OH 44870. The archival research center for the Sandusky Library, this collection also has fascinating Civil War artifacts from a former confederate officers' and soldiers' prison on nearby Johnson's Island, in addition to Victorian housewares, toys, furnishings, and clothes. A standout is a Baltimore-style quilt made in the 1840s. A visit to the widow's walk on top provides a panoramic view. Open April through December; hours vary. Free. (419) 627–9608.

WHERE TO EAT

Cedar Downs. 1935 Cleveland Road, Sandusky, OH 44870. This establishment has the distinction of being the state's only offtrack-betting enterprise. Along with putting on the feedbag for Italian and American cuisine and local favorites, you can also play the ponies "live" by watching televised events at Churchill Downs, Gulf Stream, Santa Anita, Saratoga, and others. Horseplay never tasted so good. $$-$$$. (800) 654-3364.

DeMore's Fish Den. 302 West Perkins Avenue, Sandusky, OH 44870. Home of the giant perch sandwich and featuring Lake Erie pickerel (aka walleye) and perch by the pound, this spot reinforces the tenet that it's better to feast on fins than to be fish food. Casual dining on an outdoor patio also provides prime people-watching. $-$$. (419) 626-8861.

Cameo Pizza. 706 West Monroe Street, Sandusky, OH 44870. Since 1936, this family-owned eatery has been serving up pizza with "Mama's" secret sauce and dough made daily. Along with the obvious, they also serve wings, fried chicken and shrimp, salads, and sandwiches. A wide variety of sizes, crusts, and toppings are available. $-$$. (419) 626-0187; www.cameopizza.com.

Toft's Dairy. 3717 Venice Road, Sandusky, OH 44870. This family-owned operation has been in the area since 1900 and makes its own products. The ideal place for a cone or confection after a hard day of touring. $. (800) 521-4606; www.toftdairy.com.

WHERE TO STAY

Cottage Rose. 210 West Adams Street, Sandusky, OH 44870. There's a modicum of privacy in this second-floor accommodation, which features two bedrooms, a bath, and a study. It's a bargain, considering the prime location, and you can stay as little or as long as you'd like. The home is furnished with antiques, so parents with younger children might want to consider an alternative. $. (419) 625-1285.

Wagner's 1844 Inn. 230 East Washington Street, Sandusky, OH 44870. Listed on the National Register of Historic Places, this beautiful Italianate-style B&B is filled with antiques. Three spacious guest rooms have private baths, and you're close to Lake Erie and Sandusky attractions. $$. (419) 626–1726.

Big Oak. 2501 Campbell Street, Sandusky, OH 44870. Furnished with family heirlooms, this Victorian farmhouse was built in 1879 and boasts several small gardens. The hosts, James and Jeanne Ryan, have also provided plenty of games and books, along with insider tips for visiting the area. Only one of the four bedrooms has a private bath. Breakfast brings Dutch Babies, an egg puff served with strawberries. $–$$. (419) 627–0329; www.thebigoakbb.com.

CEDAR POINT

Cedar Point is a short hop from Sandusky. Simply follow the signs for Cedar Point Causeway. You can't miss it. Its claim to fame is the largest collection of rides (sixty-eight) and roller coasters (six) in the known universe. Oh, and there are the countless shrieking people.

WHERE TO GO

Cedar Point Amusement Park. One Cedar Point Drive, Sandusky, OH 44870. The second oldest in the United States, this park has garnered almost as many awards as it has roller coasters. Standouts in the latter include Top Thrill Dragster, a 420-foot-high über-coaster that shrieks along at 120 mph, Millennium Force (92 mph over 6,500 feet of track that goes up to 310 feet high), and Raptor (an adventure in being flipped upside down and back with the sensation of having nothing under you, thanks to chairlift-type seats), among others. Milder diversions consist of hand-carved antique carousels, a railroad, paddle wheel excursions, a sky lift, and bumper cars. Extended children's programs range from Camp Snoopy, with its close encounters of the Peanuts kind, to the Gemini/Kiddy Kingdom area, which has mini-versions of the most popular rides, including a much smaller adaptation of the 24-story stomach-dropper, the Power Tower. But before you let the family loose, take advantage of the Park's Kid Track program, which provides wristbands with parental cell phone numbers in case kids get separated. Open daily mid-May through the first weekend of September; weekends September through mid-October. Best times to visit are Tuesday through Thursday in May and June. Admission is charged. (419) 626–0830; www.cedarpoint.com.

Soak City Water Park. One Cedar Point Drive, Sandusky, OH 44870. Here you can get in touch with your inner tube. This eighteen-acre complex next to the Point has slides such as the mammoth Zoom Fume, a wave pool, rafting rivers, and three children's play areas. Breakers Bay, a 22,500-square-foot, 500,000-gallon drenching experience gives new meaning to being all wet and has two 60-foot-tall speed slides and a 76-foot raft shaft. Or you can go Main Stream with a calm tube ride or get jolted and jarred while traveling down Renegade River. Staffed by certified lifeguards, this City is safe. Along with a twenty-one-and-over Bubbles Swim-Up bar, the entire family can enjoy picnic shelters for land and food breaks. Open daily from the end of May through the first weekend of September. Admission is charged. (419) 627–2350; www.cedarpoint.com.

Challenge Park. One Cedar Point Drive, Sandusky, OH 44870. Those searching for a near-roadkill experience might want to try Rip Cord, a super-bungee that involves being tethered to an aircraft cable, hoisted up a 15-story launch tower, having the rip cord released, and speeding toward the ground at 65 mph, stopping a mere 6 feet from certain pulverization. Speed racers can choose from mild to wild alternatives at the Triple Challenge Racepark. A raft of video games, a food stand, a merchandise shop, and miniature golf make this a well-rounded offering. Open daily mid-May through the first weekend of September; weekends September through mid-October. Fee depends upon option chosen. (419) 627–2350; www.cedarpoint.com.

WHERE TO EAT

Listed here are some of the many restaurants located on or near the Cedar Point property. Unless otherwise designated, most are only open when the park is operating. Unless otherwise noted, call (419) 627–2350 for more information.

Silver Dollar. Those wanting to sit down and enjoy a relaxed meal near the main midway might want to opt for this eatery, which features rib eye, huge sandwiches, salads, and more. The wide-ranging children's menu includes chicken fingers, a pot roast sandwich, and hot dogs. $$.

Bay Harbor. A bit more upscale and also next to the waterfront, the Bay Harbor serves a wide variety of fresh seafood, fish specials, steaks, and chops. Although open year-round for dinner, it's closed for lunch. No swimsuits, cutoffs, or tank tops allowed. $$$. (419) 625–6373.

Breakwater Cafe. Adjacent to the Sandcastle Suites, this waterfront site serves up three squares ranging from pasta to steak, all with a terrific view of Lake Erie. Selections are available for kids, and there's a lounge for the adults that serves cocktails along with great sunsets. $$.

The Coffee Shop. This spot, located in the Hotel Breakers, is ideal for a quick meal or late-night snack. You can choose from breakfast, sandwiches, pizza, and more. $$.

WHERE TO STAY

Greentree Inn. 1935 Cleveland Road, Sandusky, OH 44870. This hotel is about as close to the Point as you can get without actually staying on the grounds. There's something for all in the family: an indoor heated pool, whirlpool, and fitness center, plus a bowling alley with arcade games and snack bar. Bonus: Glitter Glow bowling, a laser light and sound show in the evenings. It's also home to Cedar Downs restaurant and sports bar. $$–$$$. (800) 654–3364.

Great Bear Lodge. 4600 Milan Road, Sandusky, OH 44870. In case you get really stuck for something to do—not likely if kids are involved—this hotel/indoor water park combo offers 271 luxury suites, a 4-story atrium lobby, two restaurants, and planned kids' activities to give Mom and Dad a respite. For the youngsters (and perhaps not-so) there are seven slides, five pools, two hot tubs, a twelve-level tree fort, and about one-hundred arcade games. So it can be snowing outside—or worse—and everyone can have fun. $$$. (888) 779–2327; www.greatbearlodge.com.

Radisson Harbor Inn. 2001 Cleveland Road, Sandusky, OH 44870. Unlike the other Cedar Point hotels, this 237-room resort is open year-round. Each room has a private patio, and several have great views of the bay. Other conveniences include an indoor swimming pool, whirlpool/spa, fitness center, game room, and on-property eateries. $$–$$$. (800) 333-3333.

Cedar Point Resorts. The lodgings listed here operate seasonally. The mailing address is One Cedar Point Drive, Sandusky, OH 44870. Unless otherwise noted, the phone number for reservations is (419) 627-2106. Call ahead for special weekend packages that can provide discounts.

- **Hotel Breakers.** Those looking for the turn-of-the-twentieth-century leisurely ambience need search no further. The hotel, which is rapidly approaching its first one hundred years of operation, also has amenities such as an indoor pool, a beach, and several restaurants. With 650 rooms, it's the second largest hotel in Ohio. A variety of accommodations is available, from single rooms in the main hotel to large suites with Jacuzzis in the recently added Breakers East and Tower. $$$.

- **Breakers Express.** Geared for the budget-minded family, this new lodging offers high-quality furnishings, a game room, coin-operated washers and dryers, and an outdoor pool shaped like Snoopy. The 350 rooms are nicely furnished with queen-size beds. Pricewise, it's also the best deal on the Cedar Point property. $$–$$$. (419) 627-2109.

- **Sandcastle Suites Hotel.** It's water, water, everywhere, although you can get to the Point from this far-from-the-madding-crowd property by walking. There's plenty of beach, along with tennis courts, volleyball court, sundeck, and outdoor heated pool. Each suite has its own screened-in patio or balcony. $$$.

- **Lighthouse Point.** Those who prefer to bring their own—accommodations, that is—can set up an RV at the Camper Village. Each site has electricity, a charcoal grill, and a picnic table, along with a nearby convenience store for those last-minute supplies. Or you can stay at a cabin or lakeside cottage in a cozy New England setting. An outdoor pool, recreation area, arcade, and restaurant are set near a renovated lighthouse, the oldest structure at Cedar Point and built in 1862. Campsites $; cabins and cottages, call for rates.

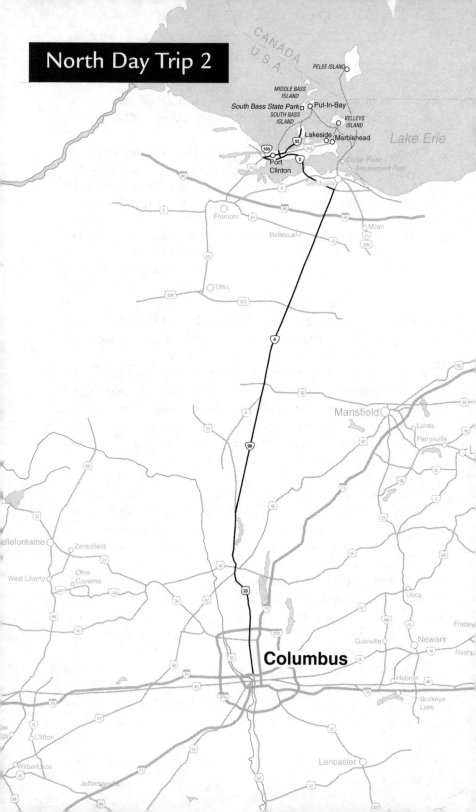

North Day Trip 2

NORTH

DAY TRIP 2

Port Clinton ·
South and Middle Bass Islands ·
Kelleys Island · Pelee Island ·
Lakeside and Marblehead

What's up, dock? Plenty, particularly if you like fishing and boating. The Lake Erie island area is a sporting paradise, even during the cold months, when ice fishing happens. Thanks to high nutrient levels and warm temperatures, its shores teem with walleye, smallmouth bass, yellow perch, freshwater drum, crappie, white bass, and more. Don't forget to purchase a fishing license (among other places, at the Ohio Division of Wildlife, 305 East Shoreline Drive, Sandusky), and be cognizant of the daily limits, which vary according to type of fish.

The area's also chock-full of bird brains: herons and egrets as well as migratory warblers to the tune of more than 300 species. Prime spots include Kelleys Island and South Bass Island. For information on "Wing Watches" and hotels accommodating birders, contact the Erie County Visitors Bureau at (800) 255-3743.

There are also enough restaurants, shopping, and historical sites to keep even the most seasoned traveler occupied. You can party at the bustling town of Put-in-Bay and on Kelleys Island, or have fun with the whole family at parks, monuments, and museums. Once you arrive, getting around the islands is made easy by a variety of bike and golf-cart rental companies, which are usually located within walking distance of the ferry.

GETTING THERE

First, however, you need to reach the island of your choice. Short of purchasing or renting a boat, ferries are the only option. Some depart directly from Sandusky, while others embark from Port Clinton (west) or Marblehead (east) just over the Bay Bridge, which splits off at Route 2. Most of the ferry services listed below operate seasonally and may not run as frequently during wintertime. Call ahead to check schedules, many of which are also available online. Ferries accepting autos and other vehicles are also noted. All charge a fee.

Island Rocket. 401 West Shoreline Drive, Sandusky, OH 44870. The fastest alternative without wheels, this ferry will propel you to Cedar Point, Kelleys Island, Put-in-Bay, and the more remote Pelee Island. (800) 854–8121; www.islandrocket.com.

Jet Express. 5 North Jefferson Street, Port Clinton, OH 43452. Hydrojet catamarans provide transportation to downtown Put-in-Bay. (800) 245–1538, www.jet-express.com.

Miller Boat Line. End of SR 53 north off SR 2 at Catawba. Mailing address: P.O. Box 239, Put-in-Bay, OH 43456. Auto/passenger trips to Put-in-Bay, South Bass Island, and Middle Bass Island. (800) 500–2421; www.millerferry.com.

Passenger and auto transportation to Kelleys Island every half hour can be found via the following:

Kelleys Island Ferry. 510 West Main Street, Marblehead, OH 43440. (888) 225–4325; www.kelleysislandferry.com.

PORT CLINTON

A key link in the Lake Erie chain, mainland-bound Port Clinton serves as a base for many excursions. The town has its own unique charm, however. The top of a restored lighthouse sits in the marina, and a picturesque stretch of sandy shore located along the main drag is a popular beach. The downtown area is also undergoing revitalization, so you might be able to get a cappuccino and bagel while waiting for the ferry.

To get to Port Clinton from Columbus, head north on U.S. 23 to SR 98, which turns into SR 4 at Bucyrus, then head west on SR 2.

WHERE TO GO

African Safari Wildlife Park. 267 Lightner Road, Port Clinton, OH 43452. Want to start your seafaring adventures on land? Here you can view giraffes, zebras, and other exotic animals from your car, ride on a camel, and even watch a pig race and other shows featuring critters. Open daily April through October. Admission is charged. (800) 521–2660; www.africansafariwildlifepark.com.

Shore-Nuf Charters. Drawbridge Marina, 247 Lakeshore Drive, Port Clinton, OH 43452. Flexible offerings allow for "walk-ins" (individuals who want to fish on a boat) as well as charter groups of twelve or more. Schedules vary, but most activities take place April through October. Fee is charged. (419) 734–9999; www.shore-nuf.com.

Fisherman's Wharf. 83 North Madison Street, Port Clinton, OH 43452. This family-owned and -operated business not only has a bait and tackle store for all the necessary supplies but also offers several different kinds of boats for larger groups and smaller expeditions. Call for schedules and times, which vary according to season. Fee is charged. (419) 734–0488; www.wecatchfish.com.

WHERE TO EAT

Mon Ami Restaurant and Historic Winery. 3845 East Wine Cellar Road, Port Clinton, OH 43452. Here you can truly "wine and dine." Built in the 1870s as a winery, it has expanded into two restaurants. Along with tastings, you can tour historic cellars and learn the secrets of making your own. Then chow down in the more casual Chalet or dine formally. Offerings range from Lake Erie catches to steak to pasta. $$$. (800) 777–4266; www.monami winery.com.

Anthony's. 102 Madison Street, Port Clinton, OH 43452. Anthony's serves up delicious Italian cuisine in a cheerful, relaxed atmosphere. Many of the locals eat here, a testament to long-term quality. Open April through October only. $$. (419) 734–5632; www.islandhouseinn.com.

Conrad's Porterhouse. 102 Madison Street, Port Clinton, OH 43452. Named after Sheriff Conrad Gernhart, builder of the Island House, this eatery offers up steaks, ribs, and chicken. Bargain hunters can chow down on the Monday prime rib special—8 ounces with a baked potato for around $5.00. And it wouldn't be "Erie" unless the menu had perch, walleye, shrimp, and other seafood and fish. $–$$. (419) 734–2166; www.islandhouseinn.com.

WHERE TO STAY

Island House Inn. 102 Madison Street, Port Clinton, OH 43452. Designed to be the most elegant "gentleman's hotel" in Lake Erie, this circa 1886 structure has been recently renovated and includes a variety of room choices, an afternoon English tea, murder mystery weekends, and even bikes for guests. Plus, there are two restaurants (Anthony's and Conrad's Porterhouse) and live entertainment. So you can have your cable and eat there, too. End of September through mid-May, $-$$; mid-May through mid-September, $$-$$$. (800) 233-7307; www.islandhouseinn.com.

SOUTH AND MIDDLE BASS ISLANDS

Put-in-Bay, on South Bass Island, started out as a sheep ranch in the 1850s. Along with several other of the Lake Erie Islands, it later became a center for grape growing and wine making. Before that it was the site of a key battle during the War of 1812, where U.S. troops were led by Commodore Oliver Hazard Perry. The area offers a variety of activities, but you can truly get away from it all at Middle Bass, particularly since the Lonz Winery, a popular drinking spot, shut down in 2000. On July 1 of that year, its last day of operation, a terrace collapsed, killing one person and seriously injuring about eighty others. It remains closed, although plans are to eventually convert it into a state park with hiking trails and camping.

WHERE TO GO

Perry's Victory and International Peace Memorial. Near the ferry ramps. Mailing address: P.O. Box 549, Put-in-Bay, OH 43456. If he who dies with the tallest monument wins, then Commodore Oliver Hazard Perry comes in third in the United States, thanks to his victory over the Brits in 1813. In order to get to the top of this 352-foot-high structure, you need to climb thirty-seven steps on a winding circular stairway to an elevator. But the view is worth the effort, especially on a clear day. A newly constructed visitor center offers interactive displays, memorabilia, a video theater, and live Web-cam shots of the monument, among other things. Open daily from mid-May to mid-October, other times by appointment. Admission is charged. (419) 285-2184.

Kimberly's Carousel. Downtown Put-in-Bay. A must for the young, no matter what age. With band organ music and a red-and-white-striped top, this Allen Herschell machine is one of the last operating carousels in the United States with all-wooden horses. It's also decorated with various scenes from around the area. Rides cost only $1.00, although that can be subject to inflation. Open seasonally.

Aquatic Resource Center. Located at Peach Point, off West Shore Boulevard. Mailing address: P.O. Box 38, Put-in-Bay, OH 43456. Operated by the Ohio Division of Wildlife, this attraction offers live fish exhibits, hands-on displays, children's activities, and (of course) free fishing on the dock. Open May through August; closed Monday. Free. (419) 287-5301 or 424-5000.

Stonehenge Estate. 808 Langram Road, Put-in-Bay, OH 43456. This restored farmhouse and winepress cottage is nestled on seven acres of landscaped grounds and furnished with antiques, photographs, and memorabilia. Visitors get a sense of wine growing during the 1800s, plus there's a cool gift shop with kaleidoscopes, bronze sculptures, porcelain signs, antique crafts, and more. Open daily during the summer. Admission is charged. (419) 285-2585; www.stonehenge-put-in-bay.com.

Lake Erie Island Historical Society. 441 Catawba Avenue, Put-in-Bay, OH 43456. Founded in 1985 by folks interested in preserving their heritage, this 6,000-square-foot center not only offers a wide variety of exhibits but provides several educational programs. Displays cover ice sailing and fishing, wineries and vineyards, ships, lighthouse lenses, ferryboat history, and more. Models, postcards, photographs, and original documents help bring the past to life. Hours vary; call ahead during the off-season. Free, but donations are welcome. (419) 285-2804; www.leihs.org.

Heineman's Winery. Box 300, Catawba Avenue, Put-in-Bay, OH 43456. Established in 1888, this business has been "all in the family" since then. Along with receiving a complimentary glass of the award-winning wines (or grape juice for the kids), you can also visit Crystal Cave, at 30 feet wide, arguably the world's largest geode. Made of bluish white celestite crystal, it was accidentally discovered a few years after the winery opened. Admission is charged. (419) 285-2811; www.ohiowine.com.

Perry's Cave. 979 Catawba Avenue, Put-in-Bay, OH 43456. This attraction has something for everyone. Discovered in 1813 by Commodore Perry, it's historically significant: His men drank from the underground lake to help cure their ills. Geologically, it's 52 feet below the surface and remains a steady 50 degrees, no matter what it's like outside. Walls, ceiling, and floor are heavily encrusted with calcium carbonate, the result of centuries of drippage, a sort of eternal Chinese water torture. After-hours lantern tours are also available, and as an added bonus, you can sift for real gems! Finds may include rose quartz, topaz, moonstone, ruby, and more. Open daily during the summer. Admission charged. (419) 285–2405; www.perryscave.com.

WHERE TO EAT

The Round House. P.O. Box 60, Put-in-Bay, OH 43456. The history of this restaurant, established in 1873, is as circuitous as its design. Some claim it was built in Toledo, while others insist it was constructed on the island. In the 1940s the circular bar was cut in half so the owner/piano player could play facing a full audience. The rollicking ambience is accentuated by red decor and murals painted by a late local artist known as Canoe Bob. $$. (419) 285–2323; www.theroundhousebar.com.

The Skyway. P.O. Box 717, Put-in-Bay, OH 43456. This restaurant caters to all preferences and budgets, from inexpensive lunches to elaborate clambakes. The martini menu includes variations such as saketinis and chocolate raspberry flavors for those who prefer liquid lunches or dinners. Dinner offers a full range of gourmet soups and appetizers, in addition to entrees. $–$$$. (419) 285–4331; www.put-in-bayskyway.com.

The Boathouse. Hartford Avenue. Put-in-Bay, OH 43456. With the same name and approximate location, this new structure offers outdoor seating, a view of the park and downtown, and a menu that is sandwich and local-catch intensive. Six original vessels are also hanging around at various points on the ceiling and above the bar, with the latter being a relatively rare "Iron Clad," which was used by the current owner's grandfather. $$. (419) 285–5665; www.theboat housebarandgrill.com.

J. F. Walleye's. 1810 Fox Road, Middle Bass, OH 43446. A recent fire gutted the original structure, and they rebuilt with a vengeance.

The snazzy-looking interior includes cathedral ceilings and light wood decor, as well as an extended menu covering salads, sandwiches, pizzas, wings, and all manner of bar food. Karaoke fans can breathe a sigh of relief: The owner plans on continuing that long-running tradition. $$. (419) 285-2739.

Hazard's Restaurant and Microbrewery. 1223 Fox Road, Middle Bass, OH 43446. When worlds collide, the result can be extremely eclectic. Along with bamboo walls, outside torches, and a tiki bar, this eatery has oak doors and wooden furnishings from Cleveland's old Municipal football stadium. $$. (800) 837-5211; www.sthazards.com.

WHERE TO STAY

Perry Holiday. 99 Concord Avenue, Put-in-Bay, OH 43456. With restaurants, tennis courts, public docks, a nine-hole golf course, and more, this fifty-two-unit hotel will round out any getaway. Plus you can walk to just about every attraction, restaurant, and shop on the island. $$–$$$. (419) 285-2107.

Park Hotel. P.O. Box 60, Put-in-Bay, OH 43456. The good news: The rooms in this restored Victorian hotel have been individually decorated and air-conditioned, and there's a large front porch where you can sit and watch all the activity downtown. The not-so-good news: There are separate men's and women's bathroom facilities on each floor, harking back to those college dorm days. $$–$$$. (419) 285-3581.

Islander Inn. 225 Erie Street, Put-in-Bay, OH 43456. This hotel caters to all ages and stages of life. Its H_2O diversions include a kids' pool with a slide, a swim-up bar, a waterfall, and a thirty-person Jacuzzi. Satellite TV and a lunch counter complete the offerings. $$–$$$. (877) 500-7829.

St. Hazards on the Beach. 1223 Fox Road, Middle Bass, OH 43446. Those searching for the Caribbean need look no further. With a fountain of dyed blue-green water, artificial palm trees, a pool, and a restaurant, this is about as close as you can get to Jimmy Buffettland without jumping aboard an island-hopper. Villas, cabins, and campsites are available; one-bedroom chateaus accommodate up to six people. You must furnish your own linens and towels; cabins lack a private bath. Villas, $$–$$$; chateaus, $$–$$$; cabins, $–$$; campsites, $. (800) 837-5211; www.sthazards.com.

KELLEYS ISLAND

Those really looking to turn down the volume might prefer Kelleys Island. Here, life is so leisurely you might have to pinch yourself to make sure you're still breathing. There are still things to see and do, however, particularly in the evening when the nightlife heats up. And although this island is bank impaired, ATMs are strategically located downtown.

WHERE TO GO

Glacial Grooves. North side of the island, off Division Street. Fans of erosion might enjoy this. One of the largest and most easily accessible geological phenomena of its type, this limestone bedrock was formed about 18,000 years ago by passing ice, resulting in a 400-foot-long, 35-foot-wide, and, in places, 10-foot-deep incision in the earth. The limestone contains marine fossils between 350 and 400 million years old. Open year-round, daylight hours. Free. (419) 797–4025.

Inscription Rock State Memorial. South shore of the island, by East Lakeshore Drive. Looking for more excitement? This flat-topped limestone rock has faint pictographs of men, birds, and animals. Archaeologists believe they were inscribed by Erie Indians between 400 and 800 years ago. Eroded by the elements, the rock is now protected by a roof and has a viewing platform. Open year-round, daylight hours. Free. (419) 797–4530.

WHERE TO SHOP

Anneliese's Treasure Chest. 212 Division Street, Kelleys Island, OH 43438. Here you can browse for gifts and memorabilia, including the popular Kelleys Island afghan, while listening to an old player piano. Selections include nautical items and the work of local artists. (419) 746–2821.

Kelleys Cove. 108 West Lakeshore, Kelleys Island, OH 43438. Specialties include Cat's Meow designs, Harbor Lights collectibles, and Ben Richmond art, along with depictions of Lake Erie in other media. Bonus: You can purchase fishing licenses and supplies here and rent a condo, if so inclined. (419) 746–2622.

Vi's Island Treasures. 125 Division Street, Kelleys Island, OH 43438. The newest, just-remodeled addition to the local gift array features everything from gold and sterling jewelry to sunglasses, with frogs by Kitty Critters, snowmen by Willaraye, American Chestnut figurines, clothing, nautical gifts, McCall's candles, and more. (419) 746–2268.

WHERE TO EAT

The Village Pump. 103 Lakeshore Drive, Kelleys Island, OH 43438. A favorite with both locals and "summer people," this watering hole offers hand-dipped onion rings, perch by the pound, and other specialties. Brandy Alexanders and mudslides made with ice cream are a favorite of the over-twenty-one set. $$. (419) 746–2281.

Bag the Moon. 109 Lakeshore Drive, Kelleys Island, OH 43438. Along with daily specials, popular offerings include ribs, steak, and perch. Thanks to live entertainment and sing-alongs, the whole family can party, although only those of legal age can partake of their signature strawberry shots. $$. (419) 746–2365.

Kelleys Island Wine Company. 418 Woodford Road, Kelleys Island, OH 43438. Spend a relaxing few hours sampling the fruits of European hybrid grapes. In addition to a nifty gift shop with gourmet and wine accessories, it also features a deli with cheese and sausage platters, sandwiches, pizza, and wraps. $–$$. (419) 746–2537

The Kelleys Island Brewery. 504 Lakeshore Drive, Kelleys Island, OH 43438. Located dockside, it's grub with a view, including hand-crafted beer; full breakfast, lunch, and dinner menus; and friendly people, not to mention great ice cream. $–$$. (419) 746–2314.

Winking Lizard Tavern. 101 Lakeshore Drive, Kelleys Island, OH 43438. Now part of a mostly Ohio-based chain of eateries, the Kelleys Island version is located in a historic building. But that hardly prevents the purveying of Lizardinis, Reptizers, soups, pizza, barbecue, chicken, fish, and more in a TV-laden, casual atmosphere. Open seasonally. $$. (419) 746–2112; www.winkinglizard.com.

WHERE TO STAY

Kelleys Island State Park. North side of the island, off Division Street. Along with a sandy beach and prime fishing and bird-watching, this park has about 150 campsites, although only a few provide electric hookups. Shower- and bathhouses are located throughout. It's first come, first served and fills up quickly during weekends and peak season. $. (419) 746–2468.

PELEE ISLAND

Those looking to wander farther north can cross over into Canadian waters to Pelee Island. This sedate 10,000-acre playground offers bicycling, water sports, hiking, and more fishing and bird-watching. Unlike the other Lake Erie Islands, "wild life" here usually involves four-legged activity rather than two. Bonus: Because it's in Canada, you can enjoy a lower exchange rate—for now.

WHERE TO GO

Pelee Island Winery. 20 East-West Road, Pelee Island, ON N0R 1M0. Open since 1979, this popular attraction not only bills itself as Canada's largest estate winery, but also hosts tours, tastings, and events, including barbecues, live bands, and (Canadian) holiday celebrations. The pavilion and vineyards are located on Pelee; the production facilities are in Canada. You can purchase their ever-expanding vintage online or on-site. Open May to mid-October. Admission charged for tours only. (800) 597–3533; www.peleeisland.com.

WHERE TO EAT AND WHERE TO STAY

Tin Goose Inn. 1060 East-West Road, Pelee Island, ON N0R 1M0. With eight individually decorated rooms, a restaurant, a cocktail hour, and full breakfast, this lodge is a stone's throw from the beach. Special packages available. $$–$$$. (519) 724–2223.

The Gathering Place. West Shore Road, Pelee Island, ON N0R 1M0. One of the Island's original limestone structures, this historic bed-and-breakfast provides a library, fireplace, and screened-in porch, as well as access to the beach. $$–$$$. (519) 724–2656.

It's Home. 1431 East Shore Road, Pelee Island, ON N0R 1M0. This relaxing bed-and-breakfast offers four bedrooms, a private sitting room, and full and continental breakfasts. You can chill out on the patio and watch the water, or participate in one of the island's many birding events. $-$$. (519) 724-2328.

The Pelee Island Hotel & Pub. 1085 West Shore Road, Pelee Island, ON N0R 1M0. One of the area's first boarding houses, it lodged politicians, bootleggers, fishermen, explorers, naturalists, and Canadian and American families. Today it has fourteen renovated rooms and three cottages, all with private baths. The restaurant serves perch, walleye, steaks, chicken, pasta, and chef specials. $$. (519) 724-9994; www.peleeislandhotel.com.

LAKESIDE AND MARBLEHEAD

Circle back to the Western tip of the U.S. mainland and you'll find Lakeside and Marblehead. Dubbed the "Walleye Capital of the World," Marblehead, which is encompassed by the area's Western Basin, harvests 80 percent of all that species caught in Lake Erie. You can also find, on the south side of Bayshore Road, a battle marker for the War of 1812. One of the few remaining Chautauquas—retreats for a Methodist-based adult education movement founded in the late 1800s—Lakeside continues to be a popular draw for individuals and families seeking spiritual and intellectual renewal. Along with plenty of waterfront activity, this small town boasts a symphony and theater.

WHERE TO GO

Marblehead Light House. Northernmost tip of Marblehead Peninsula. Mailing address: Lake Erie Islands State Park, 4049 East Moores Dock Road, Port Clinton, OH 43452. The oldest continuously operating lighthouse on Lake Erie, this 67-foot masonry and limestone landmark has been "beaconing" ships into Sandusky Bay since the early 1820s. Among its fifteen keepers were two women, including the widow of Benajah Wolcott, the original keeper. It's been restored several times and has been automated since 1958. Also surrounding the lighthouse are lakeside daisies, a tiny and rare protected species. Open Monday through Friday, June through September, and some Saturdays. Admission may be charged. (419) 797-4530.

Johnson's Island Confederate Officers Prison. Off the causeway, from the southern edge of Marblehead Peninsula. Now a cemetery for the 201 soldiers who died there, the prison housed 9,000 Confederate officers, soldiers, and civilians during the Civil War. It originally consisted of thirteen barracks and a hospital, artifacts from which are scattered around local museums and historical societies. Open year-round. Small fee charged to cross the causeway.

Teddy-Bare Charters. 8390 North Shore Boulevard, Marblehead, OH 43440. Go on a fishing expedition with coffee, doughnuts, box lunches, bait, and beer. The fleet, including 33-foot Sportcrafts, can take fifteen people, while a 27-foot sailer accommodates six standard-size sailors. Groups of up to sixty are welcome. Fee charged. (800) 837-5507; www.teddybare.com.

WHERE TO STAY

Hotel Lakeside and Fountain Inn. 236 Walnut Avenue, Lakeside, OH 43440. This property, on the National Register of Historic Places, offers a unique combination of the old and less-than-antiquated. Built during the Victorian era, the refurbished Hotel Lakeside has hosted two presidents, among other luminaries, and has many of the same furnishings used during that period. The newer Fountain Inn provides fifty-six rooms with private baths, carpeting, and air-conditioning. $$-$$$. (419) 798-4461.

Idlewyld Bed and Breakfast. 350 Walnut Avenue, Lakeside, OH 43440. This B&B has fifteen rooms, some with private baths. A large gathering/dining room is also available for workshops, meetings, or retreats. Includes a full English breakfast. $-$$. (419) 798-4198; www.idlewyldbb.com.

Keystone Guesthouse. 202 Maple Avenue, Lakeside, OH 43440. Although it was built in the late 1800s, this inn boasts full suites with kitchenettes and central air. It's also within walking distance to just about anywhere in town. $-$$. (419) 798-4263.

Rainbow House Guest Cottage & Tea by the Sea Tea Room. 115 West Second Street, Lakeside, OH 43440. The charmer offers a combination of themed guest rooms with names like Lilac, Sunflower, and Summer Breeze, and afternoon tea with assorted dainty sandwiches, fruit, sherbet, desserts, and (but of course) tea. $. (419) 798-4255; www.rainbowhouse.us.

This region's eclectic assortment highlights nineteenth-century pacesetters, railroad chronicles, a U.S. president, and glassmaking history mixed in with shopping and restaurants. Each town has a unique personality.

MILAN

Although it's mostly known as the birthplace of Thomas Alva Edison, this bright idea for a town was originally founded in 1816 as Merry's Mill, and by the middle of that century it was second only to Odessa, Russia, in wheat exportation. Milan also has the distinction of being a center of shipbuilding, a major hub for the formation of wagon trains heading west, and the home of Isaac Hoover, the area's most successful potato farmer. Hoover created and manufactured the Hoover Potato Digger (not to be confused with the vacuum cleaner of the same name, which was invented several miles east in North Canton).

This sparklingly maintained New England-inspired burg offers a nifty square with museums, antiques shops, and nearby parks for hikes and more. It's less than 100 miles north of Columbus: Take I-270 north to U.S. 23 to SR 98, which turns into SR 4 at Bucyrus, then head east on the Ohio Turnpike (I-80/90) until you get to U.S. 250, which bisects the town shortly after turning south off the Turnpike.

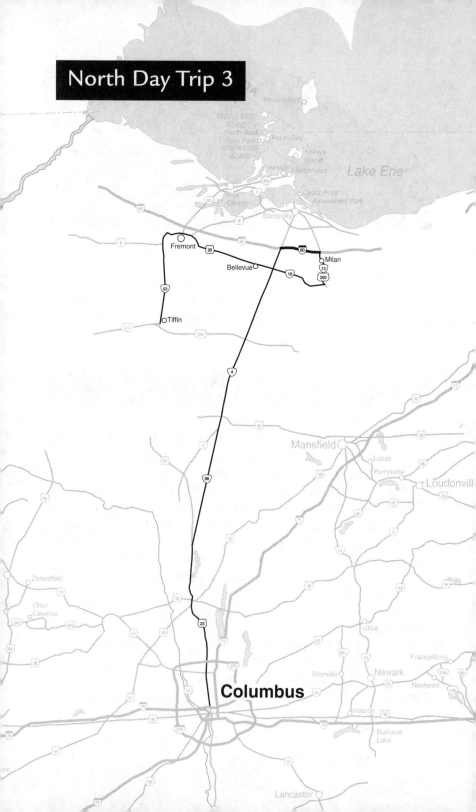

WHERE TO GO

Edison's Birthplace. 9 Edison Drive, Milan, OH 44846. February 11, 1847, was a date that changed Milan—and the world—forever. It was the day that Thomas Edison, originator of the phonograph, the light-bulb, and many more time- and labor-saving devices, was born. The museum contains rare examples of the man's early inventions, documents, and family photographs. Although the family sold the house in 1854 and moved away, Edison's sister purchased it several decades later, and Edison himself became the owner in 1906. Much of the family's furniture was lost in a fire, but it has been restored as closely as possible to its original appearance, thanks to the donations of friends and relatives. Open Tuesday through Sunday, April through October; by appointment only from November through March. Closed in January. Admission is charged. (419) 499-2135; www.tomedison.org.

Milan Historical Museum. 10 Edison Drive, Milan, OH 44846. Constructed about the same time as the Edison home, this complex consists of several buildings housing an impressive collection of glassware, dolls, and Civil War memorabilia. The fully furnished Sayles House boasts a weaving room, children's playroom, and cellar, and the Edna Roe Newton Memorial Building contains an accumulation of goodies from one world-traveling Milan family. You will also find a blacksmith shop, a carriage shed, and a fully stocked circa 1850 general store. Open Tuesday through Sunday, April through October, with special events on holidays. Small donation requested. (419) 499-2968; www.milanhistory.org.

WHERE TO SHOP

Sights and Sounds of Edison. 21 South Main Street, Milan, OH 44846. It's horns aplenty at this antiques store that focuses on old phonographs. Those with an ear for Victors, Panel Horns, and Edison Music Masters will find a veritable cornucopia of styles. (419) 499-3093.

Gingersnap Junction. One Main Street on the Square, P.O. Box 509, Milan, OH 44846. Among other things, they also peddle teddy bears, collectible and antique dolls, seasonal items, and furniture and reproductions. (419) 499-9411; www.gingersnapjunction.net.

WHERE TO EAT

Pollyanna's Tea Room. One Main Street on the Square, P.O. Box 509, Milan, OH 44846. With a name like that, it *has* to be cheerful. The menu alone should incite a smile: Along with made-from-scratch soups, chicken salad, and a specialty sandwich or salad, you can choose from such exotic blends as caramel tea, chai spice, and blue lady (grapefruit with marigold and mallow flowers). $. (419) 499–9411; www.gingersnapjunction.net.

WHERE TO STAY

Gastier Farm Bed & Breakfast. 1902 Strecker Road, Milan, OH 44846. Located on a working farm, this is a century-old lodging in wide-open spaces. Decorated in "homey country," the three rooms have a shared bath. $. (419) 499–2985.

Coupling Reserve. U.S. 250 north of Milan. Turn right on SR 13 (Mudbrook Road); park is on the right immediately after the Turnpike. Mailing address: Erie Metroparks, 3910 East Perkins, Huron, OH 44839. This is one sleeping experience you're not likely to forget. Stay in a gen-u-ine heated railroad car in a twenty-acre pastoral setting. You can also go canoeing, hiking, and sledding during the winter. Except for the occasional mouse or other small critter, you won't be bothered by noisy neighbors. $. (419) 625–7783.

BELLEVUE

Hop back on U.S. 250 south to U.S. 20 west and you'll run into Bellevue in about a half hour. Along with a railroad past and present, which includes modern-day railroad yards that still contribute to its economy, this town is home to a diverse assortment of attractions.

WHERE TO GO

Seneca Caverns. 15248 Township Road, Bellevue, OH 44811. Also known as "The Earth Crack," this unusual natural wonder, which was formed whole rather than from erosion, was discovered in 1872 and has seven different levels. At the bottom, 110 feet below the surface, you'll find Ole Mist'ry River, a crystal-clear stream that is part of a vast underground system. Bring a light jacket—it's 54 degrees year-round—and expect to do lots of walking. Open daily Memorial Day through Labor Day, weekends in May and September through mid-October. Admission is charged. (419) 483-6711; www.senecacavernsohio.com.

Sorrowful Mother Shrine. 4106 SR 269, Bellevue, OH 44811. Established in 1850 as a place to honor the Virgin Mary, these peaceful 120 acres have been visited by countless believers as well as others seeking peace. Paved walkways winding amid trees lead to the various Stations of the Cross and replicas of Lourdes and Sepulcher grottoes. There's Mass twice a day, as well as a cafeteria and religious gift shop. Open daily; closed Christmas through New Year's and on other major holidays. Donations welcome. (419) 483-3435.

Bellevue Heritage Museum. 200 West Main Street, Bellevue, OH 44811. With continually changing displays, this attraction offers something different with each visit. Focusing on items, photos, and other memorabilia relating to the town, it gives you a sense of what the community, past and present, is like. Open Sunday, Memorial Day through Labor Day; call for other times. Free. (419) 483-7376.

Mad River & NKP Railroad Society Museum. 233 York Street, Bellevue, OH 44811. Get on board for this growing accumulation, one of the state's largest collections of railroad memorabilia. Explore the many vintage cars, including the Wabash F-7 diesel engine, a PRR mail car, and the first domed model built in the United States, among others. Stationary artifacts include a watchman's tower, a depot, and a section house, which doubles as a gift shop. Uniforms, lanterns, and locks are also on display. Open daily from Memorial Day to Labor Day, and on weekends in May, September, and October. Admission is charged. (419) 483-2222; www.onebellevue.com/madriver.

Lyme Village. 5001 SR 4, Bellevue, OH 44811. This cluster of buildings spans one hundred years, beginning in 1830, although most focus on life in the nineteenth century. Some have been restored, while others contain displays. Highlights include a Victorian mansion built by John Wright, a one-room schoolhouse, a log church and homes, a post office, hardware store, and more. Open daily except Monday from June through August, Sunday only in May and September. Call for other times. Admission is charged. (419) 483–4949; www.lymevillage.com.

WHERE TO SHOP

Maplewood Gallery. 1021 U.S. 20, Clyde, OH 43410. A few miles west of Bellevue, this 14,000-square-foot facility peddles the works of local woodcrafters, painters, sewers, and other artisans. Antiques, glass, collectibles, fine art, and other treasures can also be found. Spacious aisles and uncrowded displays add to the shopping experience. (419) 547–9175.

Cherry Blossom Antique Mall. 801 West Main Street, Bellevue, OH 44811. Plan plenty of time to browse through a wide selection of antiques, primitives, glassware, and old-time wares. (419) 484–7035.

Junction Antique Mall. 127 East Main Street, Bellevue, OH 44811. Forty-five dealers display everything from soup tureens to nut dishes in more than 10,000 square feet. It's open every day, allowing for unlimited exploration. (419) 483–8227.

Lavender Meadows. 121 East Main Street, Bellevue, OH 44811. This crafts store in the historic downtown offers candles, artwork, and more. (419) 483–7737.

WHERE TO STAY

Best Western Bellevue Inn. 1120 East Main Street, Bellevue, OH 44811. This recently renovated property contains indoor and outdoor pools, whirlpool and sauna, game area, and some in-room Jacuzzis. Dinner and complimentary coffee for breakfast are also available. $$–$$$. (800) 528–1234.

FREMONT

A few miles west on U.S. 20 is Fremont, home of the nation's first presidential library. There's also lots of good eating to be found here, judging by the large number of restaurants. Routes 53 and 6 also pass through, and it's a favorite stop off the Turnpike (exit 91).

The quaint downtown, with its shops, galleries, and eateries, is good for a few hours' worth of wandering. The area is well-known for its half baker's dozen of seasonal farm markets, most notably Eshleman Fruit Farm, 1 mile northeast of U.S. 20 in Clyde on SR 101 (753 East Maple Street, 419-547-9584; www.eshlemanfruitfarm.com). June through October—when it's open—reap fresh-grown sweet cherries, blueberries, peaches, and apples, along with an activity barn, goat corral, candy scramble, putt-putt golf, wagon rides, and more. Other farm markets include Rimelspach Produce Company & Farm Market (SRs 12 and 53, 419-334-4100) and Red Barn Country Market (4148 North SR 53, 419-334-4323).

WHERE TO GO

Hayes Presidential Center. Spiegel Grove, corner of Hayes and Buckland Avenues, Fremont, OH 43420. OK, so maybe Rutherford B. Hayes hardly seems like Mr. Excitement, but the center devoted to him has lots going on. The holiday season alone could fill a calendar: Along with sleigh and carriage rides through Spiegel Grove and other happenings, there's a layout with four operating model trains weaving among late 1800s wintertime scenes. Other special events are scheduled throughout the year as well. Even without an occasion, this library, opened in 1916, offers much to see and do. The thirty-three-room mansion has the original furnishings belonging to the president and his family, while the museum consists of more than 10,000 objects and items on loan. With more than a million manuscripts, the library also has all of R. B.'s diaries and letters, in addition to family trees. You can hike on the wooded estate and visit the tombs of Hayes and his wife, Lucy, as well as stopping by carriage and guest houses, the latter being decorated in ornate Victorian style. Open daily year-round, except holidays. Admission is charged. (800) 998-7737; www.rbhayes.org.

    Fremont Speedway. 19101 Orchard Drive, Elmore, OH 43416. Those who enjoy going in circles might appreciate races at the "Track That Action Built." 410 and 305 winged sprint cars and trucks go wheel-to-wheel (as opposed to neck-and-neck) around the one-third mile of semi-banked clay oval track. Open since 1951, it has seen speed racers such as Steve Kinser, Sammy Swindell, Brad Doty, Doug Wolfgang, and current NASCAR stars Jeff Gordon and Dave Blaney. It recently became one of the first dirt track facilities in the United States to install softwalls, ensuring the drivers' safety and reducing damage to cars. Gates open at 4:30 P.M. on Saturday, April through September. Admission is charged. (419) 333-0478; www.fremontohspeedway.com.

WHERE TO EAT

Here is a sampler of Fremont's many restaurants, several of which are family owned and have been around for decades:

818 Club Restaurant. 818 Crogan Avenue, Fremont, OH 43420. This casual eatery has been serving up American cuisine for more than eighty years. Specializes in lunches and dinners. $-$$. (419) 334-9122.

Grate's Silver Top. 3939 North SR 53, Fremont, OH 43420. Looking for a drink or a quick meal? A full-range bar-food menu (wings, nachos, sandwiches) and drinks make this a solid watering/feeding stop. $. (419) 334-9250.

Kelly's Fine Food & Spirits. 3680 North OH 53, Fremont, OH 43420. Fremont's answer to fine dining comes replete with steaks, chops, chicken, and all manner of seafood (crab, salmon, Lake Erie perch, and more) with sautés, sauces, or just plained broiled. The wide-ranging menu should satisfy most appetites. $$-$$$. (419) 334-8144.

Mike & Ninfa's Bar and Grill. 1789 East State Street, Fremont, OH 43420. This family-centered food stop features multiple TVs and is especially popular during sports events. $$. (419) 355-1668.

Whitey's Diner. 216 East State Street, Fremont, OH 43420. Famous for hearty breakfasts, this reasonably priced eatery serves up large portions, no matter what the meal. $-$$. (419) 334-9183.

Chud's Grill. 1103 Napoleon Road, Fremont, OH 43420. Lunch features soups, salads, and sandwiches, while steak, chicken, and fish are what's for dinner. $$. (419) 332-9565.

WHERE TO STAY

Blessings Bed & Breakfast. 903 Birchard Avenue, Fremont, OH 43420. Along with lodging, this century-old home built in Romanesque style offers a parlor, drawing room, and dining room for conversation and relaxation. No smoking, children, or pets. $$. (419) 333-7829.

Bartlett's Old Orchard Motel. 2438 West State Street, Fremont, OH 43420. Built in 1949, this old-school–style motor inn has twenty-one rooms, about half of which have double beds. But the price is right and the staff is friendly. $. (419) 332-4307.

TIFFIN

About 20 miles south on SR 53 is Tiffin, a glassmaking center from 1888 until 1980. You can view its "sparkling" history in museums, factories, and various other exhibits, and purchase a piece for yourself in one of many shops.

WHERE TO GO

Crystal Traditions of Tiffin. 145 Madison Street, Tiffin, OH 44883. Watch glassblowing artisans at work, demonstrating sand carving, acid polishing, and other aspects of this delicate craft. The showroom offers crystal giftware as well as bargains on seconds, discontinued items, and closeouts. Open Monday through Saturday. Free. (888) 298-7236; www.crystaltraditions.com.

Tiffin Glass Museum. 25-27 South Washington Street, Tiffin, OH 44883. A full display of all original Tiffin Glass, this collection focuses on popular lines, stemware, lamps, optics, and colors. More than 2,000 pieces, arranged in oak cabinets, trace the factory's evolution and its many owners. Open year-round, Tuesday through Saturday; other times by appointment. Donations welcome. (419) 448-0200; www.tiffinglass.org.

Seneca County Museum. 28 Clay Street, Tiffin, OH 44883. Dating from 1853, this Greek Revival house museum is filled with displays relating to the history of the county. Highlights include a carriage house with antique fire equipment and horse-drawn wagons as well as (of course) Tiffin Glass. Open Tuesday, Wednesday, and Sunday afternoons; other times by appointment. Admission may be charged. (419) 447-5955.

St. Paul's United Methodist Church. 46 Madison Street, Tiffin, OH 44883. Built in 1874, this structure has the distinction of being the first public building in the world to be wired for electricity.

Bonus: Thomas Edison gifted the brass chandelier. Call for appointment. Donations are welcome. (419) 447–1743.

Ritz Theatre. 30 South Washington Street, Tiffin, OH 44883. This historic 1928 vaudeville and movie palace has been completely refurbished and now attracts top acts as well as local productions. Standouts include 30-foot hand-painted murals and a 1,200-pound Czechoslovakian chandelier. Open Monday through Friday. Free. (419) 448–8544; www.ritztheatre.org.

WHERE TO SHOP

Deerfield Station. 60 Clay Street, Tiffin, OH 44883. Gift and home decor items ranging from candles to collectibles are elegantly and spaciously arrayed in a 6,000-square-foot Queen Anne Victorian home. (419) 448–0342.

Jeffrey Jewelry. 2449 West Market Street, Wolf Creek Shopping Complex, Tiffin, OH 44883. Here you'll find diamonds, gemstones, watches, gold, and more. Extensive offerings include Lladro, Hummel, Swarovski, and Lenox. (419) 447–4515.

Something Special. 2800 South SR 100, Tiffin, OH 44883. With lots of Ohio-made crafts and Amish artwork, this store is a country-lover's delight. There's a year-round Christmas room and a large selection of collectibles, candles, florals, and pictures. (419) 448–8560.

WHERE TO EAT

Pioneer Mill of Tiffin. 255 Riverside Drive, Tiffin, OH 44883. Located along the banks of the Sandusky River, this former gristmill, built in 1822, serves a variety of foods in a casual atmosphere. Whether you're waiting for the specialty, prime rib, or other orders, you can check out the waterwheel, which still supplies electricity to the complex. $$. (419) 448–0100.

WHERE TO STAY

Fort Ball Bed and Breakfast. 25 Adams Street, Tiffin, OH 44883. Built in 1894, all parts of this Queen Anne Revival house are open for guests' use. Some rooms have private baths; others are shared. $$. (888) 447–0776.

Mad River Railroad Bed and Breakfast. 107 West Perry Street, Tiffin, OH 44883. Decorated with antiques and period furnishings, this Victorian home is located next to a walking/bike path, formerly the site of the area's first railroad. Most rooms have private bath and TV. $$. (419) 447-2222.

Zelkova Country Manor. 2348 South CR 19, Tiffin, OH 44883. This classic Georgian Revival structure is nestled amid lush hills, sprawling lawns, and country gardens. Each room is uniquely furnished, and much of the food served is grown on site. The eight guest suites have all electronic accoutrements (telephone, TV, stereo), private baths, and luxurious bedding. $$-$$$. (419) 447-4043; www.zelkovacountrymanor.com.

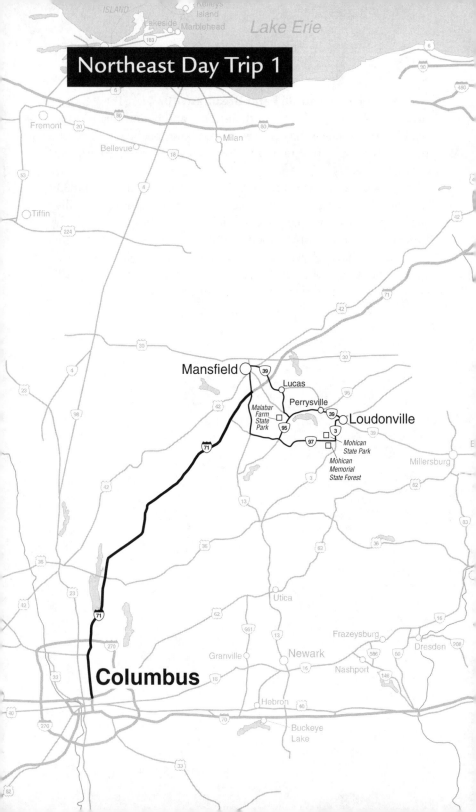

Northeast Day Trip 1

NORTHEAST DAY TRIP 1

Mansfield · Lucas ·
Perrysville · Loudonville

Two of Ohio's most charming and diverse state parks are located within a few miles of each other. Malabar Farm State Park is the world-famous home of author and celebrity-monger Louis Bromfield and offers a variety of programs and entertainment. Mohican State Park is a popular year-round recreational and outdoor mecca.

MANSFIELD

Mansfield itself has several natural—and not so natural—attractions. Carousel buffs can tour a manufacturing facility (Carousel Magic, 44 West Fourth Street; 888-213-2829), ride the first new hand-carved wooden merry-go-round built since the early 1930s (Richland Park, 75 North Main Street; 419-522-4223), and do related shopping. From Columbus, take I-71 north to exit 169, SR 13, and turn left toward Mansfield, about 70 miles total.

WHERE TO GO

Oak Hill Cottage. 310 Springmill Street, Mansfield, OH 44902. Built in 1847, Oak Hill remains one of the most outstanding examples of Gothic homes in the United States. It has seven gables and five chimneys, and Louis Bromfield played there as a child. It was the inspiration for Shane's Castle in the Bromfield novel *The Green Bay Tree*. Open April through December; other times by appointment. Admission is charged. (419) 524-1765.

Living Bible Museum. 500 Tingley Avenue, Mansfield, OH 44905. Although this attraction claims to be nondenominational, you should at least believe in *something* when you come through the door. Life-size dioramas chronicle Creation to Judgment, with special effects and audio commentary. There's a wax museum depicting miracles of the Old Testament and a collection of rare bibles, wood-carvings, American folk art, and a Christian art gallery. Open daily, April through December; weekends only the rest of the year. Admission is charged. (800) 222-0139; www.livingbiblemuseum.org.

Ohio Bird Sanctuary. 3773 Orweiler Road, Mansfield, OH 44903. This wildlife rehabilitation facility focuses on species native to Ohio. You can view our feathered friends at a birds-of-prey exhibit or hear their songs in an aviary. Hikes through marsh and old-growth forests also offer opportunities to glimpse them au naturel. Open Wednesday, Saturday, and Sunday; restricted winter hours. Admission is charged. (419) 884-4295; www.ohiobirdsanctuary.org.

Ohio State Reformatory. 100 Reformatory Road, Mansfield, OH 44906. A different kind of cage, built in 1886 for those other bird-brains, juvenile offenders. Despite the castlelike appearance, the original cell blocks and administration offices convey a grimy grim-ness. It was also the location of four major movies and is in the process of being converted to a museum with tours, a library, and special events. One tour Tuesday through Friday and two tours Sunday, mid-May through October. Admission is charged. (419) 522-2644; www.mrps.org.

WHERE TO SHOP

A Gift Horse. 101 North Main Street, Mansfield, OH 44902. Feel free to look these carousel-themed souvenirs, jewelry, books, collectibles, art, toys, shirts, and more in the mouth. (419) 524-2510.

Nooks & Crannies. 115 North Main Street, Mansfield, OH 44902. Take a break from the carousels: Along with country and French country, primitive, and Victorian items and knickknacks, they also host tea parties for children. (419) 524-3752; www.trezbaerco.com.

Carrousel Antiques. 118 North Main Street, Mansfield, OH 44902. Housed in a restored Victorian building, more than forty antiques dealers offer a wide selection of merry-go-round collectibles and more from various periods (419) 522-0230.

LUCAS

Two of Ohio's most charming and diverse state parks are located within a few miles of each other. From SR 13, in Mansfield, drive 2 miles east on Hanley Road, then turn right at Little Washington Road. Bear left at the fork onto Pleasant Valley Road. Go about 6 miles, then turn right at the entrance to Malabar Farm State Park, which is the main attraction in Lucas.

WHERE TO GO

The Big House, Malabar Farm. 4050 Bromfield Road, Lucas, OH 44843. Although the original structure is more than 150 years old, it was remodeled extensively in 1939, when best-selling author Louis Bromfield and his family moved back to his native Richland County from France. He brought the world with him in the form of famous personalities who visited him frequently, most notably Humphrey Bogart and Lauren Bacall, who married there in 1945. If going down the famous staircase to the tune of the "Wedding March" on the player piano doesn't snag your imagination, then the original furnishings, which have been unchanged since Bromfield's time, probably will. Some pieces are antiques from the 1700s. Open daily during summer hours; weekends during fall and winter. Call for appointment other times. Admission is charged. (419) 892–2784; www.malabarfarm.org.

Malabar Farm Market. 3650 Pleasant Valley Road, Lucas, OH 44843. In addition to being an internationally acclaimed man of letters, Bromfield was quite the agriculturalist. His ideas about conserving soil and sustainable farming are still in use today and are at work on the 914-acre estate, which includes the Bromfield Resource Center, an agricultural library with more than 2,500 documents. Highlights include a smokehouse, dairy barn, and petting farm. An organic produce business sells its products from May to October. You can also go fishing, hiking, ice-skating, cross-country skiing, and horseback riding (you supply the horses); wagon tours are available from time to time. Open weekends in January and February; daily except Monday the rest of the year. Depending on options chosen, admission may be charged. (419) 938–5000.

Fowler Woods State Nature Preserve. On Olivesburg-Fitchville Road. From Malabar take SR 13 north to Noble Road. Go east on Noble Road, then south one-quarter mile on Olivesburg-Fitchville Road in Lucas. Mailing address: Ohio Department of Natural Resources, 1435 Township Road, 38W, Tiffin, OH 44883. This 133-acre woodland is a mixture of old-growth woods, swamp forest, and, in the spring, abundant wildflowers. It's also a naturalist's paradise, with frogs, nesting birds, and breeding amphibians. Best times to visit are during spring, winter, and fall; mosquitoes are prevalent during summer. Open daylight only. Free. (419) 981-6319.

WHERE TO EAT

Malabar Inn Restaurant. 3645 Pleasant Valley Road, Lucas, OH 44843. There are plenty of good eats here, in the form of "farmhand dinners" (meat loaf, pot roast, potpie) as well as healthier fare (salads, vegetable lasagna, vegetarian plate). Call for winter hours. $$. (419) 938-5205.

WHERE TO STAY

Hostelling International, Malabar Farm. 3954 Bromfield Road, Lucas, OH 44843. Those looking for lodging on the Malabar Farm grounds will find "such a deal" here for less than $20 a night. Not only can you participate in the various programs but some private rooms are also available. Closed December and January. $. (800) 909-4776.

Angel Woods Hideaway. 1983 Pleasant Valley Road, Lucas, OH 44843. Visitors have a selection of several "theme" chambers, some with shared baths. Other amenities include common room with fireplace, game room, in-ground pool, hot tub, and exercise areas. $$. (888) 882-6949.

PERRYSVILLE

From Malabar Farm in Lucas turn right onto Pleasant Valley Road and follow to the stop sign. Turn right onto SR 603 and go about one-half mile, then turn left onto SR 95, which leads to SR 39 and Perrysville.

WHERE TO GO

Mohican Memorial State Forest. 3060 CR 939, Perrysville, OH 44864. Adjacent to Mohican State Park, the forest separated from the park in the late 1940s. This truly untouched terrain offers more than 20 miles of hiking and riding trails, free camping sites, a nature preserve, a war memorial shrine, and a snowmobile trail, conditions permitting. And unlike the park, hunting is permitted. Open daily. Free. (419) 938-6222.

WHERE TO EAT

Bromfield's. Mohican State Resort and Conference Center, 1098 CR 3006, Perrysville, OH 44864. Breakfast, lunch, and dinner consist of a wide variety of offerings, including steaks, seafood, Italian, salads, soups, and sandwiches. There's a kids' menu and Saturday BBQ/Sunday brunch as well. $$. (419) 938-5411; www.mohicanresort.com.

WHERE TO STAY

Mohican State Resort and Conference Center. 1098 CR 3006, Perrysville, OH 44864. A National Gold Medal winner for state parks and recreational excellence, this lodge offers private rooms, many with lake views and balconies, coffeemakers, indoor and outdoor pool, exercise room, and quick access to all park facilities. Children under eighteen can also stay free in the same room. $$-$$$. (419) 938-5411; www.mohicanresort.com.

LOUDONVILLE

Just a few miles from Perrysville, Loudonville can be reached via SR 39.

WHERE TO GO

Mohican Canoe Livery and Fun Center. 3045 SR 3 South, Loudonville, OH 44842. OK, so it isn't white-water rafting, but it is for all ages. Canoe trips down the Mohican vary in length and do offer occasional faster waters in addition to a gentle current. Choose from return transportation via bus, van, or a narrated train ride on "The Doodlebug." Open daily, April 1 through October 31. Admission is charged. (800) 662-2663; www.mohicancanoe.com.

Mohican State Park. 3116 SR 3, Loudonville, OH 44842. Formerly the hunting grounds of the Delaware Indians, this scenic wonder offers glistening waterfalls, glorious gorges (especially at Clearfork), towering hemlock forests, and the Mohican River, which supports diverse animal and plant life. Recreational opportunities abound, including fishing, hiking, picnicking, and camping. Open daily. Free. (419) 994-5125.

WHERE TO STAY

Mohican State Park Cabins and Camping. 3116 SR 3, Loudonville, OH 44842. Choose your amenities. You can pitch a tent or park an RV at one of 153 campsites with electric, sewer, or water hookups, or forget the gear and utilize a rented tepee. It's first come, first served, and communal showers and modern restrooms are included. Or you can opt for a cozy cottage with two bedrooms, a fully equipped kitchen and bath, living room, gas log fireplace, cable TV, and more. Camping, $; cottages, $$-$$$. (419) 994-4290.

Blackfork Inn. 303 North Water Street, Loudonville, OH 44842. Visitors can choose from two properties: the mailing address, an 1865 Italianate Victorian town house with six guest rooms and two suites, all with private baths, or an 1847 former saloon that's now a small antiques shop with two guest suites. Furnished with lots of Victoriana along with a large collection of Ohio-related books. $$-$$$. (419) 994-3252.

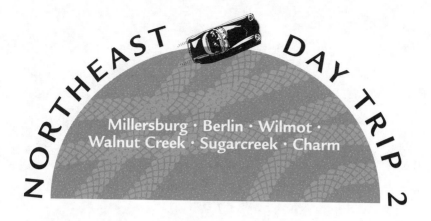

"Wilkummin" to the twenty-first century. By many accounts, Ohio has the largest concentration of Amish and Mennonites in the world. And they're well organized and savvy when it comes to tourism; some even maintain Web sites. They also have religion: Holmes County alone, our destination for this trip, contains nearly fifty churches, which has to be some kind of record for such a sparsely populated area. Not surprisingly, many things are closed on Sunday, making that traditional day of worship a less-than-ideal time to visit.

The other main activities in Amish Country are shopping, eating, and just kicking back. Specialties of the area—and many of its primary industries—include cheese, chocolates, quilts, furniture, country crafts, and every manner of baked goods. So don't be surprised if you come back from your trip with your clothes tighter than when you left.

If you're lucky, you might glimpse the "Plain People" going to services, a meeting, or school in a large group. Given their old-fashioned attire and hairstyles and the untouched rural topography, you may feel as if you've stepped back in time at least one hundred years. You're most likely to see them on one of the county's many back roads or near Old Order strongholds like Charm. However, it's best to refrain from making a fuss over them and taking pictures.

You also might find yourself behind a black buggy clop-clopping at 5 or 10 miles per hour—slower if the horse-drawn vehicle is pulling farm equipment. Because the roads have lots of auto and truck traffic, with speed limits of up to 60 miles per hour, wait until you

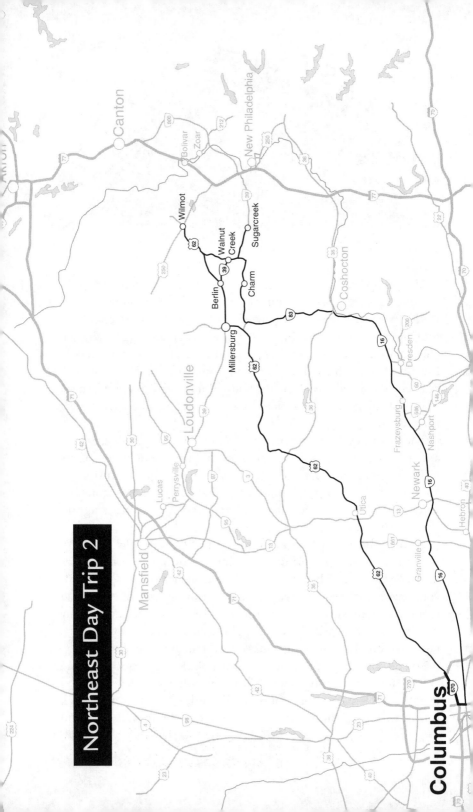

have a clear view to go around it; never pass at the top of a hill, which might result in a horrific encounter of the vehicular kind. The buggies lack turn signals, and horses tend to back up when stopped, so leave tailgating and road rage in the big city, especially during dawn and dusk hours when visibility is poorest.

MILLERSBURG

There are a couple of ways to get to Millersburg, one of the larger towns in Holmes County. From downtown Columbus, go east on SR 16 (Broad Street), until you reach SR 83, then drive north to U.S. 62. Continue north to Millersburg, about an hour and fifteen minutes from Columbus. Or you can take the scenic, winding route of U.S. 62 north from I-270, which will take considerably longer because it's on a crowded, two-lane highway.

WHERE TO GO

Victorian House Museum. 434 Wooster Road, Millersburg, OH 44654. Home of the Holmes County Historical Society, this four-floor, twenty-eight-room mansion boasts Queen Anne architecture, a white oak staircase, a ballroom, and even a sauna and steam room in the basement. Many of the furnishings and antiques have been provided by local citizens, making it a true community effort. Open daily. Admission is charged. (330) 674-0022; www.victorianhouse.org.

Yoder's Amish Farm. 6050 SR 515, Millersburg, OH 44654. This 116-acre working farm features two homes for tours, a petting zoo, buggy and hay rides, and crafts. The friendly native staff will also answer any and all questions about the Amish. Open Monday through Saturday, April through October. Admission is charged. (330) 893-2541.

WHERE TO SHOP

Shopping in Amish country can involve more than browsing, buying, and bustling out the door. Visitors get a chance to watch items being manufactured or crafted through firsthand demonstrations, videos, even murals. Many of the enterprises have been in families for generations, which provides an added personal touch. So add some extra time to your itinerary so you can enjoy such pleasant diversions. Listed here are but a few of dozens of offerings (some are open only during the warmer months, so it's best to call ahead from November to March).

Heini's/Bunker Hill Cheese. 6005 CR 77, Millersburg, OH 44654. Few escape here without ingesting several thousand calories: Along with free samples of more than fifty cheeses, cheese fudge, and other goodies, visitors can choose from sixteen flavors of ice cream. A specialty of the house is yogurt cheese, which the company claims tastes no different than the regular stuff, yet aids digestion. Other offerings include popcorn, Amish potato chips, fudge, and chocolates, and nonedibles like collectibles, Amish throws, and country home accessories. (800) 253–6636, www.heinis.com.

Guggisberg Cheese. 5060 SR 557, Millersburg, OH 44654. Home of the original Baby Swiss, this operation also welcomes visitors to view cheese-making processes. The original owner, the late Alfred Guggisberg, was trained in Switzerland and brought his expertise to Holmes County in 1947. Along with forty varieties of cheese, you'll also find cuckoo clocks and Swiss chocolates for sale. (800) 262–2505; www.guggisberg.com.

WHERE TO EAT

Chalet of the Valley. 5060 SR 577, Millersburg, OH 44654. Dine in an authentic Swiss chalet while enjoying members of the Schnitzel family: wiener (veal cutlet prepared a traditional German style), rahm (veal with creamy wine sauce), jaeger (veal marinated in wine and served with mushroom sauce), and swine, er, schwein, specially seasoned tenderized pork. More American-style dishes include chef and chicken salads, roast beef, ham steak, and spaghetti. The Black Forest cake is layered with chocolate mousse, butter icing, and marinated cherries. $$. (330) 893–2550; www.chaletinthevalley.com.

WHERE TO STAY

Bittersweet Farm. 1720 SR 60, Millersburg, OH 44654. Copied from an 1800s-style house in Connecticut, this bed-and-breakfast was built by the Amish and boasts reclaimed barn lumber, antiques collected by the owners, and a stone fireplace constructed by a local mason. Rooms include private baths, and there are chickens and peacocks on the grounds, along with the owners' cat and dog. $$. (330) 276–1977.

The Barn Inn. 6838 CR 203, Millersburg, OH 44654. Sleeping in a barn has never been so comfy. The site of a dairy in the early 1900s, this building, which retains its original beams, has been restored in Victorian style and has a spacious and elegant sitting room with a 33-foot-high fireplace. A full country breakfast consists of home-made bread, eggs, apple dumplings, and Belgian waffles with whipped cream. $$–$$$. (877) 674–7600.

BERLIN

From Millersburg, Berlin's about a 15-mile drive east on U.S. 62 until you reach SR 39.

WHERE TO GO

Schrock's Amish Farm and Home. 4363 SR 39, Berlin, OH 44610. From Millersburg, go east on 62 about 15 miles until you reach SR 39. If Walt Disney had been Amish, this might have been his vision. Along with guided home tours, including the family's, which was built in 1847, there's animal petting and feeding; a slide presentation of "The Amish Way"; crafts like quilt making, wood and furniture building, and potting; and baking, canning, and cooking. A train ride, back-road tours, a health club and spa, a restaurant, and several shops make for more than one might expect from a "Plain" culture. Open Monday through Saturday, April through October. Admission is charged. (330) 893–3232; www.amish-r-us.com.

Mennonite Information Center. 5798 CR 77, Berlin, OH 44610. A thirty-minute interpretive tour includes *Behalt*, a striking and colorful 10-by-265-foot cyclorama depicting the heritage of the Amish and Mennonite people, from their beginnings in Zurich, Switzerland, in 1525, until today. Painted by German-born artist Heinz Gaugel, the mural covers the persecution of these groups by state churches, the migration to Russia and North America, and more. Gaugel continues to paint in a studio on the premises, and there's a large selection of Amish/Mennonite-related books, crafts, and other items for sale in the gift shop. Admission is charged. Open Monday through Saturday. (330) 893–3529.

WHERE TO SHOP

Schrock's. 4363 SR 39, Berlin, OH 44610. With woodcrafts and Amish-made furniture, home and outdoor decor, snacks, antiques, pottery, and more, this is truly one-stop shopping. Bonuses: You can even purchase obscure toys and collectibles for men and boys and there's a year-round Christmas store. Shops are open year-round. (330) 893–3232; www.amish-r-us.com.

Wendell August Gift Shop and Forge. 7007 Dutch Country Lane, Berlin, OH 44610. These creators and merchants of distinctive hand-forged aluminum, bronze, and pewter items give new meaning to heavy metal. Selection ranges from plates and cups to bookmarks and more. Bonus: They also claim to have the world's largest buggy. (330) 893–3713; www.wendellaugust.com.

Lehman's Mt. Hope. One Lehman Way, Mt. Hope, OH 44660. Hitch your horse up to the rail and rub shoulders with "real" Amish while they shop for hand-powered kitchen supplies like butter churns, homesteading tools, composting toilets, oil lamps—anything without a wire or plug. Many items date back to the 1800s; nevertheless, there's an online catalog for those who prefer to browse via the Web. (888) 438–5346 or (330) 674–7474; www.lehmans.com.

Stone Barn Furnishings. 8613 Township Road 635, Mt. Hope, OH 44660. Two floors of handmade Amish furniture and accessories contain home accents, gifts, upholstered and hardwood furniture, mattresses, and more. Nearly every room and function is covered, from free-standing sinks to coat trees to entertainment centers to computer desks. (330) 674–2064; www.stonebarnfurnishings.com.

WHERE TO EAT

Dutch Harvest Restaurant. Intersection of SRs 39 and 62, P.O. Box 346, Berlin, OH 44610. Along with a wide assortment of soups, sandwiches, and hearty dinners, there's Bag Apple pie, a confection consisting of apples, cinnamon, and sugar, topped with a thick cookie crust. Ice cream is optional. $$. (330) 893–3333.

WHERE TO STAY

Zinck's Inn. 4703 SR 39, Berlin, OH 44610. Options in the forty-six available rooms include nice views of farmlands, a king- or queen-size bed, refrigerator, Jacuzzi, and free continental breakfast. It's also within walking distance of many of the town's shops and restaurants. $-$$. (877) 435-6600; www.zincksinn.com.

    A Day in the Country. 4744 SR 49, Berlin, OH 44610. Spend more than a day, if you'd like. Also close to town, this cozy B&B has rooms with private showers, a whirlpool suite, and a large front porch where you can sit on a rocker and watch the world go buy, uh, by. The hosts will also ply you with hot cocoa and cookies, if you're game. $$. (888) 893-7017.

WILMOT

From Berlin, continue northeast on U.S. 62 to U.S. 250 in Wilmot.

WHERE TO SHOP

Alpine-Alpa Cheese Co. 1504 U.S. 62, Wilmot, OH 44689. The home of the world's largest cuckoo clock, this enterprise also peddles many of its smaller cousins and has a large assortment of Black Forest timepieces. Given the decor, you might even think you've been beamed into Switzerland. And, of course, there's cheese and cheesemaking. (800) 546-3572; www.alpine-alpa.com.

    1881 Antique Barn. 927 U.S. 62, Wilmot, OH 44689. Along with furniture, glass, tools, and pottery, you can purchase antique kitchen collectibles, Depression toys, advertising pieces, and more in a novel setting. (330) 359-7957; www.amishdoor.com.

WHERE TO EAT

Alpine-Alpa Restaurant. 1504 U.S. 62, Wilmot, OH 44689. The cuisine consists of Swiss, German, and Amish cooking, although there's a modern-style salad bar and large Sunday buffet. $$. (800) 546-3572; www.alpine-alpa.com.

Amish Door. 1210 Winesburg Street, Wilmot, OH 44689. Along with the traditional fried, breaded, and gravied items, this menu also features heart-healthy meals and salads. You can also work off some calories at the adjacent shops. $$. (800) 891–6142; www.amishdoor.com.

WHERE TO STAY

Hasseman House. 925 U.S. 62, Wilmot, OH 44689. This Victorian home is loaded with antiques, stained-glass windows, and intricate woodwork, and has a "honeymoon" attic suite. All rooms come with private baths. Breakfast is at the nearby Amish Door restaurant. $$–$$$. (330) 359–7904; www.amishdoor.com.

WALNUT CREEK

Back track on U.S. 62 to SR 515. Turn left and head south to reach Walnut Creek.

WHERE TO SHOP

Troyer's Trail Bologna. 6530 SR 515, Dundee, OH 44624. On your way from Wilmot to Walnut Creek, stop and pick up a home-made favorite, made here since 1912. Troyer's has added a slimmed-down version in the form of turkey bologna. Offerings are in an old-fashioned general store, which also peddles an assortment of jams, jellies, noodles, and more food and other stuff. (330) 893–2407.

Holmes County's Amish Flea Market. P.O. Box 172, Walnut Creek, OH 44687. With more than 100,000 square feet, 500 shopping areas, and hundreds of vendors, this is a universe of collectibles, crafts, and quilts, to mention a few items. A restaurant and elevators are especially useful for breaks (the former) and when loaded down with purchases (the latter). (330) 893–2836; www.amishfleamarket.com.

WHERE TO EAT

Der Dutchman. 4967 Walnut Street, Walnut Creek, OH 44687. Here you can enjoy home-style Amish cooking in a relaxing atmosphere. The restaurant and deck overlook the Genza Bottom Valley, and there are plenty of rocking chairs on the front porch. Stop by the bakery and take home fattening mementos of your trip. $$. (330) 893-2981, www.derdutchman.com.

SUGARCREEK

To get to Sugarcreek, take SR 39 southeast until you reach SR 93.

WHERE TO GO

Alpine Hills Historical Museum. 106 West Main Street, Sugarcreek, OH 44681. This museum, which depicts the merging of the Swiss and Amish cultures, has a bit of everything: a reproduction of an early cheese factory, an Amish kitchen, turn-of-the-twentieth-century woodworking and printing shops, an 1895 Sugarcreek Fire Department display, and more. There are three floors of antiques and artifacts, plus videos about cheese making, area industry, and Amish life. Open April through October. Free. (888) 609-7592.

WHERE TO SHOP

Swiss Village Quilts and Crafts. 113 South Broadway, Sugarcreek, OH 44681. Here you'll find Amish quilts, wall hangings, pillows, and tablecloths, in addition to hand-fashioned dolls, pinewood crafts, and other farm toys. (330) 852-4855.

WHERE TO EAT

Dutch Valley Restaurant. 1343 Old Route 39, Sugarcreek, OH 44681. The specialty of the house is family-style dinners of panfried chicken, ham, or roast beef. And of course, there are all the fixin's: "real" mashed potatoes (none of that gussied-up yuppie fluff), gravy, corn, stuffing like Grandma used to make, homemade breads, pies, and a salad bar if you still haven't had enough. A country breakfast buffet is served daily. $$. (330) 852–4627.

CHARM

Charm can be reached by driving south on SR 93 from Sugarcreek, then west on SR 557.

WHERE TO SHOP

Keim Lumber. 4465 SR 557, Charm, OH 44617. This hardware-lover's heaven features a 30,000-square-foot tool display along with an amazing array of wallpaper, kitchen cabinets, vanities, lights, and more. If you want to build it, you will come. (800) 362–6682; www.keimlumber.com.

WHERE TO STAY

The Charm Countryview Inn. P.O. Box 100, Charm, OH 44617. With private baths, handmade quilts, solid oak furniture, and evening snacks, charmed you might surely be. This lodging, which has fifteen rooms, serves full breakfasts Monday through Saturday and a continental offering on Sunday. $$–$$$. (330) 893–3003; www.charmcountryviewinn.com.

New Philadelphia · Zoar ·
Bolivar · Canton

Despite being in the middle of America's heartland, Ohio has had its share of mavericks and do-gooders, many of whom settled here. Iconoclastic religious groups share geography with Revolutionary War ruins and a diverse assortment of museums and memorials.

NEW PHILADELPHIA

To get to New Philadelphia from Columbus, take I-70 east to I-77. Travel north to exit 81, then go east on SR 39. It's a drive of less than 100 miles.

WHERE TO GO

Schoenbrunn Village. 1984 East High Avenue, New Philadelphia, OH 44663. Founded in 1772 as a Moravian mission to the Delaware Indians, this was the first Christian settlement in Ohio, which established the first civil code, Protestant church, and school in the state. At its peak, Schoenbrunn had more than 300 residents, sixty structures, and eighty fields, although pressures from encroaching settlers and British-aligned Indians forced its abandonment in 1777. The original cemetery and eighteen reconstructed log structures are maintained in the restored village, with men and women dressed in period clothing demonstrating crafts and customs. There are also artifacts and an instructional film. Open daily from Memorial Day through Labor Day; weekends only from Labor Day through October. Admission is charged. (800) 752-7211.

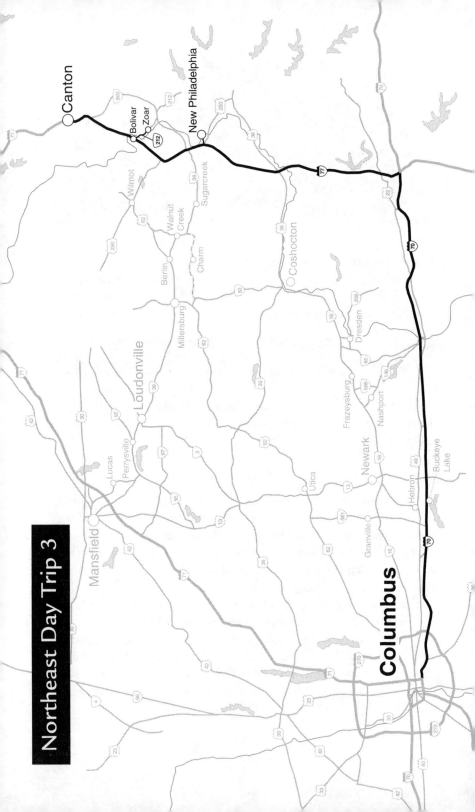

Northeast Day Trip 3

WHERE TO EAT

Fly Boys Grill. 110 South Broadway, New Philadelphia, OH 44663. Located in the heart of the downtown, this local institution serves up steaks, pasta, seafood, salads, and more. $$. (330) 343-7896.

Michael's Restaurant. 134 East High Avenue, New Philadelphia, OH 44663. Although it may sound like an upscale eatery, this diner serves unadorned breakfast and lunch with daily soup specials, along with salads, sandwiches, and burgers. $-$$. (330) 343-8670.

Hog Heaven. 1290 West High Avenue, New Philadelphia, OH 44663. Go "Hog Wild" with appetizers, sandwiches, salads, and (but of course) barbeque ribs, chicken, skewers, and combos. The adventuresome can go for the hog balls or prehistoric hog eggs. $-$$. (330) 308-8040; www.hogheaven-bbq.com.

WHERE TO STAY

The Schoenbrunn Inn. 1186 West High Avenue, New Philadelphia, OH 44663. This sixty-six-room lodge boasts a variety of room choices; an indoor pool, hot tub, and sauna; a pub for sandwiches and beverages; a fitness room; and continental breakfast. With Amish-style decor, it's the best of the Old and New Worlds. $$. (800) 929-7799.

ZOAR

In 1817 a small society of German Separatists who had their own mystical brand of worship and leader purchased 5,500 acres in the Tuscarawas River Valley. They named their settlement Zoar, after Lot's biblical town of refuge, and adopted a seven-pointed star of Bethlehem and a "Tree of Life," a huge Norway spruce representing Christ, as their emblems. Individual property and earnings became communal, and men and women possessed equal political rights, two unheard-of concepts back then. The commune thrived until the mid-1800s, when the leader died. By 1898 it was dissolved, and all assets reverted to the original families. Take I-77 12 miles north from New Philadelphia to exit 93. Zoar is located 3 miles east on SR 212.

WHERE TO GO

Zoar Village. Box 404, Zoar, OH 44697. This 12-block historic district consists of renovated private residences as well as small shops, restaurants, B&Bs, and museums populated by costumed interpreters. Listed here are some of the highlights. Unless otherwise noted, all are open daily in April and May; Wednesday through Sunday from Memorial Day through Labor Day; Saturday and Sunday in September and October; other times by appointment. Admission is charged. (800) 262–6195.

- **Zoar Store.** Constructed in 1833, this hotbed of village life—which was used as a community center by the locals and whose products attracted outside buyers as well—is still a post office, ticket center, and gift shop. You can also see an introductory video about the society.

- **Number One House, Magazine and Kitchen.** This two-story Georgian-style abode served as the home of leader Joseph Baumeler (who later changed his name to Bimeler) and two other families and is loaded with original furniture and crafts. Food for the entire commune was stored in the cellar; it was distributed via the magazine.

- **Garden and Greenhouse.** The biblically inspired design of the garden features a "Tree of Life" layout with twelve apostle trees that represent direct routes to Christ and eternal life. The warm months bring an awesome display of asters, larkspur, zinnias, petunias, and more.

- **Bimeler Museum.** This 1868 residence was remodeled after the society dissolved; however, it's been furnished to re-create the commune's last few years. Open Monday through Friday, March through May and September through December; Monday and Tuesday, June through August. Free.

- **Bakery.** Members of the commune came here to receive their daily bread, as much as they needed, for free. The brick ovens still work: Loaves, pretzels, and other comestibles are produced for demonstration purposes.

- **Tin/Wagon/Blacksmith Shops.** In one two-room structure, the tinsmith created cups, buckets, pitchers, and milk pails for sale in the main store. Down the street, the village smithy and wheelwright toiled next to each other so the buggies and farm tools could quickly and conveniently be fitted with iron parts.

WHERE TO EAT

Zoar Tavern. 162 Main Street, Zoar, OH 44697. A full-service menu offers two squares (lunch and dinner), from bar munchies and salads to German cuisine and vegetarian entrees to good ol' American burgers and steaks. Specialties include salmon burger and beer-batter whitefish. Desserts, sandwiches, seafood, and pasta are also served. $$. (888) 874–2170.

WHERE TO STAY

The Inn at Cowager House. 197 Fourth Street, Zoar, OH 44697. You can take your pick from an 1817 log cabin, an 1833 post-and-beam manor, or an Amish oak cottage. All rooms are comfortably furnished and accompanied by a full country breakfast. Dinners available by reservation. $$–$$$. (800) 874–3542; www.zoarvillage.com.

Cobbler Shop Inn. 121 East Second Street, Zoar, OH 44697. Restored and furnished with period antiques, this accommodation offers five guest rooms, two with private baths and a screened porch that overlooks the gardens. Breakfast can be purchased, and you're within walking distance of attractions. $$–$$$. (800) 287–1547.

Zoar Tavern. 162 Main Street, Zoar, OH 44697. Although this lodge is small, it's a mighty good deal. Five rooms have hand-hewn beams, brick and stone walls, antiques, a private bath, and room service. Continental breakfast is included in the cost. $$. (888) 874–2170.

BOLIVAR

From Zoar, go west on SR 212, crossing I–77 to the petite burg of Bolivar, about 15 miles away.

WHERE TO GO

Fort Laurens State Memorial. Route 1, Box 442, CR 102, Bolivar, OH 44612. Harking back to the days when Ohio was a remote outpost, this was the only American fort built during the Revolutionary War. Constructed with available timber, it featured corner bastions and a blockhouse and was the site of much suffering, including starvation and attacks by hostile Indians who supported the Brits. Abandoned in 1779, most of the original structure has decayed. However, a museum and Tomb of the Unknown Patriot, which holds the remains of an anonymous soldier who died on the grounds, were erected in the 1970s. The museum contains a crypt with the bodies of others who perished there as well as artifacts and weapons of the era. On a more cheerful note, the memorial is also a favorite site of Revolutionary War reenactments. The park is open daily from April through October. The museum is open daily from Memorial Day through Labor Day; weekends only in September and October. Admission is charged. (800) 283-8914.

WHERE TO STAY

Spring House Bed and Breakfast. 10903 SR 212 NE, Bolivar, OH 44612. Smack-dab in the middle of a fifty-five-acre cornfield, this Greek Revival farm was originally constructed in 1857 as a family homestead. Managed by former entertainment professionals, it also features bathrobes and hair dryers in each room, a full gourmet breakfast, and even an in-room TV/VCR and limited transportation to attractions. A newly renovated kitchen and two friendly cats add to the ambience. $$–$$$. (800) 796-9100; www.springhousebnb.com.

CANTON

Any place founded by a man with the name of Bezaleel Wells is bound to be eclectic. So it's no surprise that this small city is the home of a sports hall of fame, a First Ladies' center, a vacuum cleaner museum, a presidential memorial, and some of the yummiest candy around. From Bolivar, go back north on I-77; Canton is about a fifteen-minute drive.

WHERE TO GO

Pro Football Hall of Fame. 2121 George Halas Drive NW, Canton, OH 44708. From the moment you step inside until you walk out of the museum store, it's all football, all the time. In between, you'll learn about the origins of the game and various other leagues that challenged the NFL, test your skill in calling various plays, and get an up-close and personal view of training camps and the Super Bowl in an interactive stadium exhibit, among other diversions. A new Hall of Fame Gallery pours even more adulation on the 200-plus enshrinees via bronze portrait busts and includes a Game Day Stadium rotating theatre to relive not-so-instant replays. Open daily except Christmas. Admission is charged. (330) 456–8207; www.profootballhof.com.

Hoover Historical Center. 1875 Easton Street NW, North Canton, OH 44720. Devices, rather than humans, suck it up in this recently refurbished museum, which bills itself as the only known collection of vacuum cleaners in the world (perhaps there's another in a rain forest somewhere?). It's also the boyhood home of the company founder, William H. Hoover. Highlights include the first Hoover model made in 1908; a bowling-ball-shaped Constellation canister from the '50s that floats on an airstream above the carpet; and non-Hoover appliances such as a 1910 Kotten suction cleaner, which required the user to stand on a platform and rock, so as to activate the device. Open Tuesday through Sunday; closed major holidays. Free. (330) 499–0287; www.hoovercompany.com.

McKinley Museum and National Memorial. 800 McKinley Monument Drive NW, Canton, OH 44708. OK, so not *everything* has to do with the twenty-fifth president, even though this attraction bears his name. But there is a classic Greek memorial honoring McKinley as well as animatronic figures of him and his wife describing their personal effects, the largest accumulation of McKinley memorabilia in the world. You can also observe live plants and animals on Ecology Island, encounter a robotic dinosaur at a natural history display, and learn about the outer limits at Space Station Earth. A planetarium and an industrial hall tracing Canton developments round out the exhibits. Open daily, May through August; closed Sunday the rest of the year. Admission is charged. (330) 455–7403; www.mckinleymuseum.org.

Canton Classic Car Museum. Market Avenue at Sixth Street SW, Canton, OH 44702. More than forty vehicles from 1907–81 include Amelia Earhart's 1916 Pierce-Arrow, a 1939 Lincoln believed to have been used by England's Queen Mother, and a 1981 DeLorean driven by Johnny Carson, among others. The large selection of artifacts includes petroliana, toys, period clothing, and highway history displays. The museum is located in one of the country's earliest Ford dealerships. Open daily. Admission is charged. (330) 455–3603; www.cantonclassiccar.org.

National First Ladies' Library. 331 Market Avenue S, Canton, OH 44702. The home of former First Lady Ida McKinley, this structure has been restored with great attention to period detail and accuracy. It also contains a comprehensive bibliography of books, manuscripts, diaries, journals, and other materials related to First Ladies and is developing and expanding its education programs and holdings. Open Tuesday through Saturday for historical tours by advance reservation only; other times by appointment. Admission is charged. (330) 452–0876; www.firstladies.org.

MAPS Air Museum. 5359 Massillon Road, North Canton, OH 44720. Located in a 16,000-square-foot facility next to (where else?) the airport, this accumulation's displays range from a Polish MiG–17 to a rare Martin B–26 Marauder to a Douglass Dauntless Dive Bomber. There are also documents, paintings, and memorabilia, along with more than 800 handbuilt aircraft. Open Monday, Wednesday, and Saturday. Admission is charged. (330) 896–6332; www.mapsairmuseum.org.

Harry London Candies. 5353 Lauby Road, North Canton, OH 44720. With more than 20,000 square feet, a state-of-the-art factory, and family recipes used since 1922, this establishment makes Willy Wonka look like a dilettante. The tour encompasses the Chocolate Hall of Fame, and there are lots of free samples, including eleven sugar-free (but not calorie-free) varieties. And few can resist the temptation of the gift shop. Open daily. Admission is charged. (800) 321–0444; www.londoncandies.com.

WHERE TO SHOP

Westfield Shoppingtown. 4230 Belden Village Mall NW, Canton, OH 44718. This is one of the more diverse shopping arenas around and includes more than one hundred retail stores. Dillard's, Kaufmann's, Sears, American Eagle, Victoria's Secret, the Disney Store, and many others can be found here. (330) 494–5490.

Lazar's Art Gallery. 2490 Woodlawn Avenue NW, Canton, OH 44708. Browsers can choose from the work of more than 700 craftspeople. There's handblown glass, pottery, Judaica, sculpture, jewelry, porcelain, and more. (800) 400–8351; www.lazarsartgallery.com.

WHERE TO EAT

The Stables Restaurant and Hall of Fame Grille. 2317 Thirteenth Street, Canton, OH 44708. Those whose appetites for the gridiron have been whetted by the Pro Football Hall of Fame need only go a few blocks to this former horse barn, which continues the tradition with a statue and memorabilia. There's also a game and entertainment room as well as outdoor dining. Menu items include hickory grilled steaks, seafood, burgers, and salads. $$–$$$. (330) 452-1230.

356 Fighter Group Restaurant. 4919 Mt. Pleasant Road, North Canton, OH 44720. Ditto for folks visiting the MAPS Air Museum (wonder what a vacuum-cleaner-themed restaurant would be like?). Located at the airport, this restaurant serves American chow amid 1940s flier and other types of souvenirs, artifacts, and music. $$–$$$. (800) 994-2662; www.starcom2.com/356thFG.

Walther's Restaurant. 1836 Maple Avenue N, Canton, OH 44704. This reasonably priced eatery caters to families and large groups and even sells Ohio lottery tickets. Specialties include frog legs and broasted chicken (some might say the former tastes like the latter), and breakfast is served all day. $$. (330) 452-0785.

WHERE TO STAY

Glenmoor Country Club. 4191 Glenmoor Road, Canton, OH 44718. With seventy-four luxuriously appointed rooms, each of which is decorated differently, a presidential suite, a Jack Nicklaus–designed golf course, and several gourmet dining options, this lodging should satisfy the most discriminating tastes. There's also a full-service spa for those who wish the pampering to continue. $$$. (888) 456-6667; www.glenmoorcc.com.

Heatherwood Farms. 9320 Kent Avenue, North Canton, OH 44721. This B&B's amenities include hot tub, airport shuttle, and full breakfast. However, the two rooms have a shared bath. No animals are allowed. $$. (888) 637-6763.

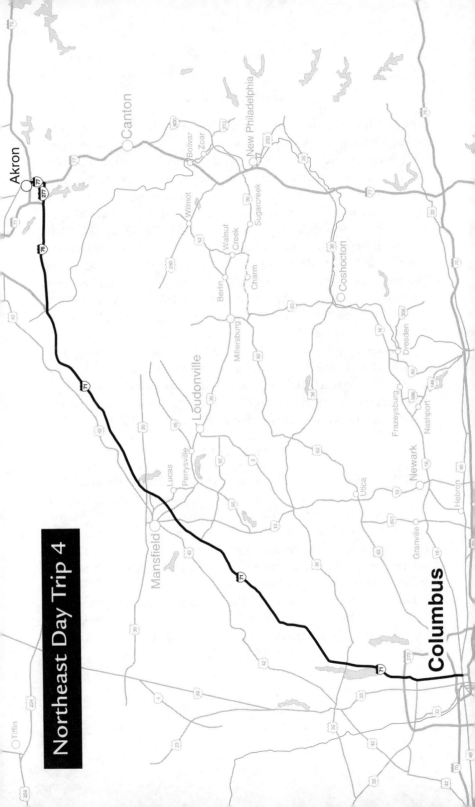

Akron

AKRON

One of the nation's first canal towns, which eventually became the home of Quaker Oats and a rubber hub (manufacturer B. F. Goodrich was drawn by the easy railroad access and the large water supply), Akron is an eclectic mix of old-time industrialism, nouveau culture, and high-tech innovation. On one hand are diverse manufacturing plants and their curious accoutrements and on the other are artistic draws such as Blossom Music Center (1145 West Steels Corners Road, Cuyahoga Falls, OH 44223; 330-945-9400, www. blossommusic.com), which attracts top musical acts from around the world and is the summer home of the Cleveland Orchestra. Much of the city's economy revolves around the development of polymers; in fact, the University of Akron has an internationally noted program in that particular science.

From Columbus, Akron is a straight shot of about 125 miles: Take I-71 north to I-76 east, which leads directly to downtown.

WHERE TO GO

Goodyear World of Rubber. 1144 East Market Street, Akron, OH 44316. Here you'll learn that vulcanization does not always relate to Mr. Spock and was, in fact, a process discovered by Charles Goodyear. Also on display are Goodyear's personal mementos, descriptions of how products are made with rubber components, and Indianapolis 500 race cars. Of special interest is a discussion of the glory years of blimps, which peaked in the 1930s with elaborate and luxurious airships. Open Monday through Friday. Free. (330) 796–7117.

Lockheed Martin Airdock (Blimp Hangar). Take I–76 east to I–277 east to U.S. 224; continue east past SR 8 to the Airdock on the left. Mailing address: Lockheed Martin Tactical Defense Systems, 1210 Massillon Road, Akron, OH 44315. At twenty-two stories high and as long as two Washington Monuments, this fascinating structure is the world's largest building without interior supports. It even has its own climate, occasionally creating a lightning system or fog. Built by Goodyear in 1929 to construct blimps, it's now used to manufacture aerospace products. Drive by only, unless you have security clearance to get inside. (330) 796–2800.

National Inventors Hall of Fame. 221 South Broadway, Akron, OH 44308. Want to get a handle on your inner genius? The Inventor's Workshop includes a laser area for creating mazes and sounds; fiber optics to experiment with color mixing, translucence, and composition; microscopics for an up close and personal view of objects; strobes and animation; and more. Learn and be inspired by the multitiered tribute to hundreds of men and women who helped shape life as we know it today. Open daily except Monday. Admission is charged. (800) 968–4332; www.invent.org.

Stan Hywet Hall. 714 North Portage Path, Akron, OH 44303. Eat your heart out, Martha Stewart. This exquisite sixty-five-room Tudor Revival manor boasts richly carved paneling, stained-glass windows, and sumptuous furnishings. Other opulent excesses include walls and fireplaces imported from England; hidden telephones, radiators, and closets; Persian rugs handwoven for the house; and various "theme" rooms (e.g., Chinese, music) furnished with authentic period pieces. Exterior touches include formal gardens, a lagoon, and a greenhouse. All this was patched together in 1898 by tire magnate Frank Seiberling, cofounder of Goodyear Tire and Rubber. Open daily, April through January; closed Monday in February and March. Admission is charged. (330) 836–5533; www.stanhywet.org.

Hower House. 60 Fir Hill, Akron, OH 44325. Before Stan Hywet, there was this Second Empire Italianate mansion constructed in 1871, some areas of which are, oddly, octagonal. Inhabited by industrialist John Hower and his descendants for 102 years, this twenty-

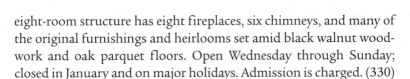

eight-room structure has eight fireplaces, six chimneys, and many of the original furnishings and heirlooms set amid black walnut woodwork and oak parquet floors. Open Wednesday through Sunday; closed in January and on major holidays. Admission is charged. (330) 972–6909.

Perkins Stone Mansion/John Brown House. 550 Copley Road, Akron, OH 44320. Even farther back in time are these two abodes, which are across the street from each other. Built in the 1830s by Colonel Simon Perkins Jr., namesake son of Akron's founder, the former is a well-preserved example of Greek Revival architecture and contains period pieces and other displays depicting local history. The John Brown home was the abolitionist's residence from 1844 to 1846 and includes an exhibit tracing the insurrection at Harper's Ferry and the antislavery movement. Open Tuesday through Sunday; closed in January. Admission is charged. (330) 535–1120.

Dr. Bob's Home. 855 Ardmore Avenue, Akron, OH 44302. This is the spot where stockbroker William Wilson helped Akron resident Dr. Robert Smith sober up and began Alcoholics Anonymous in 1935. This "dynamic duo" then continued to hold meetings to help other alcoholics at this residence, which has many of the original furnishings. Open daily. Free. (330) 864–1935; www.drbobs.com.

WHERE TO SHOP

Mustard Seed Market & Cafe. 3885 West Market Street, Akron, OH 44333. Aisles of organic produce, handcrafted breads, a supplement section with herb and homeopathic remedies, and a full line of cruelty-free body-care products help back up its claim as Ohio's largest natural-food store. A full-service cafe, extensive deli, and gourmet foods and wines section round out the offerings. (888) 476–2379; www.mustardseedmarket.com.

Rolling Acres Mall. 2400 Romig Road, Akron, OH 44322. The largest mall in Akron is home to five department stores: Sears, Kaufmann's, JC Penney Outlet, Dillard's Clearance Center, and Target, as well as more than fifty specialty shops. Events and activities and a food court add to consumers' delight. (330) 753–5045; www.rollingacresmall.com.

Summit Mall. 3265 West Market Street, Akron, OH 44333. Anchored by Dillard's and Kaufmann's and with more than 120 specialty stores, this shopping arena includes Ann Taylor, Banana Republic, The Disney Store, Eddie Bauer, Brookstone, Gymboree, Victoria's Secret, Williams-Sonoma, and Zany Brainy. (330) 867–1555; www.shopsimon.com.

Don Drumm Studio and Gallery. 437 Crouse Street, Akron, OH 44311. The largest showroom of contemporary crafts in the state, this two-building emporium offers up glass, jewelry, ceramics, sculpture, wood, and graphics from more than 500 artists. (330) 253–6268.

West Point Market. 1711 West Market Street, Akron, OH 44313. Even folks who dislike grocery shopping might want to stop by. You'll find an amazing selection of chocolates, cheese, prime meats, imported foods, fine wines, and more and may leave understanding why regular customers come from as far as 50 miles away. (800) 838–2156; www.westpointmarket.com.

WHERE TO EAT

Carousel Dinner Theatre. 1275 East Waterloo Road, Akron, OH 44306. A favorite of all generations and the largest entertainment center of its kind in the United States, this merry-go-round name-sake combines sit-down dining with live performances. Offerings range from comedies to musicals to drama. With a 60-foot prosce-nium stage, everyone has a good view. $$$. (includes show). (800) 362–4100; www.carouseldinnertheatre.com.

West Market Grill at Tangier. 532 West Market Street, Akron, OH 44303. This unique Akron institution that fed and entertained presidents, celebrities, and even foreign heads of state has undergone a makeover in both its menu (from Moroccan to beef, seafood, and pasta) and decor (New York steakhouse). But reminders of its glory days remain in touches of exotica around the bar and in photos of famous patrons. $$$. (330) 376–7171; www.thetangier.com.

Whistle Stop Tavern. Quaker Square, 135 South Broadway, Akron, OH 44308. Originally the cellar of the original Quaker Oats factory, this 1800s structure boasts 3-foot-thick walls and stained-glass windows from now-defunct area churches. It also has a stair-case from the home of the Schumachers, one of the factory's founders. Enjoy a wide selection of appetizers, sandwiches, salads, steaks, and seafood amid dozens of kinds of beer and multiple TVs. $$. (330) 762–9333.

Trackside Grille. Quaker Square, 135 South Broadway, Akron, OH 44308. All aboard for a restaurant built around the 1930s-era Broadway Limited Railroad run from New York City to Chicago. Sit in an original Pullman car surrounded by antiques and memorabilia while enjoying sandwiches, entrees, and salads. There are also luncheon specials and a large and varied Sunday brunch. $$–$$$. (330) 253-4541.

Papa Joe's/Iancomini's. 1561 Akron Peninsula Road, Akron, OH 44313. Established in 1932, the family-owned enterprise specializes in Italian entrees, steaks, seafood, and salads. Although the founder passed away in 1998, his daughter and children continue the culinary tradition. $$–$$$. (330) 923-7999.

WHERE TO STAY

Crowne Plaza Quaker Square. 135 South Broadway, Akron, OH 44308. If you've ever wondered what it's like to sleep in a Quaker Oats box, albeit a luxurious one, this is the place for you. Not only are all the rooms round but the rest of the hotel is as well. Of particular interest is the lobby, a striking combination of modern art and company memorabilia. Make sure you remember your room number because it's easy to get confused. $$$. (330) 253-5970.

Portage House. 601 Copley Road, Akron, OH 44320. This large home was built in 1918 as part of the Perkins family farm and is near Simon Jr.'s home (see Perkins Stone Mansion). Located on the second floor, sleeping quarters consist of four bedrooms and two baths. Guests can also relax downstairs in the living room on the first floor. $–$$. (330) 535-1952.

O'Neil House. 1290 West Exchange Street, Akron, OH 44313. Built in the 1920s, this Tudor mansion offers an expansive living room, a well-stocked library, and four bedrooms, all with private baths. The home of William O'Neil, founder of General Tire, it can serve as a warm-up for a visit to Stan Hywet Hall. Gourmet breakfast, one dog, and two cats included. $$. (330) 867-2650.

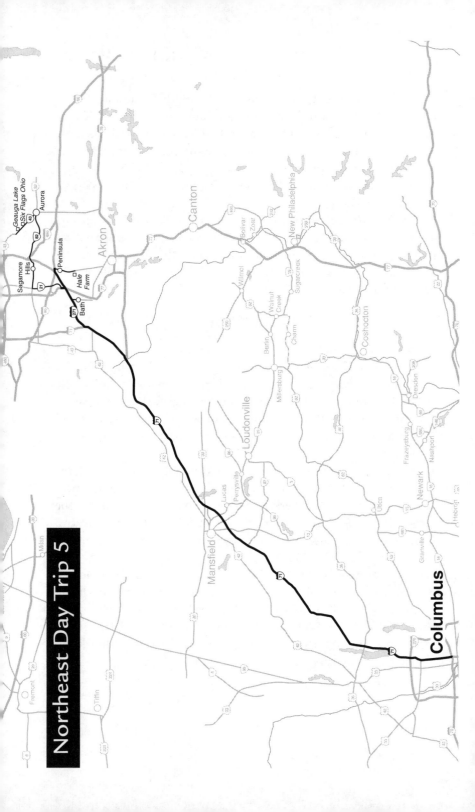

Northeast Day Trip 5

Bath · Peninsula ·
Sagamore Hills · Aurora

This region has both the old and the new: Amish history, skiing, shopping (crafts and outlets), amusement parks, and more. The recent absorption of Sea World into Six Flags amusement park makes it even easier for travelers who prefer one-stop thrills.

BATH

Far from being all washed up, this tiny town boasts the Hale Farm and Village, located in the picturesque Cuyahoga Valley. A drive of about an hour and a half, Bath can be reached by heading north from Columbus on I–71 to exit 218. Turn right (east) on SR 18 and continue approximately 5 miles to Cleveland-Massillon Road. Turn left on Cleveland-Massillon Road, heading north, and turn right on Ira Road to Oak Hill Road.

WHERE TO GO

Hale Farm and Village. 2686 Oak Hill Road, Bath, OH 44210. This attraction allows you to experience the attitudes and beliefs of 1848 Amish culture without worrying about taking out a buggy with your vehicle or having your ringing cell phone or teenager's attire offend Old Order sensibilities. Populated with townspeople-cum-actors who discuss the struggles, triumphs, and rewards of pioneering the Western Reserve, the land was originally settled in 1810 by Jonathan Hale, who constructed a three-story redbrick house on the grounds.

A glassblower, candle maker, potter, and blacksmith also demonstrate the early trades of the region. Open daily May through October. Admission is charged. (800) 589–9703.

PENINSULA

Situated in the heart of the Ohio Valley, the charming shop-, antiques-, and gallery-loaded village of Peninsula is a short hop north of Bath on I–271. Get off at SR 303 and turn right (east).

WHERE TO GO

Cuyahoga Valley Scenic Railroad. 1630 West Mill Street, Peninsula, OH 44264. This ninety-minute round-trip excursion runs through 26 miles of the Cuyahoga Valley National Recreation Area. Relax in climate-controlled vintage coaches circa 1939–40; you can also take a guided tour with a park ranger through the area. Other round-trip destinations include Hale Farm and Village, Stan Hywet Hall, Quaker Square/Inventure Place, and others. Dates and times vary. Closed in January. Admission is charged. (800) 468–4070; www.cvsr.com.

  Boston Mills/Brandywine Ski Resort. 7100 Riverview Road, Peninsula, OH 44264. With nineteen slopes and eighteen chairlifts, you can plow through a plethora of skiing, snowboarding, and tubing activities. When the weather fails to cooperate, there's snow-making equipment, so you can still get the drift. Lessons are available, as are locker and equipment rental, shuttle bus service, and sale of apparel. Hours vary, depending on weather conditions. Fee varies. (800) 875–4241; www.bmbw.com.

WHERE TO SHOP

Fine Art Services. 1770B Main Street, Peninsula, OH 44264. This custom framing shop is also a full-service art gallery that features the works of internationally recognized photographer Luciano Duse. There's a continually changing selection of photography, paintings, sculpture, and gift items, as well as "Meet the Artist" receptions. (330) 657–2228.

Elements Gallery. 1619 West Mill Street, Peninsula, OH 44264. You can watch craftspeople at work, creating bowls and other pottery. The studios of Bures Pottery, this shop also showcases the work of other artists. (330) 657-2788.

The Ewe Tree. 61 Geoppert Road, Peninsula, OH 44264. Owned by two sisters, this enterprise creates fine woven clothing, rugs, and bags. Wool, yarns, spindles and other equipment, and books are available at the supply barn adjacent to the studio. Call before coming. (330) 650-6777; www.ewetree.com.

Heritage Farms. 6050 Riverview, Peninsula, OH 44264. Here you can find that perfect Christmas tree in December, pick out a pumpkin in October, or view more than 250 varieties of daylilies in the summer. The area's oldest family-run farm, it's been operational since 1848 and has covered bridges and a barn with a stone fireplace big enough to stand in. (330) 657-2330; www.heritagefarms.com.

Century Cycles Peninsula. 1621 Main Street, Peninsula, OH 44264. Talk about a prime location: This cycle shop is next to a 25-mile towpath. You can rent or buy a bike or get your bike repaired here. (330) 657-2209; www.centurycycles.com.

Many antiques stores are located within walking/close driving distance of the town. Call for hours and availability and type of merchandise.

The Antique Roost. 1455 West Hines Hill Road (330) 657-2687.

Antiques Etc. 1593 Main Street (330) 657-2700.

The Buggy Step. By appointment. (330) 657-2915.

Downtown Emporium. 1595 Main Street (330) 657-2778.

Innocent Age Antiques. 6084 North Locust Street (330) 657-2915.

Olde Players Barn. 1039 West Streetsboro Road (330) 657-2886.

WHERE TO EAT

Winking Lizard. 1615 Main Street, Peninsula, OH 44264. With "Reptizers" such as Lizard Lips (fried chicken strips), Sandweggies, and "Creek and Roadkill Grill" (fish and meat entrees), the menu alone is a feast for the mind. $$. (330) 657-2770.

SAGAMORE HILLS

Sagamore Hills is located on SR 82, off I–271 about twenty-five minutes north of Peninsula.

WHERE TO GO

Dover Lake Waterpark. 1150 West Highland Road, Sagamore Hills, OH 44067. With slippery mountain slides, speed slides, tubing rides, a waterwhirl, rolling river tubing, a wave pool, and a lake with a sandy beach, this is wet and wild-to-mild. Non-H_2O activities include a 30-foot-high bag slide, a kiddie coaster, fire engine ride, miniature golf, video games, batting cages, softball, volleyball, and more. There are also picnic and changing facilities. Open daily early June through late August. Admission is charged. (800) 372–7946; www.doverlake.com.

WHERE TO STAY

Inn at Brandywine Falls. 8230 Brandywine Road, Sagamore Hills, OH 44067. Part of a recreational area that includes a waterfall, this 1848 restored Greek Revival home boasts six luxurious rooms, each with private bath. Other amenities include gourmet foods, exercise facilities, and Ohio historic decor. $$$. (888) 306–3381; www.innat brandywinefalls.com.

AURORA

Established nearly 200 years ago, this well-maintained New England–style town has enjoyed increased tourism along with a respectable growth in population and industry. Diversions range from amusement parks to shopping to getaways. There is also some good eatin', mostly in shopping areas and lodges. Aurora is accessible from major interstates such as I–271 and I–480. From Sagamore Hills, go east on SR 82 about 15 miles and turn left (north) on SR 306.

WHERE TO GO

Six Flags Ohio. 1060 North Aurora Road, Aurora, OH 44202. This amusement park has ramped up its coaster lineup to ten, the most recent being X-Flight, which involves soaring up a 115-foot hill, then inverting into a 180-degree twist. Other gut-benders include Batman Knight Flight, arguably the world's longest "floor-less coaster," Superman Ultimate Escape, which claims to be the world's first vertical spiraling coaster; and the Villain, which aspires to be world-class by climbing 120 feet, reaching 60 mph, and then continuing with twelve successive drops. Or you can do the Time Warp by catapulting 50 feet, tumbling toward the earth, then being tossed up again (not recommended after a heavy meal). Take a walk on the milder side with the kids to the Thriller Bee gondolas, the starfish tilt-a-whirl, and separate Starcastle and Pirate Flight voyages. Boat rides, a carousel, and shows round out the diversions. Among the latter are four Bengal tigers who strut their stuff, a tropical treasures bird show, a 3-D interactive pirate movie, and fireworks. And the usual Looney Tunes suspects—Bugs Bunny, Daffy Duck, Sylvester, and others—perform at the Palace Theatre and can be found at certain times and locations. With a nod to its Sea World roots, there are dolphins, otters, and a "killer whale" as well. Open daily end of May through end of August; weekends only in early May, September, and October. Admission is charged. (330) 562–8303; www.sixflags.com.

WHERE TO SHOP

Aurora Premium Outlets. 549 South Chillicothe Road, Aurora, OH 44202. This is the place for close encounters of the bargain kind. More than seventy outlet stores are housed in an early American–style village and include Polo, Ralph Lauren, Off 5th–Saks Fifth Avenue, DKNY Jeans, Ann Taylor, Big Dog, and more. There are also shoes, children's things, luggage and leather goods, gift and specialty items, home accessories, and more, as well as restaurants and a food court. (330) 562–2000; www.premiumoutlets.com.

    Dankorona Winery and Lounge. 155 Treat Road, Aurora, OH 44202. Visitors can choose from several reds, rosés, and whites; some vintages have won awards. Purchases are available by the glass, bottle, or case. Along with regular spaghetti and fish dinners, they also host special and seasonal events. Call for information on tours. (330) 562-9245.

WHERE TO STAY

Inn at Six Flags. 800 North Aurora Road, Aurora, OH 44202. This accommodation is just a quarter mile from the park bearing the same name and includes a free shuttle there and to other area attractions. Amenities include an indoor pool, kiddie jungle gym, arcades, miniature golf, eatery, and bar. $$$. (330) 562-9151.

Aurora Inn. 30 East Garfield Road, Aurora, OH 44202. This nineteenth-century lodging resides in beautiful downtown Aurora and is an excellent example of Western Reserve architecture. Guests can indulge in indoor and outdoor pools, sauna, Jacuzzi, and tennis courts. Restaurant offerings range from country cooking to lighter fare. $$-$$$. (800) 444-6121.

Walden Country Inn and Stables. 1119 Aurora Hudson Road, Aurora, OH 44202. This exclusive getaway is located on 1,000 acres that would do Thoreau proud. Thirty-two Arabian horses graze the property, and riding is available. Suites come with cedar-paneled ceilings and a variety of fireplaces, and the beds boast fine Italian linens. Jacuzzis, full kitchens, and fine to casual dining options may tempt you not to leave the grounds. $$-$$$. (330) 562-5508; www.waldenco.com.

Bertram Inn and Conference Center. 600 North Aurora Road, Aurora, OH 44202. With 156 rooms, an exercise facility, and several restaurants and bars, this lodging suits travelers from business to pleasure. High-speed Internet access, Play Station, and premium cable TV will satisfy the high-tech junkie. $$$. (877) 995-0200; www.thebertraminn.com.

Mario's International Spa and Hotel. 35 East Garfield Road, Aurora, OH 44202. This is the spot for reasonably priced pampering. The nationally recognized facility offers elegant accommodations, fine and casual dining with a variety of cuisine (low-cal and up), even limousine service. Most rooms have a private whirlpool; other public areas contain cozy fireplaces. There's a large menu of spa services as well: skin and beauty care; body and water therapies, scrubs, and masks; and hand and foot treatments. Spa days and retreats are also available. $$-$$$. (330) 562-9171; www.mariosspa.com.

Six Flags Camping Resort. 250 Treat Road, Aurora, OH 44202. At the other end of the spectrum—but perhaps not as much as one would think—are these grounds, which offer water, electric, and sewer hookup for the tenter and RVer as well as cabins for those who just like to think about camping. A heated pool, three lakes, and children's playground complete the scenario. Located just minutes from Six Flags, the resort also supplies free shuttle service. $–$$. (330) 562-9151.

Northeast Day Trip 6

Cleveland

CLEVELAND

Once called the "Mistake on the Lake" and the butt of national jokes because of pollution, financial instability, and race riots, Cleveland certainly has come a long way, baby. Along with city fathers (and mothers) and various industries, citizens pulled together and revitalized areas, building such attractions as the Rock and Roll Hall of Fame and the Great Lakes Science Center and making the Lake Erie waterfront area habitable and safe. Public and private sectors also combined forces to spiff up downtown, the Flats, and other urban districts, so bars, restaurants, shops, and other businesses could move in.

Three major sports teams (four, if you count soccer) and well-kept arenas add to the appeal, especially for folks who make an excursion for that big game. Culture buffs can choose from Severance Hall (11001 Euclid Avenue; 216-231-1111; www.clevelandorchestra. com), home of the renowned Cleveland Orchestra; the Playhouse Square Center (Euclid at East Seventeenth, 216-241-6000; www.playhousesquare.com) with five magnificently restored theaters and the largest venue of its kind outside of New York City; the Cleveland Opera (1422 Euclid Avenue; 216-575-0903; www.clevelandopera.org); the locally based Cleveland Playhouse (8500 Euclid Avenue; 800-278-1274; www.cleveplayhouse.org), and more. With nightclubs, coffee shops, and jazz and blues bars, as well as major performers who make Cleveland a regular gig, nightlife is ubiquitous. The ethnic blend of the city—African-American, German, Italian, Jewish, Polish, and more recently, Latino—lends flavor and individuality to various neighborhoods such as Little Italy and Ohio City, which have become draws in themselves.

When visiting Cleveland, it's always difficult to choose what to do. The only way around this is to return, again and again, because there's always something new and different. Although Cleveland's about 140 miles from Columbus, it's a straight shot up I-71 and you can make it in a little more than two hours without getting pulled over by those guys with sirens who frequent highway turnarounds.

WHERE TO GO

Trolley Tours. 1831 Columbus Road, Cleveland, OH 44113. On rigs with names such as Lolly the Trolley and Gus the Bus, you're in for an entertaining ride. This is a good way to get oriented and learn about the city, its history, and landmarks. Reservations are required. Admission is charged. (800) 848-0173; www.lollytrolley.com.

Rock and Roll Hall of Fame. One Key Plaza (East Ninth Street, at Lake Erie), Cleveland, OH 44114. Not only is this 150,000-square-foot facility visually stunning with its cantilevered spaces and glass "tent," but the interactive exhibits, intimate performance spaces, and rotating costume and artifact displays make it a treat for other senses

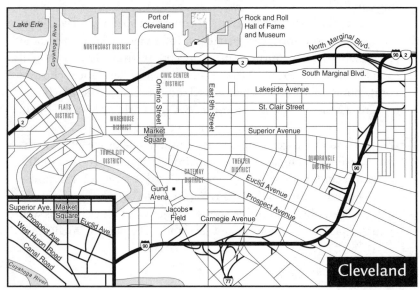

as well. Listening to songs and oral histories and seeing genuine objects that shaped so much popular culture can be awe-inspiring for any age. Where else can you view Buddy Holly's high school diploma, Jim Morrison's Cub Scout uniform, or diverse, rotating exhibitions on everything from U2 and Jimi Hendrix to the music of Ohio? Plus, there's a really cool gift shop. Open daily except Thanksgiving and Christmas. Admission is charged. (888) 764-7625; www.rockhall.com.

Great Lakes Science Center. 601 Erieside Avenue, North Coast Harbor, Cleveland, OH 44114. With more than 340 hands-on exhibits and an OMNIMAX cinema, this attraction, which focuses on science, environment, and technology, makes learning fun. There's an indoor tornado, a static-electricity generator that literally makes your hair stand on end, and a "Shadow Room" that just cries out for you to leap in the air for that special effect. You can pilot a blimp, experience virtual reality, and visit "sick Earth" in a hospital bed or a house "haunted" by toxic chemicals and pollutants. Open daily. Admission is charged. (216) 692-2000; www.greatscience.com.

Steamship *William G. Mather.* 1001 East Ninth Street Pier, Cleveland, OH 44114. In its previous life, this 1925 vessel was a Great Lakes freighter carrying millions of tons of ore and coal. Now a museum and completely restored, the *Mather* consists of cavernous cargo holds, a shipshape pilot house, and a four-story engine room. It also boasts classy guest and dining accommodations (and not-so upscale cribs for deckhands), as well as captain's quarters. An exhibit details the history of Great Lakes shipping; a video is also available. Open Friday through Sunday, May through October. Admission is charged. (216) 574-6262.

Goodtime III. 825 East Ninth Street Pier, Cleveland, OH 44114. OK, so it's not sailing the Bahamas, but this quadruple-deck, 1,000-passenger luxury cruise ship offers two-hour narrated tours as well as fun and/or romantic luncheon and dinner options. The ship has an enclosed, heated/air-conditioned lower deck and a topside that allows for sunning. Snacks and drinks are available. Open daily from Memorial Day through Labor Day, limited hours in May and September. Admission is charged. (216) 861-5110; www.goodtimeiii.com.

Cleveland Browns Stadium Tours. 1083 West Third Street, Cleveland, OH 44113. See Cleveland's lakefront jewel, which opened in 1999, without the crowds. You'll visit the locker room, the Dawg Pound where the most rabid fans sit (think diehards in canine masks or painted faces and bodies), and the Browns Hall of Fame, among other spots. The Browns Team Shop offers the largest selection of team-related gear and souvenirs around, and there's a bar and grille and Hall of Fame as well. Tours at specified hours, April through December, except on game days. Admission is charged. Reservations required. (877) 746–9326 or (440) 824–3361; www.cleveland browns.com.

Cleveland Museum of Art. 11150 East Boulevard, Cleveland, OH 44106. Those searching for more highbrow endeavors will find cultural satisfaction at what the *New York Times* calls "one of the nation's premier collections." More than 30,000 works of art encompass 5,000 years, from Egyptian vase paintings (3500 B.C.–A.D. 300) to Medieval and Islamic Art (A.D. 300–1500) to Old Master paintings (thirteenth through eighteenth centuries), nineteenth-century European portraits, and contemporary art and photography. In between you'll find a collection of armor and other weapons of war; sculpture, decorative arts, and textiles; and Asian art, among other items. Open daily. Admission is charged. (888) 262–0033; www.clevelandart.org.

HealthSpace Cleveland. 8911 Euclid Avenue, Cleveland, OH 44106. The first of its kind in the Western Hemisphere and formerly called the Health Museum, HealthSpace was founded in 1936 by a gaggle of doctors and community leaders. It's been renovated twice since and has addressed such issues as HIV/AIDS, Alzheimer's disease, obesity, child abuse prevention, smoking, and reproductive health. It was home of the circa 1950 icon Juno the Transparent Woman. Completed in 2003, a new 81,000-square-foot facility boasts a soaring atrium, loads of natural light for various exhibits, and a 40-foot-wide waterfall. Follow the Road to Good Health, which features places to play and learn via a "walk" through life's stages. Feed your mind with Head First!, a giant guess-what with an interactive theater. The Frohring Education Center offers everything from cooking classes to Junior Medical Camp to a fitness evaluation. Open daily. Admission is charged. (216) 231–5010; www.healthmuseum.org.

Western Reserve Historical Society. 10825 East Boulevard, Cleveland, OH 44106. This complex houses the Crawford-Auto Aviation Museum and the History Museum and Library. The former highlights more than 200 autos and aircraft, with special focus on turn-of-the-twentieth-century and Cleveland-made cars. There's also an early 1900s Curtis Hydroplane flown by local aviator Al Engel.

The History Museum features a mansion built in 1911 and is home to the Chisolm Halle Costume Wing, which has more than 30,000 items for rotating exhibitions. Open daily. Admission is charged. (216) 721-5722; www.wrhs.org.

NASA Glenn Research Center. 21000 Brookpark Road, Cleveland, OH 44135. Opened to the public in 1976, this facility had been conducting aerospace research since the early '40s. Its six galleries consist of displays on innovative engines and space communications and a tribute to local hero John Glenn. There's also an Apollo command module that was used on *Skylab 3,* a microgravity laboratory with a drop tower, and a launch center where you can conduct your own countdown sequence. Far out! Open daily except major holidays. Free. (216) 433-2001; www.grc.nasa.gov.

Cleveland Metroparks Zoo and RainForest. 3900 Wildlife Way, Cleveland, OH 44109. What a zoo. Along with claiming to be the home of the largest collection of primate species in North America, its 165 rolling acres include an Australian adventure featuring koalas, kangaroos, kookaburras, and kowaris (marsupial rats). The other residents hail from Asia (bears), Africa (giraffes), Chile (flamingos), and lots of other places (elephants, zebras, cheetahs, and more, oh my!). The indoor rain forest re-creates that vital but dwindling atmosphere and contains 600 animals and 10,000 plants from three continents. Additional draws are a seasonal exhibit of exotic butterflies, Waterfowl Lake, the Pachyderm Building, and others. Open daily except Christmas and New Year's. Admission is charged. (216) 661-6500; www.clemetzoo.com.

WHERE TO SHOP

Tower City Center. 230 West Huron Road, Cleveland, OH 44132. A former train depot, this $400 million downtown redevelopment project has 52 stories and 115 shopping, dining, and entertainment venues. Options range from Abercrombie & Fitch to WaldenBooks and include a Hard Rock Cafe and a cinema. Bonuses: a leapfrog fountain where water shoots up unexpectedly, an observation deck on the forty-second floor, and several parking lots. A fitness center and ampitheatre/performance space round out the offerings. (216) 771-0033 or 623-4750; www.towercitycenter.com.

Westside Market. 1995 West 25th Street and Lorain Avenue, Cleveland, OH 44113. On Mondays, Wednesdays, Fridays, and Saturdays an outdoor arcade and a vintage grand hall fill with more than 115 vendors. Hailing from all over the world, they peddle meat and dairy products, baked goods, fruits and vegetables, ethnic foods, and more. The building also has lots of nifty stone carvings of foodstuffs in doorways and interior arches. (216) 664-3387, www.westsidemarket.com.

Shaker Square. Corner of Shaker and Van Aken Boulevards. Mailing address: 11811 Shaker Boulevard, Room 206, Cleveland, OH 44120. Constructed in 1927, this historic spot is Ohio's first and the nation's second oldest shopping center and has been redeveloped, attracting purveyors such as Ann Taylor and upscale ethnic restaurants, all housed in classic Georgian-style architecture. Just 1 block north is Larchmere Boulevard, a mix of antiques shops, specialty boutiques, fine and folk art galleries, and more. (216) 421-2100.

Beachwood Place. 26300 Cedar Road, Beachwood, OH 44122. Located in a suburb on the east side of Cleveland, this is worth a few extra miles of driving, especially if you like upscale shopping. Saks Fifth Avenue, Nordstrom, the Galleries of Neiman Marcus, and Dillard's are but a few of the 150 options with which to max out your charge card. It's Beverly Hills with a change of seasons. (216) 464-9460; www.beachwoodplace.com.

Legacy Village. 23220 Chagrin Boulevard, Cleveland, OH 44122. Within spitting (well, almost) distance of Beachwood Place is this brand-new, self-proclaimed "lifestyle" center, which features many retailers and restaurants that will be breaking ground (and bread) in the area for the first time. Among the open-air fountain and bricked walkways you'll find Brio Tuscan Grille, Cheesecake Factory, California Pizza Kitchen, Flemming's Prime Steak House and Wine Bar, Expo Design Center, Crate & Barrel, Z Gallerie, Coldwater Creek, Anthropologie, and more. (216) 378-0066; www.legacy-village.com.

WHERE TO EAT

Nautica Queen **Cruise Dining Ship.** 1153 Main Avenue, Cleveland, OH 44113. Enjoy a lavish buffet in plush splendor while perusing Cleveland's ever-changing skyline. Afterward you can relax on the observation decks or see the sights from inside the ship. Cruises are from April through New Year's Eve. $$$. (800) 837–0604; www.nauticaqueen.com.

Watermark. 1250 Old River Road, Cleveland, OH 44113. This is one of the most popular seafood places in the Flats. Gourmet entrees, including fresh- and saltwater fish as well as beef and chicken, are served in a pre–Civil War shipping warehouse with open-beam ceilings and lots of natural light. Or you can chow down in the garden room, recently glassed-in for year-round use. $$–$$$. (216) 241–1600; www.watermark-flats.com.

Corbo's Golden Bowl. 12312 Mayfield Road, Cleveland, OH 44106. With entrees like stuffed scampi, sea bass and risotto, and more, plus salads, soups, and appetizers, this Little Italy staple lives up to its namesake cuisine. The garden is a favorite spot in warm weather, but be prepared to wait. $$–$$$. (216) 721–4850; www.corbos.com.

Great Lakes Brewing Company. 2516 Market Avenue, Cleveland, OH 44113. Located in Ohio City, this eatery is Cleveland's first micro-brewery and the first brewpub in the state since Prohibition ended. Solid food offerings range from beer-battered fish to pretzel chicken to pizza. A wide variety of salads and sandwiches, Stilton-cheddar cheese soup (also made with beer), and a gift shop and tours are other highlights. $$. (216) 771–4404; www.greatlakesbrewing.com.

Corky & Lenny's. 27091 Chagrin Boulevard, Cleveland, OH 44122. One of the few "real" (i.e., Kosher-style) delis in the state of Ohio, menu items range from traditional Jewish favorites like towering corned beef sandwiches, matzo ball soup, lox and eggs, outrageous desserts, and, of course, bagels. $$. (216) 464–3838.

WHERE TO STAY

The city offers a plethora of choices, from the Super 8 to the Ritz Carlton and beyond. In general, however, hotel and motel accom-modations are more expensive here than in the rest of the state, with even moderately priced rooms being in the $150 range. Below are some inns and bed-and-breakfasts that may be less costly.

Edgewater Estates. 9803–5 Lake Avenue, Cleveland, OH 44102. Located on the coast of Lake Erie, this remodeled, antique-filled 1910 English Tudor–style home is close to major attractions. You can enjoy the benefits of a big city in a room with a private bath and also get a full breakfast. $$–$$$. (216) 961–1764.

The Brownstone Inn. 3649 Prospect Avenue, Cleveland, OH 44115. This renovated and elegantly furnished Victorian Italianate town house is both an official Cleveland landmark and on the National Register of Historic Places. There's a choice of rooms (medium to large) and sherry or port in the evening. It's also centrally situated in midtown. $$–$$$. (216) 426–1753; www.brownstoneinndowntown.com.

The Glidden House. 1901 Ford Drive, Cleveland, OH 44106. This University Circle–based accommodation was originally constructed for the founder of the Glidden Paint Company in 1910; the family resided there until the early '50s. It's been restored to its original French Gothic grandeur and boasts a restaurant and light dining options. You can even chow down in the former library. Suites have a sitting room and wet bar. $$. (216) 231–8900; www.gliddenhouse.com.

Crest Bed & Breakfast. 1489 Crest Road, Cleveland, OH 44121. With antique-filled rooms and a shared bath, this lodging, on a residential tree-lined street, is ideal for families. Also included are a continental breakfast, a living room with a piano, and an afternoon glass of wine for those twenty-one and older. $$. (216) 382–5801.

Bourbon House. 6116 Franklin Boulevard, Cleveland, OH 44102. This Victorian-style home has retained much of its original ambience and includes an old-fashioned receiving room, a parlor with pump organ, and a large fireplace with window seats. Suites are available; the cost includes breakfast. There's a generous supply of books about Cleveland, and you can learn about the genealogy of European royal families from the innkeeper. $$–$$$. (216) 939–0535.

Granville · Hebron ·
Buckeye Lake · Utica

The village of Granville and surrounding area offer plenty of activities, from history to the outdoors. Along with shopping and dining, the friendliness of the natives and beautiful architecture make for a well-rounded excursion.

GRANVILLE

Founded in 1805, the quiet New England–style village of Granville was named by the folks who settled there from Granville, Massachusetts. Although it harks back to a simpler, slower era, it's got the added torque of a prestigious college in the form of Denison University (100 South Road, Granville 43023; 800–336–4766; www.denison.edu), which provides an upscale academic flavor thanks to professors, an ever-changing cast of students, and well-to-do alumni who love to visit.

About 30 miles from Columbus, Granville can be reached by going east on I-70 and getting off at exit 126, Granville-Lancaster (SR 37). Go north on SR 37 until you reach Broadway, then turn right into town.

WHERE TO GO

Robbins Hunter Museum. 221 East Broadway, Granville, OH 43023. Can you say toga? This 1842 Greek Revival home was built by

East Day Trip 1

Alfred Avery, one of Granville's founders. It's been added to over the years and was a private residence for various branches of the Avery family until 1903, when it was turned over—perhaps *turned loose* might be a better term—to the Phi Gamma Delta and Kappa Sigma fraternities. This lasted until 1956, when local historian Robbins Hunter purchased the property as a combination domicile and antiques business. Upon his death in 1979, it was converted to a museum and opened two years later. Although there's plenty of eighteenth- and nineteenth-century American and European furniture, paintings and sculptures, oriental rugs, and more, perhaps the truly amazing thing is that the home survived in decent condition. Open Tuesday through Sunday and by appointment; closed January through March. Depending on the program, donations may be required. (740) 587–0430.

Granville Life Style Museum. 121 Main Street, Granville, OH 43023. At minimum, this collection is a tribute to pack rats everywhere. Hubert and Oese Robinson, who lived in the home from 1918 until their respective deaths in 1960 and 1981, kept everything that four generations of the family owned. Some objects are accompanied by a photograph taken at the time of their use, but the real charm lies in the story as to how they obtained such an eclectic accumulation. Other standouts include Oese's garden, which is full of old-fashioned flowers; needlework and rose potpourri programs; and "Victorian Flirts" and "Victorian Undergarment" demonstrations, featuring attractive high school and college students, which undoubtedly bring in their fair share of male visitors. Open Sunday, mid-April through October, other times by appointment. Free. (740) 587–0373.

Granville Historical Society. 115 East Broadway, Granville, OH 43023. Dedicated to preserving the town's heritage and genealogy, this building—the oldest structure in Granville—houses pioneer collections dating from 1805. These include hand tools and furniture from early settlers, as well as an exhibit chronicling local agriculture. Open Friday through Sunday, April through October; other times by appointment. Donations are welcome. (740) 587–3951.

Alligator Mound. End of Bryn Du Drive, Granville, OH 43023. A gigantic sculpture of a four-footed creature made of mounded earth and small chunks of burned and broken rock, this structure was built by prehistoric Indians between 1200 and 800 B.C. Although it loosely resembles an alligator (hence its name), other guesses have ranged from opossum to panther to salamander. What it *isn't* is a burial ground. Open daily. Free.

The Granville Golf Course. 555 Newark-Granville Road, Granville, OH 43023. Designed in 1924 by course guru Donald Ross, this spot has been top-rated by *Golf Digest* and boasts fully irrigated tees, fairway, greens, and rough. You can hone your game with lessons or at the driving range and rent any necessary equipment. There's also a fully equipped pro shop for all those wild-looking pants and shirts, among many other items. Open year-round. Call for tee times and fees. (740) 587-4653; www.granvillegolf.com.

WHERE TO SHOP

Scrapbookery. 939 River Road, Granville, OH 43023. It's to "die" for: a $20,000 cutting center that allows you to create unique mementoes from hundreds of designs. Cashing in on the major trend of scrapbooking, this store offers equipment, supplies, and accessories as well as a sewing center and classes for all levels of skill. (740) 587-1555; www.scrapbookery.com.

Kussmaul Gallery and Flower Market. 140 East Broadway, Granville, OH 43023. Known among locals as the "Koos," this shop not only sells all kinds of flowers but also provides frame jobs of the picture kind. There's also a continuously changing array of jewelry, paintings, prints, and other objets d'art. (740) 587-4640; www.kussmaulgallery.com.

Greystone Country House. 128 South Main Street, Granville, OH 43023. Specializes in antiques and gifts, as well as other accessories that add that "country" touch. (740) 587-2243.

Granville Cherry Traditions. 1630 Columbus Road, Granville, OH 43023. Here you'll find antiques and art alongside period furniture. Refinishing is also available. (740) 587-3414.

River Road Coffee House. 935 River Road, Granville, OH 43023. An ideal spot for a shopping break, this emporium specializes in gourmet coffee and baked goods. (740) 587-7266.

WHERE TO EAT

Granville Inn. 314 East Broadway, Granville, OH 43023. This restaurant is a destination in itself. It has fine oak paneling, a copper-hooded fireplace, and colorful stained-glass windows. Menu items vary from full-course meals to light snacks, and the Sunday brunch buffet serves up something to please every palate. $$-$$$. (740) 587-3333; www.granvilleinn.com.

Buxton Inn. 313 East Broadway, Granville, OH 43023. With nifty dining rooms, a more casual tavern, and a beautiful porch area filled with greenery, this eatery has atmosphere to spare. You can choose from appetizers, soups, and salads, as well as more unusual fare like baby beef liver, coquille of seafood, wild mushroom stroganoff, and other gourmet and American offerings. $$-$$$. (740) 587-0001; www.buxtoninn.com.

Victoria's Olde Tyme Deli & Cafe. 134 East Broadway, Granville, OH 43023. A favorite of locals, this eatery specializes in soups, sandwiches, and other quick snacks. $-$$. (740) 587-0322.

Brew's. 128 East Broadway, Granville, OH 43023. Along with specialty beers and an upstairs that has free live music on weekends, big-screen TV, and a pool table, this restaurant offers a fun and diverse menu. You can choose from fried 'n' fattening starters, a wide assortment of salads and sandwiches, and pasta or pizza. $$. (740) 587-024; www.brewscafe.com.

WHERE TO STAY

Granville Inn. 314 East Broadway, Granville, OH 43023. Set amid tall, sheltering maples with a native sandstone exterior, this seems more like an English country house than a hotel. But the recently redecorated rooms have individual themes, along with modern amenities (yes, you can check your e-mail). Continental breakfast is included. (Note: If you try to book accommodations during Denison's fall Parents or Graduation Weekends, you're out of luck, unless you get picked by a lottery.) $$-$$$. (740) 587-3333; www.granvilleinn.com.

Buxton Inn. 313 East Broadway, Granville, OH 43023. Built in 1812 as a tavern to service a stagecoach crossing, the Buxton is Ohio's oldest operating lodging in an original building. Somewhere along the way, it also picked up a ghost or two. So, along with two-story porches, formal gardens, period antiques, and all the contemporary conveniences (including refrigerators and coffee/tea service) you might encounter a lost soul. Or not. $$. (740) 587-0001; www.buxtoninn.com.

Follett-Wright House. 430 East Broadway, Granville, OH 43023. This historic residence, constructed in 1860, offers two guest rooms with queen-size beds and private baths. Breakfast consists of Danish rolls, coffee cake, and other caloric comestibles. $$. (740) 587-0941.

Porch House. 241 East Maple Street, Granville, OH 43023. This turn-of-the-twentieth-century home with a large front porch provides quaint and charming guest rooms, each with private bath and air-conditioning. Breakfast is included; if you want an additional bed, you'll need to pay a nominal fee. $$. (800) 587-1995; www.porchhouse.com.

Fraley House. 257 Clouse Lane, Granville, OH 43023. This circa 1800s replica of a colonial home features four working fireplaces and many antiques as well as modern amenities like air-conditioning, swimming pool, and communal TV/VCR. A full breakfast is included, and there's a patio as well. $$. (800) 578-0611.

HEBRON

Ten miles from Granville, Hebron can be reached by driving south on SR 37, then east on old U.S. 40.

WHERE TO GO

Buckeye Central Scenic Railroad. Old U.S. 40, 2 miles east of SR 37. Mailing address: P.O. Box 61, Hebron, OH 43025. This picturesque ninety-minute trip through gently rolling central Ohio countryside is enhanced by a ride in vintage passenger coaches powered by an authentic diesel locomotive. Visitors can also explore the 1870s-era station, various types of operating equipment, three cabooses, a Chessie system, a C&O model, and others. Open Saturday and Sunday, Memorial Day through

October. Admission is charged. (740) 928-3827; www.buckeye centralrailroad.org.

Hebron State Fish Hatchery. 10517 Canal Road, Hebron, OH 43025. This site contains sixty surface acres of water and produces 3.5 million fish a year. Two and a half miles of nature trails provide a variety of bird-watching opportunities, to the tune of 250 species. Open Monday through Friday, year-round. Free. (740) 928-8092.

BUCKEYE LAKE

From Hebron, go a couple miles south on SR 79 (from I-70 east, take the SR 79 exit and go south) to reach Ohio's oldest state park.

WHERE TO GO

Buckeye Lake State Park. Mailing address: 2095 Liebs Island Road, Millersport, OH 43046. This natural pond started out as a salt spring that attracted deer and bison, making it popular among Native Americans in search of fast food. It later underwent an enlargement procedure by palefaces, who made it part of the Ohio-Erie Canal System. Today it offers a 32-mile shoreline and 3,800 surface acres for water-related recreational opportunities. Boating, swimming, fishing and hunting (in season only, and designated areas), and picnicking can be enjoyed here, but there are no overnight facilities. You can also visit Cranberry Marsh, an ancient bog, a remnant of Ohio's glacial period from more than 17,000 years ago. Open daily. (740) 467-2690; www.ohiostateparks.org.

WHERE TO EAT

Papa Boo's. 11356 Avondale Road, Thornville, OH 43076. This self-proclaimed "Lake Place" serves up a sense of humor along with bar food, sandwiches, sides, and pricier entrees. There's trivia, karaoke, and other regular entertainment, and the daily specials are a good deal. $$. (740) 928-2667; www.papaboos.com.

WHERE TO SHOP

Nautical & Nice. 4894 Walnut Road, Buckeye Lake, OH 43008. Located in a lighthouse, this store has a large assortment of original artwork, home decor, and gifts with a (but of course) nautical theme. Pictures, sculpture, tapestries, and other items share space with l'il lighthouses and wooden yard anchors. There's even a boat ramp for shopping sailors. (740) 928-0117 or (866) 928-0117; www.nautical andnice.com.

WHERE TO STAY

Buckeye Lake/Columbus East KOA. P.O. Box 972, Buckeye Lake, OH 43008. Take your pick: stay in your own camper, pitch a tent, or opt for one of fifteen "Kamping Kabins" equipped with beds, electricity, heat, and air-conditioning but no linens (bring your own). More than forty acres offers plenty of trees and open space along with access to three bathroom/shower facilities. $. (800) 562-0792.

UTICA

Although it's about 20 miles from Buckeye Lake, Utica is a straight shot north on SR 13.

WHERE TO GO

Ye Old Mill. 11324 SR 13, Utica, OH 43080. This is one sweet historic site. Built in 1817, the mill was a traditional gathering place and is now the home of a museum, ice cream parlor and restaurant, and picnic area owned by the Velvet Ice Cream Company. Originally one of the largest of its kind in the Ohio frontier, it was utilized as a gristmill and has been reconstructed, the last version being completed after the Civil War. The wide selection of flavors is also complemented by special events, such as an ice-cream festival and crafts. Open daily, May through October. Free. (800) 589-5000; www.velveticecream.com.

At the turn of the last century, factory worker J. W. Longaberger, who created baskets in his spare time while supporting a wife and twelve children, found his handiwork replaced by paper bags and plastic containers. In the early 1970s his fifth son, Dave, became convinced that consumers desired well-crafted items from a bygone era. He started hawking the hampers at $10 a pop, marketing them via direct sales associates. Soon Dave, who passed away in 1999, and his two grown daughters had woven themselves an $850 million a year company, the largest manufacturer of handmade baskets in the United States.

The venture pumped prosperity into Dave's economically depressed hometown of Dresden. The Longaberger family also played a key role in developing the village and surrounding area, funding schools, social services, and businesses. Dresden and environs have not only become a basket-lover's mecca but a major tourist draw, which includes the Longaberger Homestead in Frazeysburg.

The region itself is loaded with golf courses, recreational areas, and some of the best paths in Ohio. Walkers, bikers, joggers, and birders can go for miles and enjoy the topography, no matter what the season.

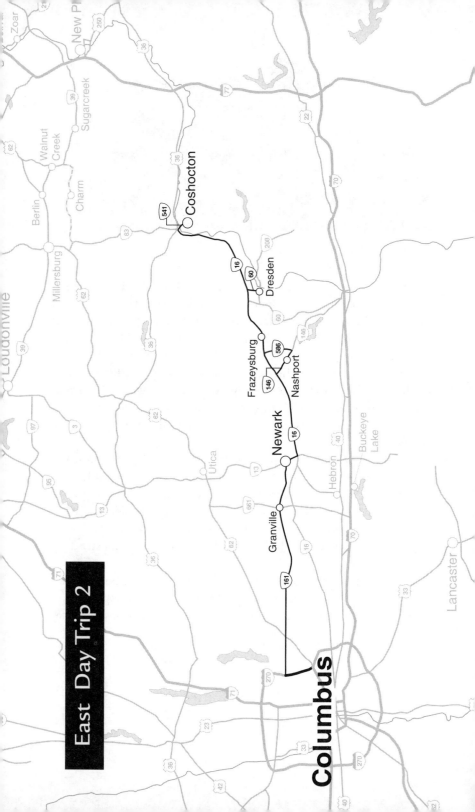

NEWARK

About an hour from downtown Columbus, Longaberger country is reached via I-270 to SR 161 east, which eventually turns into SR 16 about 6 miles west of Newark.

WHERE TO GO

Longaberger Home Office. 1500 East Main Street, Newark, OH 43055. You'll see this one coming and going: It's a seven-story basket that, rather than being the purveyor of a gargantuan picnic, contains employees who work in the corporate office. Along with receiving local and national media attention, the vast vessel boasts a 30,000-square-foot atrium, which provides a light, airy feel, and two 75-ton handles on the roof with heated humidity sensors to prevent the formation of ice. Much of the big basket's woodwork and trim was harvested and milled from Longaberger properties, keeping the construction within the family, so to speak. Inside are offices as well as educational tours and displays of company offerings. Ants are optional. Open daily except major holidays. Free. (740) 322–5000; www.longaberger.com.

Blackhand Gorge. 5213 Rock Haven Road SE, Newark, OH 43055. With 970 acres and an awesome, huge abyss cut by the Licking River, this is a *gorge*-ous experience, especially in the spring when wildflowers abound. Along with old locks of the Ohio and Erie River Canal and a tunnel of the Interurban railway, there's a 4.3-mile bike trail to explore, plus hiking, canoeing, and bird-watching. Open daily. Free. (614) 265–6495.

Dawes Arboretum. 7770 Jacksontown Road SE, Newark, OH 43056. Founded in 1929, this 9.5-mile stretch of greenery traverses accumulations of hollies, crab apples, rare trees, and horticulture. There's a Japanese garden, a nature center, and the Daweswood House museum, summer home of the family that donated the land, plus a variety of educational programs. A bonsai collection and bird-watching garden are other highlights. Should you forget the name of the place, it's spelled out in one of the world's largest lettered hedges. Open daily except Thanksgiving, Christmas, and New Year's. Free. (800) 443–2937; www.dawesarb.org.

The Great Circle Earthworks. 99 Cooper Avenue, Newark, OH 43055. Built by the Hopewell culture nearly 2,000 years ago, this earthwork is nearly 1,200 feet in diameter. Used as a ceremonial center and part of a larger system of such mounds, this is one of the few remaining remnants of prehistoric Ohio. Open Sunday through Wednesday, Memorial Day through Labor Day; weekends, Labor Day through October. Admission is charged. (800) 600–7174.

WHERE TO STAY

A Place Off the Square. 50 North Second Street, Newark, OH 43055. With 117 guest rooms, on-site shopping featuring Longaberger products, and an indoor swimming pool, this property mixes big-city luxury with small-town amenities. Full-service restaurant; continental breakfast included. $$–$$$. (740) 322–6455, www.longaberger.com.

Cherry Valley Lodge. 2299 Cherry Valley Road, Newark, OH 43055. This relaxing and elegant retreat offers 200 rooms, some with Jacuzzis; indoor and outdoor pools; exercise room; restaurant and lounge; game room; and more. Set on eighteen wooded acres, this is the only hotel in North America to claim its own arboretum. $$–$$$. (800) 788–8008; www.cherryvalleylodge.com.

NASHPORT

Down the road a ways is Nashport. Turn south on SR 146 from SR 16, about 10 miles east of Newark.

WHERE TO GO

Longaberger Golf Club. One Long Drive, Nashport, OH 43830. An avid duffer, Dave Longaberger hired architect Arthur Hills (really!) to design an eighteen-hole, par 72 course set amid rolling inclines, heavily wooded areas, and ponds. Named one of the "top ten you can play" in *Golf* magazine, the facility also offers a full-service clubhouse with grill room, a pro shop, and lockers, in addition to space for banquets, business meetings, and bar mitzvahs. Open daily. Greens fees. Call (740) 763–1100 to arrange tee times.

FRAZEYSBURG

Get back on SR 16 and go east about 10 more miles to get to Frazeysburg, where you can learn everything there is to know about baskets.

WHERE TO GO

Longaberger Homestead. 5565 Raiders Road, Frazeysburg, OH 43822. While Dad's out pretending to be Tiger Woods, the rest of the family can spend the day at the thirty-four-acre Longaberger Homestead. This multifaceted entertainment complex has shopping, eateries, classes, and special events. Decorating ideas can be found at Longaberger at Home, two stories of fully accessorized rooms that simulate an average house. Demonstrations provide suggestions as to how to best utilize the company's products, along with other innovations. Everything is for sale, of course. A replica of Dave Longaberger's family home and the original workshop where J. W. created baskets for farmers and potters are also found here. You might even run into Dave's brothers or sisters or another relative; the family is accessible and friendly and always willing to sign a basket or twelve. The kiddies will be amused in the Teddy Bear playroom, which is full of toys and activities. They can also hang out (figuratively and literally) at the life-size Tree House, or take short side trips to local points of interest. Open daily, except holidays. Free. (740) 322-5588.

    Crawford Barn. 5565 Raiders Road, Frazeysburg, OH 43822. Located within the Homestead complex, this barn was built in the 1890s and is one of the largest structures of its kind. Guests can learn about arts and crafts, ride in a hay wagon in the fall, try their feet at square dancing, and listen to reenacters describe growing up on a farm. Focus is on old-timey skills: wrought-iron products, pottery, rubber stamps, and the creation of pillows, rags, and chair pads. Then you can go for cow pies—ice cream, that is—at Flossie's or have a warm beverage at the Tea Garden. Open daily, except holidays. Free. (740) 322-5588.

    Manufacturing Campus. 5563 Raiders Road, Frazeysburg, OH 43822. Shuttles will take you from the Homestead to the nearby manufacturing campus. During the self-guided tour, employees demonstrate how baskets are woven and show a video on the production process. Then it's on to the glassed-in mezzanine with its bird's-eye view of the creation of thousands of baskets, an impressive if somewhat noisy sight. The next stop is the staining, quality assurance, and shipping departments, and then the school of basket-making. There are plenty of photo and shopping opportunities, and you might even get a chance to help put together a basket of your own. Open daily, but it's best to come before 1:00 P.M. on weekdays, the usual hours of production. Free. (740) 322–5588.

WHERE TO EAT

Heartland Deli. 5565 Raiders Road, Frazeysburg, OH 43822. A good place for a quick snack; specialties include salads, breakfast foods, and overstuffed sandwiches. The lemon almond chicken salad is a favorite. Located at the Homestead, in the Crawford Barn. $$. (740) 322–5588.

Longaberger Homestead Restaurant. 5565 Raiders Road, Frazeysburg, OH 43822. This is rapidly becoming a destination eatery for those searching for healthful, delicious, and reasonably priced home-cooked food. Along with the broasted chicken, salads, and a wide assortment of veggies, the fattening-but-worth-it category includes sweet country biscuits and homemade whipped potatoes. And then there's the apple basket: With warm apple slices, vanilla ice cream, and caramel sauce fenced in a waffle bowl, it's comfort food, Longaberger style. $$. (740) 322–5588.

Terrace Cafe. 5565 Raiders Road, Frazeysburg, OH 43822. The Italian menu includes antipasto salad, portabello-stuffed ravioli, and more. Entrees are served outside on the patio in nice weather, or you can eat inside. $$. (740) 322–5588.

DRESDEN

Now that you've bought your baskets, you'll need to accessorize, and Dresden is the place to do it. From Frazeysburg, take SR 16 east and go south on SR 60, a drive of approximately 15 minutes.

WHERE TO GO

World's Largest Basket. Corner of Fifth and Main Streets, Dresden, OH 43821. Now a misnomer, thanks to the behemoth bin in Newark, this 48-foot-long, 11-foot-wide, 23-foot-high structure with two swinging handles is still quite the conversation piece. Made from ten hardwood maple trees and requiring 2,000 hours of work, it was carted around to the Ohio State Fair, Columbus Convention Center, and Longaberger corporate offices before being set down permanently in the center of town. It's always open and available for photos, no matter what the weather.

WHERE TO SHOP

With more than fifty shops, this quasi-quaint village has everything from basket accessories and minutiae to crafts and collectibles; there's even an emporium devoted to rubber stamps (Basket-A-Stamps, 700 Main Street, 740-754-1544; www.basketastamps.com). Most stores are within walking distance of each other.

Aimee's. 622 East Main Street, Dresden, OH 43821. With basket liners, liner patterns, and protectors as well as socks, brushes, cookie cutters, sweatshirts, and basket-themed silver and gold jewelry, aficionados will barely be able to "contain" themselves. You can also order custom floral arrangements for your basket, and there's a wide selection of primitive and country accessories. (740) 754-6233; www.aimeesofdresden.com.

Olive Oyl's. 511 Main Street, Dresden, OH 43821. More than 300 baskets, along with tie-ons, basket stands and hangers, basket-themed shirts, canisters, and dishes can make choices difficult (what would Popeye's girlfriend do?). Cheesecake, gourmet coffee, umbrellas, and more are thrown into the mix as well. (740) 754-6778; www.oliveoyls.com.

Dresden Pottery. 721 Main Street, Dresden, OH 43821. One of the first shops to open due to the influence of Dave Longaberger, it carries American- and European-made pottery, Stevens linens, and all manners of collectibles. There's also basket jewelry in 14-karat gold, sterling, and pewter. (740) 754-3000; www.dresdenpottery.com.

The Patio Shops. 606 Main Street, Dresden, OH 43821. This basket-accessory mother ship not only offers products highlighted at the Longaberger Homestead but also peddles pewter items, apparel, collectible bears, and scented candles. (740) 754-2518.

WHERE TO EAT

Popeye's Soda Shop. 416 Main Street, Dresden, OH 43821. Oddly enough, this restaurant bears Dave Longaberger's childhood nickname, something most people might want to forget. But when he was alive, Dave loved the place and visited there often. And with good reason: Sandwiches, salads, and dinner entrees are served up in a spotless, fun '50s decor. Favorite menu items include onion rings, milk shakes, and red velvet cake. $$. (740) 754-5730.

WHERE TO STAY

Adams House Inn. 700 Main Street, Dresden, OH 43821. Built in 1835, this structure was the residence of Samuel B. Adams (no relation to the beer), a founding father of Dresden. It's been restored to its former splendor, with modern conveniences, of course. These include suites with private baths, kitchens, and verandas overlooking Main Street. $$. (800) 471-6621; www.adamshouseinn.com.

Hemlock House. 42 West Dave Longaberger Avenue, Dresden, OH 43821. Constructed in 1820, this former farm is one of the oldest homes in the area. It boasts large rooms with queen-size beds, private baths, and a quiet country setting that's a few blocks from shops and restaurants. The hosts, Jean and Tom Elliott, will regale you during breakfast with tales of and information about the town. $$. (740) 754-4422.

The Inn at Dresden. 209 Ames Drive, Dresden, OH 43821. With only ten spaces, this lodging reinvents the concept of intimate (it had originally been designed for corporate guests of Longaberger). Each room has its own theme, from "City Lights" to "Hideaway." Extras include kitchenettes, hot tubs, fireplaces, and private deck, plus a full breakfast with evening snacks and desserts. $$–$$$. (800) 373-7336; www.theinnatdresden.com.

Mollies Rock B&B. 1505 Mollies Rock Road, Dresden, OH 43821. With proprietors who name the rooms after their daughters, this lodging has to be run with deep devotion. Accommodations are spacious and have private baths, and a fitness facility, tanning bed, several decks, and a screened porch are available. $$. (740) 754-9195 or (866) 245-5433; www.molliesrock.com.

Sarah's House on Main. 1015 Main Sreet, Dresden, OH 43821. Located within walking distance of beautiful downtown Dresden, this four-bedroom house was built circa 1860. Today it boasts four rooms with private baths, air-conditioning, and a full breakfast. $$. (740) 754-2097; www.sarahshouse.com.

COSHOCTON

Just 15 minutes northeast of Dresden, Coshocton can be reached by taking SR 16 north (which turns into SR 83) and going east on SR 541.

WHERE TO GO

Roscoe Village. 381 Hill Street, Coshocton, OH 43812. Feeling buried in baskets? Near the junction of U.S. 36 east and SR 83 is a bit of living history. The storied and lovingly restored streets and buildings of this former canal town provide a taste of nineteenth-century Ohio. Costumed interpreters, a village smithy, an 1800s printing press, and a one-room schoolhouse add to the authenticity. Open daily except Thanksgiving, Christmas, and New Year's. Admission is charged. (800) 877-1830; www.roscoevillage.com.

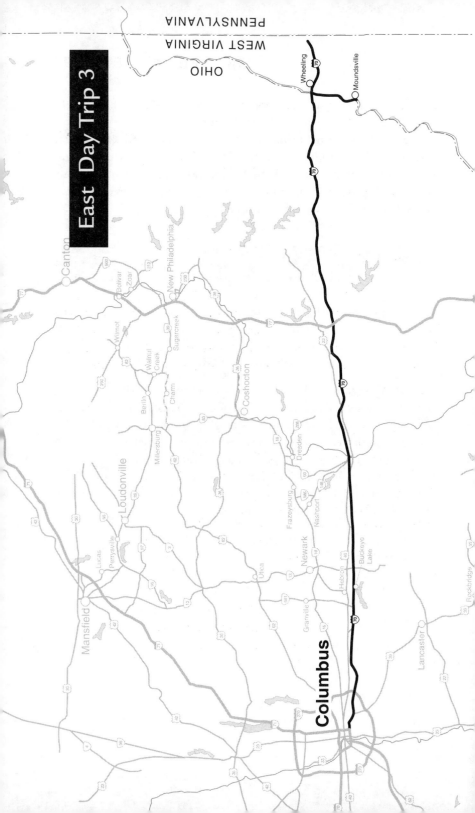

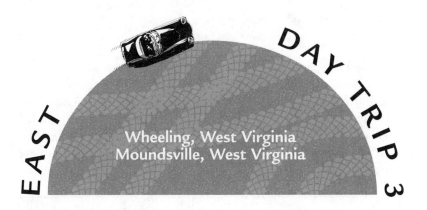

Wheeling, West Virginia
Moundsville, West Virginia

WHEELING

Wheeling, West Virginia, has a little bit of everything: gambling, culture, sports activities, shopping, and more. It calls itself the Friendly City—as opposed to Rude Town, which could be any number of places—and is manageable to navigate, despite the plethora of activities. If you go during the holiday season (Thanksgiving to New Year's), you are treated to a Christmas light show of dazzling proportions put on by both the city and Oglebay Resort and Conference Center. A candy cane wreath, dinosaur den, polyhedron star, and more brilliant works of art should bring a smile to even the most insurgent Scrooges.

Settled in 1769, Wheeling was established as a city in 1836 and, with its abundance of coal and natural gas, developed into a manufacturing and commercial center producing steel, chemicals, ceramics, glass, and textiles. Located on the site of a 1774 fort, it also became the western terminus for the National Road.

From Columbus, Wheeling is about 125 miles, a straight shot east on I-70. Cross the Ohio River and you're there. You can also explore a 150-year-old suspension bridge off Tenth Street, (1 block south of the I-70 overpass) that for many years was Wheeling's link to the rest of the world.

WHERE TO GO

Wheeling Island Race Track and Gaming Center. 1 South Stone Street, Wheeling, WV 26003. Those looking for some "reel" (aka slot

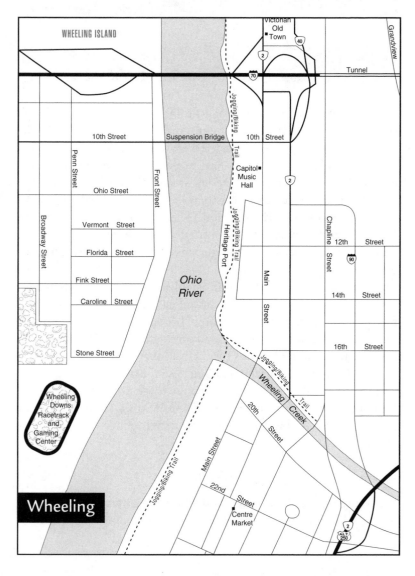

machine) excitement need search no further. "Drop in a coin, pull the handle, and wait for the sound of coins dropping," states the brochure. Well, at least the first two will happen. Keno, video blackjack, and poker are also offered, and the facility recently added 30,000 square feet of gaming space and a hotel, among other amenities. Along with a simulcast parlor that allows participants to wager on various televised racing events, there's also live greyhound racing

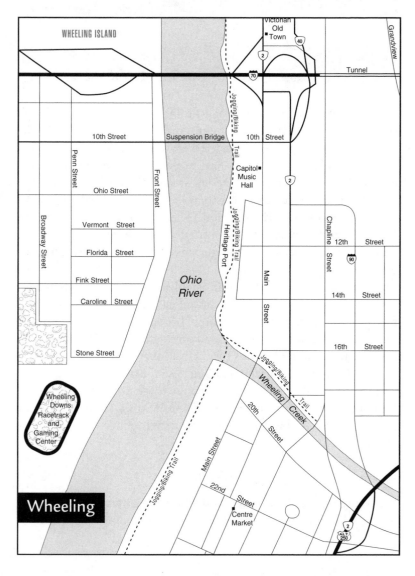

six days a week. Call ahead or check the Web site for the schedule. Open daily. Free, if you resist putting in that first quarter. (800) 946-4373; www.wheelingdowns.com.

Oglebay Resort and Conference Center. Route 88 North, Wheeling, WV 26003. This is one massive resort/park. Its 1,650 acres encompass tennis, fishing, and swimming; three golf courses, including one designed by Robert Trent Jones and another from Arnold Palmer; full formal gardens; a science lab and theater; horse stables and riding; even a zoo. There's a mansion and glass museum (see below), along with a train ride. And that's in addition to the usual accommodations and cottages (see Where to Stay), shopping, and dining. Open daily. Admission is charged. (800) 624-6988; www.oglebay-resort.com.

Mansion & Glass Museums. Oglebay Resort, Route 88 North, Wheeling, WV 26003. Originally built in 1846, this was a farmhouse that grew up into a mansion. It went through seven owners before being purchased by the Oglebay family, who made it their summer estate. Inside it's furnished with antiques as well as early pioneer furniture and Wheeling artifacts. The Glass Museum contains arguably the world's largest collection of glass manufactured in Wheeling, including pieces by such artisans and manufacturers as Sweeney, Hobbs-Brockunier, Central, and Northwood. A standout is a mammoth Sweeney punch bowl. There are also glassblowing and decorating demonstrations. Open daily. Admission is charged. (304) 242-7272.

Henry Stifel Schrader Environmental Education Center. Oglebay Resort, Route 88 North, Wheeling, WV 26003. This entity focuses on environmental education. The building itself is a lesson in ecology, as it was constructed using earth-friendly products and processes. An EarthTrek exhibit hall, nature art gallery, bird observation area, children's awareness room, and forest canopy walkway round out the offerings. You can also explore 3-mile or 5-mile trail systems, observing waterfalls, birds, and other wildlife; and visit gardens consisting of butterfly-attracting landscaping, plants, and herbs. Open daily. Depending on activity, admission may be charged. (304) 242-6855.

West Virginia Independence Hall. 1528 Market Street, Wheeling, WV 26003. The completion of this structure coincided with the start of the Civil War, which presented a real pickle for local leaders, who were hotly divided on the issue of slavery. What resulted was the independent state of West Virginia (seceded from Virginia), which sided with the Union. Displays, restored architecture and furnishings, and costumed guides provide insight into America's most divisive war. Open daily, except state holidays; closed Sunday in January and February. Admission is charged. (304) 238–1300.

Eckhart House Tours. 810 Main Street, Wheeling, WV 26003. Before the Civil War, Wheeling was the second largest city in Virginia, and it continued to prosper for nearly three decades afterward. Thus it became a draw for the wealthy and successful, who built stately Victorian abodes. You can tour four of these, three owned by the Victorian Wheeling Landmarks Foundation, and the Eckhart House, which, with its hand-painted florals, pocket doors, Queen Anne windows, ornate chandeliers, and more, was built to impress. Open Saturday and Sunday, May through December, other times by appointment. Admission is charged. (888) 700–0118; www.eckharthouse.com.

Kruger Street Toy & Train Museum. 144 Kruger Street, Wheeling, WV 26003. What a combo: More than 100,000 toys 'n' trains housed in a restored Victorian school. Standouts include the circa 1963 "Big Loo" Robot, with battery-powered eyes, a crank-operated voice, and Ping-Pong ball firing capability; a Disney Carry-All Dollhouse from 1972; and an amazing collection of trucks. And those are only the playthings manufactured by the Marx company, which had a plant near Wheeling from the 1930s until the '70s. Hours vary. Admission is charged. (877) 242–8133; www.toyand train.com.

WHERE TO SHOP

Eckhart House Victorian Gift Shoppe. 810 Main Street, Wheeling, WV 26003. This is the place to go for Victorian memorabilia. You'll find dolls, florals, candles, stained glass, prints, and lamps, to mention but a few. (888) 700–0118.

Antiquitus Jewelers. 1010 National Road, Wheeling, WV 26003. Authentic antique jewelry ranges from micromosaics and cameos to mourning pieces and Edwardian designs. Plenty of estate and costume trinkets are also available. (304) 232–3488; www.antiquitus.com.

Wheeling Artisan Center. Fourteenth and Main Streets, Wheeling, WV 26003. Handcrafted creations by West Virginia and regional artists encompass pottery, jewelry, fabric arts, woodworking, and more. Plus there's a great selection of West Virginia glass and food products and historic souvenirs in a restored building. (304) 232-1810.

Antiques on the Market. 2265 Market Street, Wheeling, WV 26003. This three-story multidealer antiques mall is located in Historic Centre Market. Antiques from the nineteenth and twentieth centuries include glassware, art pottery, furniture, jewelry, quilts, linens, and accessories. (304) 232-1665.

Hughes Gift Gallery. 600 National Road, Wheeling, WV 26003. Along with design services and even gift wrapping, this store proffers baby items, dinnerware, jewelry, lamps, furniture, stationary, floral arrangements, and accessories. Displays of The Thymes, Crane's Fine Papers, and Vera Bradley share space with products from Chelsea House, Faith Walk Designs, GuildMaster, Mariposa, Mesa International, and more. (304) 232-2424; hughesdsgn.com.

Nini's Treasures. 8 Hyde Park Drive, Wheeling, WV 26003. This is definitely a "chic(k)" store: They claim to have the largest selection of Brighton products in the state, along with clothing by designers from California, New York, and Miami; unique jewelry and watches; and hats, purses, wallets, scarves, sunglasses, belts, and more. (304) 232-6464.

WHERE TO EAT

Ernie's Esquire Restaurant and Lounge. 1055 East Bethlehem Boulevard, Wheeling, WV 26003. Open since 1956, this fine-dining establishment specializes in fish, beef, lamb, veal, pasta, and more. Steaks are cut to order, the seafood's guaranteed fresh, and some entrees are prepared tableside. Plus, there's entertainment on weekends, harking back to the days of supper clubs. $$-$$$. (304) 242-2800.

Generations Pub at the Swing Club. 338 National Road, Wheeling, WV 26003. Owned and operated since 1914 by four generations of the Duplaga family, this eatery offers three meals, seven days a week. Appetizers, sandwiches, salads, burgers, ribs, chops, and other items are on the menu. Plus, there are eight TVs if conversation ever becomes a problem, along with a game room, outdoor deck, and entertainment. $$. (304) 232–7917.

Uncle Pete's. 753 Main Street, Wheeling, WV 26003. Ideal for those who like casual dining with a view of the river. What's cooking is wings, hoagies, and other daily specials as well as the three S's: soups, salads, and sandwiches. $–$$. (304) 234–6701.

River City Ale Works. 1400 Main Street, Wheeling, WV 26003. Located in the Wheeling Artisan Center, the state's largest brewpub features a wide variety of handcrafted beers along with a varied menu. $$. (304) 233–4555.

WHERE TO STAY

Wilson Lodge (Oglebay). Route 88 North, Wheeling, WV 26003. With 212 rooms and suites, an indoor pool, Jacuzzi, sauna, fitness facility, and even a tanning bed and in-room massage, this is the area's most popular accommodation. So if you want to stay here, be sure to make reservations early. $$–$$$. (800) 624–6988; www.oglebay-resort.com.

Cottages at Oglebay Resort. Route 88 North, Wheeling, WV 26003. Ideal for families or larger groups, these cottages have all the usual amenities from color TV to air-conditioning, yet provide additional privacy. You're expected to keep the place clean, as daily maid service is not included. $$–$$$. (800) 624–6988.

Ramada Plaza City Center Hotel (formerly the McClure House). 1200 Market Street, Wheeling, WV 26003. Before its present incarnation as a Ramada, this was the area's oldest functioning hotel. It contained a watering trough and hitching post for horses, and registration was on the second floor because the first was a muddy mess due to travelers. Today, it has all the goodies you'd expect from a full-service hotel: central location, restaurants, free parking, gift shops, room service, and more. $$–$$$. (866) 223–9330.

Stratford Springs. Oglebay Drive, Wheeling, WV 26003. Situated on thirty acres of rolling, wooded hills, this bed-and-breakfast is listed on the National Register of Historic Places. It offers tennis, swimming, and more, in addition to a restaurant that's a heavy local and tourist draw. $$–$$$. (304) 233–5100.

Bonnie Dwaine Bed & Breakfast. 505 Wheeling Avenue, Glen Dale, WV 26038. Located 7 miles south of Wheeling in Glen Dale (junction of State Routes 2 and 86), this lodging has amenities ranging from a fireplace to a whirlpool tub/shower in each room to a candlelight gourmet breakfast in the formal dining room. Decorwise, you can choose from romantic Victorian, cozy country, classic charm, or a honeymoon suite. $$-$$$. (888) 507-4569; www. Bonnie-Dwaine.com.

MOUNDSVILLE

About 12 miles from Wheeling, Moundsville can be reached by taking SR 2 south from I-70 or I-470.

WHERE TO GO

The Official Marx Toy Museum. 915 Second Street, Moundsville, WV 26041. Among some age groups, these toys were more popular than the movie brothers by the same name. From 1919 to 1980, Louis Marx & Co. was one of the largest toy manufacturers in the world. A short distance from the original factory, this museum provides blasts from the past for several generations—metal toys and trains, dollhouses, Army figures, Johnny West figures, Big Wheels, and more. Original footage of a factory tour and a series of black-and-white commercials from the 1950s may trigger memories. Open Thursday through Saturday, April through December. Admission is charged. (304) 845-6022; www.marxtoymuseum.com.

Grave Creek Mound Historic Site. 801 Jefferson Avenue, Moundsville, WV 26041. The creation of the largest of the Adena burial mounds required the movement of more than 60,000 tons of earth. The mound was constructed from about 250 to 150 B.C. Artifacts and exhibits interpreting the lifestyle of the Adena people are displayed at the adjacent Delf Norona Museum. The museum also features a gift shop, theater, and a gallery with fine art. Open daily. Admission is charged. (304) 843-4128.

Prabhupada's Palace of Gold. RD 1 NBU# 24, Moundsville, WV 26041. OK, so it's not really gold, but it's close enough: An ornate exterior with thirty-one stained-glass windows, crystal chandeliers, and mirrored ceilings is set amid lush gardens, sculptures, and water fountains. Fifty-two varieties of marble and onyx were imported for floors and walls, and furniture is carved teakwood from India. You can stay one day or several and hang out with the members of the religious order who built the palace as a tribute to Srila Prabhupada, a prolific proponent of Eastern arts and culture. Open year-round. Admission is charged. (304) 843–1812.

West Virginia Penitentiary Tours. 818 Jefferson Avenue, Moundsville, WV 26041. Here's a chance to "do time" without actually breaking the law. Options include a ninety-minute tour and monthly "ghost hunts," which involve spending the night (a perhaps ideal deterrent for criminals-in-training). With towering walls and an imposing brick exterior, this ten-acre Civil War–era facility served as a maximum security prison for more than 120 years. Open daily, except Monday, April through November; other times by appointment. Admission is charged. (304) 845–6200; www.wvpentours.com.

Logan · Rockbridge

Few locales can claim beauty year-round, but the Hocking Hills are such a place. Winding roads reveal frozen waterfalls and pristine snow in the winter; verdant, leafy coolness and gushing gorges in the summer; a riotous palette in fall so dazzling that one hardly knows where to look first; and dewily abundant flowers, trees, and wildlife in spring. Although quaint and casually structured towns such as Logan seem out of step with today's frantic pace, they fit in with the Hills' slower tempo. So turn off the cell phone, computer, pager, and electronic organizer and explore what nature had in mind during Earth's early years.

LOGAN

Located about 60 miles from downtown Columbus, Logan and the Hocking Hills can be reached in about an hour and fifteen minutes, depending on traffic, by going east and south on SR 33 from I-270. Many of the local roads are winding and narrow, however, so allow extra time for travel when visiting various sites.

WHERE TO GO

Hocking Hills State Park. 20160 SR 664, Logan, OH 43138. This mother of all parks boasts several main attractions (see below) and was forged from sandstone and shales deposited more than 350 million years ago. Terrain ranges from the soft, loosely cemented

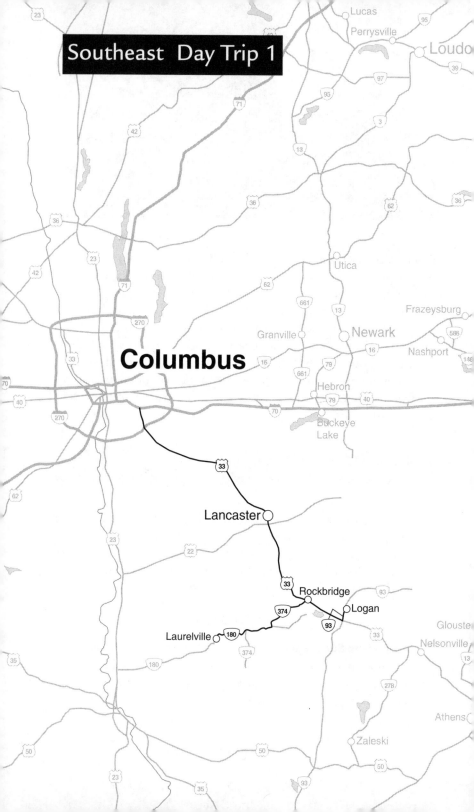

grainlike dirt found in Ash Cave to razor-sharp hard layers at Cantwell Cliffs. The effect of the glaciers can still be felt in certain regions of the park that have retained a moist, cool environment. Hours vary; some portions may be open seasonally. Free. (740) 385-6841; www.ohiostateparks.org.

- **Old Man's Cave.** The most well-trodden of all the Hocking sites, this area has deep-cut gorges, impressive waterfalls, and in one section, a 150-foot-thick slice of rock that allows visitors to look into the earth's subsurface. In the late 1700s and early 1800s, it was also inhabited by two brothers, then by an elderly hermit, all of whom are buried there. Although recently renovated, the trails still require climbing and are a honeycomb of rocks and carved steps.

- **Ash Cave.** The largest recess of its kind in the state—700 feet from end to end and 100 feet deep—this cave is surrounded by hemlocks, beech trees, and hardwoods, as well as wildflowers. Named after the ashes found by the original settlers, it remains in use today for various gatherings, thanks to excellent acoustics and handicapped accessibility. Pulpit Rock, at the entrance, was once used for Sunday worship, and there's a spectacular water geyser toward the back.

- **Rock House.** The only "true" cave in the park, this natural phenomenon consists of a 200-foot-long, 25-foot-wide tunnel-like passage with a 25-foot-high "ceiling." Man-made additions like water troughs and nooks for cooking can also be found. Native Americans, explorers, and even horse thieves and bootleggers camped here; at one point it had the nickname "Robber's Roost."

- **Cantwell Cliffs.** Located in the more remote northern area of the park, these cliffs have narrow passages (one of which is called the politically incorrect "Fat Woman's Squeeze"), deep valleys, and a rock shelter underneath. The varied and colorful terrain is accented by reddish brown sandstone and commanding views.

- **Cedar Falls.** What a misnomer: Early settlers mistook the surrounding hemlock trees for cedars. The most voluminous waterfall in the Hocking Region, it was once harnessed for power by a mill to produce grain. Cedar Falls remains one of the park's most picturesque sites and boasts a well-tended picnic area.

- **Conkles Hollow.** This rugged, rocky gorge is considered the steepest around. Ferns and wildflowers carpet the floor of the valley, while birch, hemlock, and other hardwoods dominate the top portion.

Lake Logan State Park. 30443 Lake Logan Road, Logan, OH 43138. This prime fishing hole offers pike, bass, bluegill, crappie, catfish, and more. Swimming and boating are other options; those who prefer dry land will find scenic picnic areas, secluded walking paths, and lots of plant and animal wildlife. Open daytime only. Free. (740) 385-6842; www.ohiostateparks.org.

Hocking Canoe Liveries. Both of the following offer canoe, kayak, and raft rentals in addition to organized trips, from a few hours to overnight, depending on skill level and preference. Specialized excursions can be tailored toward various spots in the Hocking Hills

- **Hocking Hills Canoe Livery.** 12789 Route 664 South, Logan, OH 43138. Open April through October. Fee is charged. (800) 634-6820 and (740) 385-0523; www.hockingriver.com.
- **Hocking Valley Canoe Livery.** 31251 Chieftain Drive, Logan, OH 43138. Open during the season; call for dates and times. Fee is charged. (800) 686-0386; www.canoerental.com.

Stone Valley Ranch. 31606 Fairview Road, Logan, OH 43138. Geared toward new riders and families with children, participants can explore the Hocking Hills area as well as a bit farther afield at Wayne National Forest and Zaleski State Forest. Private trails on 480 acres are also available. Open daily. Fee is charged. (800) 866-5196; www.hockinghillshorses.com.

WHERE TO SHOP

Artisan Mall. 703 West Hunter Street, Logan, OH 43138. The first floor offers handmade crafts; homemade jellies, candy, and other foodstuffs; and gift items and souvenirs. Antiques, Amish-made oak furniture, and other collectibles can be found on the lower level. (740) 385-1118; www.artisanmall.com.

Logan Antique Mall. 12795 SR 664 South, Logan, OH 43138. This spot has everything from advertising memorabilia to cookie jars, from military items to Victorian collectibles. More than eighty dealers can be found in a 10,000-square-foot retail space; a reference library and black light are available for verification of authenticity. (740) 385-2061; www.loganantiquemall.com.

Great Expectations. 179 South Market Street, Logan, OH 43138. A bookstore with an old-fashioned flair, this enterprise offers a wide variety of current and children's literature as well as used books. Individual selections are displayed on tables and shelves, rather than being arranged in piles on large racks. Jewelry, handblown glass, pottery, and other crafts are also for sale. (740) 380–9177.

Wind Chime Shop. 29205 Ilesboro Road, Logan, OH 43138. This array, arguably the largest in the state, should ring a bell with anyone who likes tinklers. Offerings include forty-five different lines of chimes, with an running inventory of almost 2,000. (740) 385–9537; www.windchimeshopsales.com.

WHERE TO EAT

Those willing to wander a bit more might do well to check out the diverse and excellent cuisine in Athens, 2.5 miles southeast via U.S. 33 (see Southeast Day Trip 2).

Great Expectations Cafe. 179 South Market Street, Logan, OH 43138. Here you'll find panini sandwiches and an espresso bar in a casual atmosphere. Other selections include salads, smoothies, and desserts with such enticing names as Lively Lemon Berry Bash and Milkyway Cheesecake. $. (740) 380–9177.

Olde Dutch Restaurant. 12819 SR 664 South, Logan, OH 43138. This eatery offers something for everyone: Amish-style dinners, full dinner menu, sandwiches, a weekend breakfast buffet, and children's and seniors' selections. Specialties include broasted chicken as well as variations of same, along with turkey, pork, ham, and your basic spaghetti and meatballs. $$. (740) 785–1000; www.oldedutch.com.

WHERE TO STAY

Dozens of bed-and-breakfast, cabin, lodge, and camping options abound. The Hocking Hills Tourism Association (13178 SR 664 South, Logan, OH 43138; 800–462–5464) can provide a complete listing, which is also found at www.1800hocking.com.

Ravenwood Castle. 65666 Bethel Road, New Plymouth, OH 45654. From Logan and U.S. 33, take SR 93 south about 14 miles. Travel back in time to medieval England at this one-of-a-kind lodging that has all the comforts of the twenty-first century. You can opt for a room or suite in the main castle (the Sherwood Forest complete with "trees," a "dungeon" with a chain-link lighting fixture, and so forth) or motif cottages. Full breakfast included; special English-themed programs and weekend packages available. $$–$$$. (800) 477–1541; www.ravenwoodcastle.com.

The Inn at Cedar Falls. 21190 SR 374, Logan, OH 43138. Choose from antique-laden rooms or secluded 1840s cabins, all refurbished with modern amenities but lacking telephones and televisions. Gourmet meals are served in a nineteenth-century double log house or outside on the patio during clement weather, with many ingredients grown on-site. A cookbook and cooking classes are also available. $$–$$$. (800) 653–2557; www.innatcedarfalls.com.

Bear Run Inn—Cabins and Cottages. 8260 Bear Run Road, Logan, OH 43138. This B&B/cabin combo has a five-person hot tub, private fishing ponds, and 500 acres where deer, rabbit, and turkey—but no bear—roam. Continental breakfast included. $$–$$$. (800) 369–2937; www.bearrun.com.

ROCKBRIDGE

Rockbridge is actually closer to Columbus and can be reached from Logan by going north on U.S. 33 about 10 miles. It's a nice place to tarry on the way back.

WHERE TO GO

Clear Creek Metro Park. 99935 Possum Hollow Road, Rockbridge, OH 43139. Located at U.S. 33 and CR 114 (Clear Creek Road), this park offers 5,000 acres of hickory, oak, mesophytic, and bottomland forests mixed with rugged valleys, ridges, and sandstone cliffs. More than 800 flowering plants have been identified, including many that are rare or endangered in Ohio, and some forty species of ferns. Other unnatural habitats are a nesting trail for prairie warblers, which are typically indigenous to Canada, and fly- (in more ways than one) fishing for trout in steep, cold-water gorges. Open daily. Free. (740) 385–1834; www.metroparks.net.

Hocking State Forest. 19275 SR 374, Rockbridge, OH 43149. These 9,000 acres consist of sandstone cliffs, waterfalls, birch, and hemlock in addition to abandoned homesites and fallow corn, wheat, and hay fields, all of which date from the 1800s. Although the park is managed for plant and animal habitat, forestry research, and nursery seed and soil protection, certain areas are available for rock climbing, rappelling, hunting, fishing, hiking, and horseback riding. Open daily. Free. (740) 385-4402.

Happy Trails Horseback Rides. 25851 Big Pine Road, Rockbridge, OH 43149. Along with exploring many sites at Hocking Hills State Park, visitors will get an up close and personal view of lesser-known caves, waterfalls, and rock formations. Trails are available for beginners, intermediates, and experts. Open Monday, Tuesday, Thursday, Saturday, and other times by arrangement. Fee is charged. (740) 380-6372; www.hthorsebackrides.com.

Spotted Horse Ranch. 17325 Deffenbaugh Road, Laurelville, OH 43135. Located off SR 180, this facility is BYOH (bring your own horse), or one can be supplied. Along with trail treks and cattle drives, supervised corral rides for young children are also available. There's a lighted outdoor arena as well as campgrounds and cabin. Call for reservations. Fee is charged. (877) 992-7433; www.thespottedhorse ranch.com.

WHERE TO EAT

Shaw's Restaurant and Inn. 123 North Broad Street, Lancaster, OH 43130. This destination eatery is located about 20 miles north on U.S. 33 in Lancaster. A great place to dine on your way home, it has been recommended by the Zagat Survey, Mobil Guide, *Wine Spectator,* and AAA. The menu changes daily, but specialties include ribs, steaks, fresh fish flown in from Boston, chicken, pasta, and more. $$-$$$. (800) 654-2477.

Grouse Nest Restaurant. 25780 Liberty Hill Road, South Bloomingville, OH 43152. The menu changes seasonally with gourmet selections ranging from barbecue chicken quesadillas to white bean chili to peach-glazed pork. Pasta, seafood, and vegetarian items are also offered, and in nice weather, you can eat on the patio outside. $$-$$$. (800) 222-4655; www.ashcave.com.

WHERE TO STAY

Thunder Ridge Cabins Bed & Breakfast. 11309 Starner Road, Rockbridge, OH 43149. Visitors can relax in luxurious one-room cabins with gourmet breakfasts served in the main house. Each accommodation has a kitchen with microwave and table for those wishing to prepare their own meals; there's also a communal fire pit for star gazing and marshmallow roasts. $$-$$$. (800) 600-0584.

Ash Cave Cabins. 25780 Liberty Hill Road, South Bloomingville, OH 43152. Located between Rockbridge and Logan, off SR 664. Guests can choose from cozy "love bug" cabins with TV/VCR, charcoal grills, balconies, and gas fireplaces, or larger, secluded vacation homes that are ideal for groups or families. Special programs, such as photography weekends, are also offered. Breakfast is available and there's a full gourmet restaurant on-site. $$$. (800) 222-4655; www.ashcave.com.

Glenlaurel Inn. 14940 Mt. Olive Road, Rockbridge, OH 43149. This could go under the classification "expensive, but worth it," especially for those looking to rekindle or ignite a relationship. Set on 140 acres that more closely resemble Scotland than mid-Ohio, this accommodation offers several choices of rooms, cottages, hot tubs, and fine dining packages. Wooded walking trails, rock cliffs and waterfalls, and the Inn's old-world elegance are designed to restore whatever sanity might have been lost in everyday living. $$$. (800) 809-7378; www.glenlaurel.com.

Nelsonville · Athens · Glouster

OK, so it's not New York City or even Dayton, but Athens County has a lot going on for an area of its size and population. Along with a truly diverse array of restaurants and some interesting shopping, there's Ohio University (no street address, just Athens, OH 45701; 740-593-1000; www.ohiou.edu), a highly rated academic institution with a reputation for partying hearty. Several beautiful parks can also be found amid the green, gently rolling Appalachian foothills.

NELSONVILLE

Nelsonville is a straight shot southeast on U.S. 33, about 67 miles from Columbus, halfway between Logan and Athens.

WHERE TO GO

Hocking Valley Scenic Railway. 33 Canal Street, Nelsonville, OH 45764. This train, made from bits and pieces of historical locomotives, runs round-trip from Nelsonville to Haydenville or East Logan. The Haydenville excursion takes around an hour and a half and is 14 miles long; the East Logan circuit is longer (22 miles, two and a half hours). Both include a stop at Robbins Crossing, a restored pioneer village in Nelsonville "populated" by Hocking College students who are being trained as historical interpreters. And you thought these people were just extremely well preserved. Open Saturday and

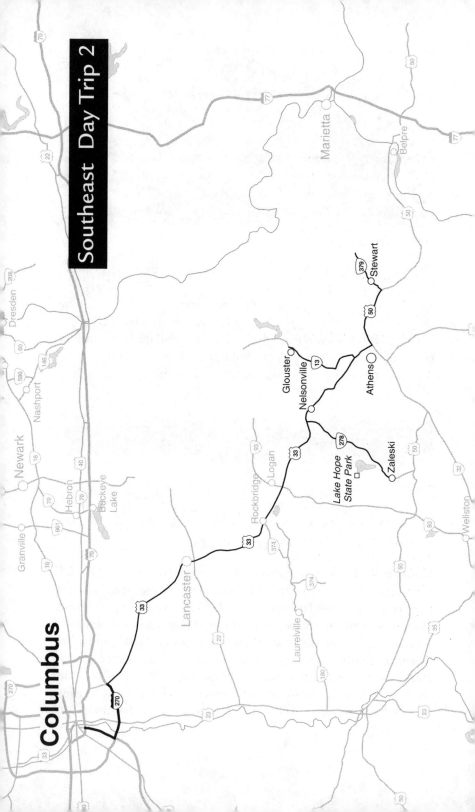

Southeast Day Trip 2

Columbus

Marietta

Belpre

Stewart

Athens

Glouster

Nelsonville

Zaleski

Lake Hope State Park

Rockbridge

Logan

Lancaster

Laurelville

Wellston

Newark

Hebron

Buckeye Lake

Granville

Nashport

Dresden

Sunday, Memorial Day through mid-November. Admission is charged. (800) 967–7834; www.hvsr.com.

Stuart's Opera House. 34 Public Square, Nelsonville, OH 45764. This second-story theater—storerooms are at street level—was constructed in 1879 with handmade bricks from local surface clay. Originally home to melodrama, vaudeville, medicine shows, comedies, and assorted musicals, it has been renovated recently. Hours and performances vary. Admission is charged. (740) 753–1924.

Lake Hope State Park. 27331 SR 278, McArthur, OH 45651. Take SR 278 south from U.S. 33 in Nelsonville. This rugged, heavily forested region offers steep gorges, constricted ridges, and unique sights such as ancient Indian burial mounds and abandoned mines. Formerly the site of an iron-smelting industry, much of the land has reclaimed its original topography. Reminders of the Civil War–era endeavor can be found in the few standing remains of the Hope Furnace. Hiking, horseback riding, nature programs, camping, swimming, and boating are also available. Open daily. Free. (740) 596–5253; www.ohiostateparks.org.

Zaleski State Forest. P.O. Box 330, SR 278, Zaleski, OH 45698. Just west and directly adjoining Lake Hope is the Zaleski State Forest, 28,000 acres of untouched land ideal for the serious sportsperson. The main trail loops around 23.5 miles; there's also a 10.5-mile option. Other highlights include a horse campground (and one for riders), 50 miles of bridle trails, a hunter's campground, a shooting range, a grouse-management area (the animals, not human complaints), and a sawmill. Open daily. Free. (740) 596–5781; www.ohiostateparks.org.

WHERE TO SHOP

Rocky Shoes and Boots Factory and Outlet Store. 39 East Canal Street, Nelsonville, OH 45764. Established in 1932, this factory-outlet store features a complete selection of boots and waders along with casual and rugged outdoor and occupational footwear. There's also a clearance center for the serious (bargain) hunter. (740) 753–3130; www.rockyboots.com.

WHERE TO STAY

Because of its proximity to Hocking Hills, hundreds of cabins and bed-and-breakfasts are just a short drive away (see Southeast Day Trip 1). Contact (800) HOCKING or Web sites such as BBonline.com or Ohioparks.net for a complete listing and recommendations.

ATHENS

Athens is around 13 miles farther on U.S. 33, a quick drive when students aren't moving into or out of dorms and apartments. Traffic and overcrowding are also an issue during special university events such as Mom's, Dad's, or Siblings Weekend or graduation as well as during unauthorized gatherings around Halloween and, in the spring, Daylight Savings weekend. The latter two honor a long-standing tradition of wandering around with or without costumes or clothes and protesting the bars closing an hour early, respectively. Then you might wish you were stuck on the subway in the Big Apple.

WHERE TO GO

Hockhocking Adena Bikeway. 667 East State Street, Athens, OH 45701. This 17-mile route, formerly the Columbus and Hocking Valley Railroad bed, winds through Ohio University, Hocking College, abandoned "company" towns from mining endeavors, historic buildings, and Wayne National Forest. High cliffs, rock outcroppings, birds, wildlife, spring flowers, and fall foliage add to the "peak" experience. Open daily. Free. (800) 878–9767.

The Dairy Barn Southeastern Cultural Arts Center. 8000 Dairy Lane, Athens, OH 45701. Rather than being dedicated to the preservation of cows, this venerated arts center milks exhibitions and cultural events from all disciplines and geographical areas. Emphasis is on arts, crafts, and cultural heritage in Southeastern Ohio. Highlights include the summer Quilt National (odd years) and Bead International (even years), with a variety of media during other months. Closed Monday. Admission is charged. (740) 592–4981; www.dairybarn.org.

Kennedy Museum of Art. Lin Hall, Athens, OH 45701. Located in what was once the administrative building of the former Athens Mental Health Center, this renovated venue has extensive Southwest Native American and contemporary print collections on permanent display. Rotating/traveling exhibitions range from Remington bronzes and contemporary Chinese American artists to the work of Western artist Walt Kuhn and a display of fifth-grade weaving projects. Closed Monday. Free. (740) 593–1304; www.ohiou.edu/museum.

WHERE TO SHOP

Companion Plants. 7247 North Coolville Ridge Road, Athens, OH 45701. More than 600 varieties of herb plants and seeds from all over the world are on display from the end of March through November. People wanting to learn about or purchase offerings can check out the Web site or request information via mail. (740) 592–4643; www.companionplants.com.

Import House. 70 North Court Street, Athens, OH 45701. Those who think the '60s are over should stop at this place, which carries a full line of, uh, paraphernalia (called "tobacco accessories") as well as shoes, clothing, candles, and incense. In tune with the times, the selection of jewelry also includes piercing items. (740) 593–5155.

Beads and Things. 8 North Shafer Street, Athens, OH 45701. Located in a red house under a shade tree, this unique emporium peddles beads, from antique to new, as well as other doodads with which to create great wearables. You can purchase ready-made items or take lessons in doing it yourself. (740) 592–6453.

Glasshouse Works Greenhouse. Church Street, P.O. Box 97, Stewart, OH 45778. From U.S. 33 in Athens, take U.S. 50 east to SR 329 north, a drive of about 12 miles. With 10,000 species, cultivars, and hybrids, this is flora nirvana. You can see tropical specimens in a small conservatory or perennials in a garden. Offerings are displayed in ponds, bamboo stands, rockeries, bog areas, and containers. (800) 837–2142; www.glasshouseworks.com.

WHERE TO EAT

Because so many patrons are college students, entree prices are generally lower here than in other places (servers light up when they see an over-twenty-one, because they know they'll get a reasonable tip). Still, the quality of food in Athens is high, and although there's a fair amount of caloric stuff, always good for late-night study sessions, fine dining is available as well.

Bagel Street Deli. 27 South Court Street, Athens, OH 45701. Enjoy a variety of sandwiches on bagels, focaccia, pretzel bread, and kaiser rolls. The menu also includes omelettes and vegetarian entrees served in a brick-and-wood modern decor. $. (740) 593-3838.

Red Brick Tavern. 14 North Court Street, Athens, OH 45701. Yeah, most of the entrees are fried, but with Athens memorabilia, old photos, and upside-down (fake) cows, this clubby bar is a fun place. Specialties include buffalo wings, french fries prepared with garlic, with chili and cheese, and with skins on, and plenty of sandwiches. Soups and salads are also available. $-$$. (740) 594-2077.

Burrito Buggy. Corner of Court and Union Streets, Athens. Those wanting to recapture campus memories should opt for this truly unique experience, which consists of ordering items from a camperlike trailer and then eating them wherever. Along with the usual Mexican fare, there are some low-fat items and during the warm months, even caffeine-free iced tea. Open for lunch and dinner. $. (740) 593-6065.

Casa Nueva. 4 West State Street, Athens, OH 45701. Along with daily specials, combo platters, and vegan items, this worker-owned Mexican restaurant offers a full bar (including Ohio brews), organic coffee, and live entertainment, from poetry readings to bands. $-$$. (740) 592-2016; www.casanueva.com.

Goodfella's. 6 West Union Street, Athens, OH 45701. Pizza toppings range from the usual pepperoni and Italian sausage to pineapple, artichoke hearts, capicolla ham, and roasted red peppers. You can purchase it by the slice; subs and salads are also available. The atmosphere may be basic campus, but it's a favorite of students and alumni. $-$$. (740) 592-1572.

Lui Lui. 8 Station Street, Athens, OH 45701. This eatery offers seafood, pasta, and chicken with an Oriental flair. During fall and winter, personal pizzas are baked in wood-burning ovens. Menu items change throughout the year. $$. (740) 594-8905.

Oak Room. 14 Station Street, Athens, OH 45701. The place for steaks and ribs, this restaurant offers a vast array of foodstuffs, from inexpensive sandwiches to pricier salads, chicken, and fish. $-$$$. (740) 593-8386; www.oakroom.net.

The Pub. 39 North Court Street, Athens, OH 45710. With a bar/restaurant that opens at 10:30 A.M., seven days a week, it's no surprise this establishment has been voted as having the most popular burger in town. Daily specials, soups, salads, sandwiches, and friendly service make this a local favorite. $-$$. (740) 592-2699.

Purple Chopstix. 371½ Richland Avenue, Athens, OH 45701. This fine-dining experience is located off the beaten path and over-looks a creek and wooded area. It's also somewhat of a misnomer. Rather than Chinese grub, several different international cuisines are used to prepare inventive dishes. $$$. (740) 592-4798.

Seven Sauces. 66 North Court Street, Athens, OH 45701. Entrees run the gamut from Thai-style trout, prime rib, and shrimp and artichoke linguine to manicotti and West Indian vegetable curry. With elegant decor and an extensive wine list, it's a favorite spot to take parents, so reservations are recommended. $$. (740) 592-5555.

Union Street Cafe. 102 West Union Street, Athens, OH 45701. Here you can get breakfast anytime, which is just about 24/7. Sand-wiches, salads, dinner entrees, and appetizers are also served. Those who are feeling especially adventuresome can go into the biker bar down the street (Smiling Skull Saloon, 108 West Union Street, 740-592-9688) for an aperitif. $-$$. (740) 594-6007.

WHERE TO STAY

The Ohio University Inn. 331 Richland Avenue, Athens, OH 45701. Athens's only full-service hotel, it offers an outdoor swim-ming pool, fitness center, two restaurants, and complete facilities for business travelers. All rooms have been renovated. It's the most prox-imate lodging to the college and within mooing distance of the Dairy Barn. $$-$$$. (740) 593-6661; www.ohiouniversityinn.com.

GLOUSTER

Glouster is 17 miles north of Athens. Take U.S. 33 northwest to SR 13, then drive north to SR 78 in Glouster.

WHERE TO GO

Burr Oak State Park. 10220 Burr Oak Lodge Road, Glouster, OH 45732. This remote and rustic location boasts miles of forested ridge and hollows; wildlife such as white-tailed deer, grouse, and beaver; and plenty of woodland wildflowers, hardwoods, and majestic oaks and hickories. Recreational opportunities include hiking, backpacking, and picnicking, as well as swimming and boating at 664-acre Burr Oak Lake. Open daily. Free. (740) 767-3570; www.ohiostateparks.org.

WHERE TO STAY

Burr Oak State Park Lodge. 10660 Burr Oak Lodge Road, Glouster, OH 45732. Although it has only sixty rooms, the lodge offers a full dining room and lounge, boat launch, beach, tennis courts, indoor pool, and more. Or you can opt for an amenity-filled family cottage with cable TV, air-conditioning, complete kitchen, eating area, and screened-in porch overlooking the lake. Camping is also available and much less expensive. $$-$$$. (800) 282-7275; www.burroakresort.com.

Marietta · Belpre

Founded in 1788, Marietta was the first organized settlement in the Northwest Territory. With its redbrick streets and cobblestone levee, this small but elegant city boasts Victorian architecture with leaded glass windows and doors, a lively downtown, and thirteen museums. The area also has plenty of riverboat action for Twainees and shopping for aficionados of art glass, dolls, and pasta.

MARIETTA

With an average temperature of 39.9 degrees in January and 75.2 in July, Marietta is in one of Ohio's balmier regions. Located at the confluence of the Ohio and Muskingham Rivers, the city is about 125 miles east from Columbus. Take I–70 east to I–77 south.

WHERE TO GO

Bizantz-Bosworth House. 316 Third Street, Marietta, OH 45750. This might be the ideal first stop: The offices of the Marietta Convention and Visitors Bureau and Chamber of Commerce are located here and can supply information and directions. A historic home built in 1868, it is typical of the architecture found throughout the city. It has been partially restored so visitors can get a glimpse of life in nineteenth-century Marietta. Open daily. Free. (800) 288–2577; www.mariettaohio.org.

    Trolley Tours. 127 Ohio Street, Marietta, OH 45750. This tour hits all the high points: downtown, churches, museums, and historic

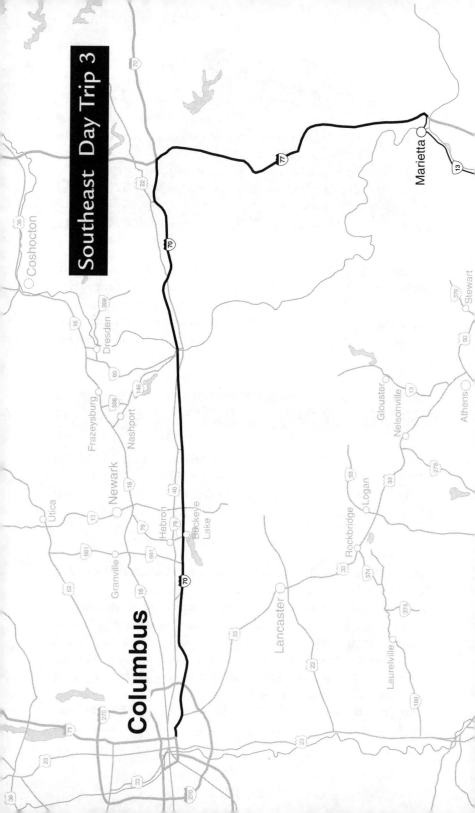

homes. Custom packages are also offered, such as the Underground Railroad. The trolley originates and ends at the Levee House Cafe. Hours of operation and times vary seasonally. Admission is charged. (740) 374-2233.

Valley Gem Stern-wheeler. 123 Strecker Hill, Marietta, OH 45750. Except for the air-conditioning and glass-enclosed lower deck, the largest stern-wheeler between Pittsburgh and Cincinnati is reminiscent of those from the height of the riverboat era. Touring options abound and range from educational one-hour trips and dinner cruises to overnight and specialized excursions. For instance, you can spend a delightful three hours floating down the Muskingham River to Lock #2 at Devol's Dam, America's last hand-operated lock system. Call for times and schedule. Admission is charged. (740) 373-7862.

Underground Railroad Tour. 127 Ohio Street, Marietta, OH 45750. With a photo exhibit, maps, and books, the Levee House Cafe is the logical starting point for this exploration. Both the Ohio and Muskingham Rivers served as major routes for fugitive slaves crossing from Virginia. Of the original sixteen underground railroad stations, six sites are available to view, including Henderson Hall Plantation (Route 2, Williamstown, WV 26187), Blennerhasset Island Plantation (137 Juliana Street, Parkersburg, WV 26101), Putnam House in Harmar Village (519 Fort Street, Marietta, OH 45750), and the John Stone House (110 Stone Road, Belpre, OH 45714), among others. Hours for sites vary; admission may be charged. Tours are conducted by historian Henry Robert Burke, (800) 288-2577 or (740) 374-2233.

Showboat Becky Thatcher Theatre. 237 Front Street, Marietta, OH 45750. This permanently moored floating song-and-dance act has been a Marietta staple for more than a quarter of a century. Entertainments range from vaudeville revues to melodramas to musicals. You may be required to sing along, although lip-synching is always an alternative. Dining is available on the second deck. June through August; call for show times. Admission is charged. (800) 746-2628.

Harmar Village. 100 Block of Maple Street, Marietta, OH 45750. Originally a fort, this area on the west side of Marietta was physically linked to the town in 1859 via a railroad bridge, which is now a walkway to shops, museums, restaurants, and historic sites. You can

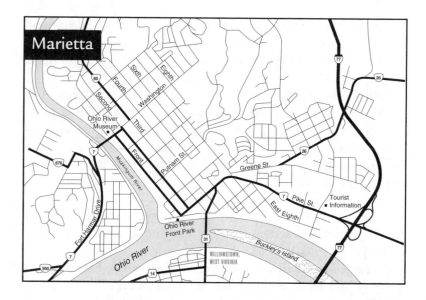

visit a Civil War–era post office (222 Gilman Avenue), a French historic marker (corner of Gilman Avenue and Virginia Street), and several museums, including the two listed below. Open daily, although many businesses are closed Monday. Admission may be charged. (800) 288-2577.

- **Marietta Soda Museum.** 118 Maple Street. This collection dispenses tin signs, coolers, clothing, paper items, vintage machines, and more. A '50s and '60s-style soda fountain features hot dogs, milk shakes, and 10-cent Cokes. And there's stuff for sale, such as the counter stools so popular during those "happy" days. (740) 376-2653.

- **The Henry Fearing House.** 131 Gilman. This example of Federal-style architecture was built in 1847 for businessman Henry Fearing. An 1870 Italianate addition and several Victorian artifacts and antiques re-create middle-class Marietta during that era. Fearing supported the temperance movement, and donated the land for what today would be called a shelter for women. (740) 373-9437.

Campus Martius Museum. 601 Second Street, Marietta, OH 45750. Spanning almost two centuries, this comprehensive collection covers the three waves of migration essential to the development of Ohio. The first floor focuses on the settling of the Marietta area, which was originally called Fort Campus Martius in the late 1700s. The display includes the home of General Rufus Putnam, one of the original leaders, among other artifacts. The lower level concentrates on the emigration from farms into the cities between 1850 and 1910 and the exodus from Appalachia to Ohio from 1910 to 1970. Other highlights are the Ohio Company Land Office, created by Revolutionary War veterans, and hands-on activities of weaving, candle dipping, and more. Open daily, May through September; closed Monday and Tuesday other months and during holidays. Admission is charged. (800) 860–0145.

Ohio River Museum. 601 Front Street, Marietta, OH 45750. Also operated by the Ohio Historical Society, this collection of riverboat-era memorabilia includes the *W. P. Synder Jr.,* a real mouthful as America's sole surviving steam-powered stern-wheel tugboat (whew!). There's also a full-scale reproduction of a flatboat and one of the oldest steamboat pilothouses around, circa 1885. Boat building tools, cabin furnishings, models, and art round out the offerings. Open daily, May through September; closed Monday and Tuesday other months and during holidays. Admission is charged. (800) 860–0145.

The Castle. 418 Fourth Street, Marietta, OH 45750. One of the best examples of Gothic Revival architecture in the state, this nineteenth-century abode boasts an octagonal tower, trefoil attic window, and stone-capped spires. Inside you'll find ornate fireplaces and moldings, floor-to-ceiling shutters, and furnishings appropriate to the era. The Castle is also home to classes in tatting and herbs, as well as Victorian teas and tours. Hours vary; call for programs. Admission is charged. (740) 373–4180.

Covered Bridges of Washington County. Tour maps available at Bizantz-Bosworth House, 316 Third Street, Marietta, OH 45750. Of Ohio's nearly 2,000 covered bridges, nine remain in the Marietta/Washington County area. This driving tour encompasses the Mill Branch Covered Bridge (circa 1832) to the Henry Covered Bridge (circa 1892). Many, such as the Bell, Shinn, Root, and Hildren Hills bridges, were constructed in the 1880s. Free; photographer not included. (800) 288–2577.

Broughton Nature and Wildlife Education Area. 3177 Cambridge Road, Marietta, OH 45750. This 500-acre retreat has trails, ponds, a natural stream, and waterfall, as well as abundant wildlife. Bird-watching, nature studies of flora and fauna, and hiking can be enjoyed here. Call for hours. Free. (740) 376-0831.

Wayne National Forest. Route 1, Box 132, Marietta, OH 45750. SR 26 runs into the forest a few miles east of I-77. The Marietta unit, part of this sprawling national forest system, offers primitive camping, hiking, fishing, and hunting. You can also do an informal circuit of historic sites, such as the Walter Ring House and mill, abandoned oil rigs, several of the previously mentioned covered bridges, and more. Call for hours. Free. (740) 373-9055.

WHERE TO SHOP

Rossi Pasta Retail Family Outlet. 114 Greene Street, Marietta, OH 45750. With nearly twenty flavors of pasta as well as accompanying sauces, this establishment has plenty of twists and turns. Gourmet food items, pasta-making accessories, cookbooks, cutting boards, even dining music make for a tasty (and even low-fat) exploration. (800) 227-6774; www.rossipasta.com.

American Flags and Poles. 276 Front Street, Marietta, OH 45750. For the patriot in the family, this store specializes in—guess what—flags and accessories as well as specialty banners, wind socks, yard sculptures, chimes, and more. (800) 262-3524.

Doll Showcase. 104 Front Street, Marietta, OH 45750. Dolls are big business for children of all ages and either gender (consider the popularity of G.I. Joe, for instance). This store peddles 'em all: Madame Alexander, Lee Middleton, Royal Vienna, Boyds Bearstones, Russ and Victorian Bears, and on and on. If that's not enough, doll accessories include tea sets, stands, cases, furnishings, wagons, beds and cradles, tables. . . (740) 374-6638.

Hartel Shipyard. 116 Maple Street, Marietta, OH 45750. Huck himself might be right at home in this eclectic emporium, which has stern-wheeler folk art, slates, railroad ties, hand-painted rowing shells, and more. (740) 374-7447.

Rinky Dinks. Route 7 South, Marietta, OH 45750. Named after an old Rinks Department store, this flea market is the largest in the area and has bargains galore, although only on weekends (Friday through Sunday). (740) 373-4797.

Salem Candles. 110 Putnam Street, Marietta, OH 45750. With 120-plus scents and dozens of colors and fifty candlemakers represented, this can be an illuminating experience. They also carry candle accessories, wreaths, and oils. (740) 376–0611.

Schafer Leather Store. 140 Front Street, Marietta, OH 45750. This fifth-generation family-owned enterprise carries such varied manufacturers as Swiss Army, Brighton, Montana Silversmith, and Tilley as well as manicure sets, wallets, belts, and portfolios. Their extensive luggage and travel accessories selection ranges from briefcases to Healthy Back Bags, and they have more than 2,500 pairs of boots in stock. (740) 373–5101.

Antiques and Needful Things. 177 Front Street, Marietta, OH 45750. Although items such as oak curved-glass china closets, pedestal tables with four leaves, barrister bookcases, and drop front secretaries hardly seem essential for survival, they are lovingly refurbished and for sale here. Plantation desks, clocks, quilts, glassware, and more are also available, and the proprietors purchase entire estates or single pieces. (740) 374–6206.

Fenton Art Glass Company. 700 Elizabeth Street, Williamstown, WV 26187. Located off I–77, just over the bridge that links Marietta to West Virginia. Along with a fine selection of discounted hand-blown "preferred seconds" and "retired firsts," you can tour the factory for free, watching artisans in action, and visit the Fenton Museum. Oh, and there's a large selection of Fenton Glass as well. (304) 375–6122; www.fenton-glass.com.

WHERE TO EAT

Becky Thatcher Restaurant. 237 Front Street, Marietta, OH 45750. Enjoy dining on a gen-u-ine riverboat, either in conjunction with the show or independently. Full lunch and dinner menus include freshwater fish, daily specials, sandwiches, appetizers, and more. $$. (740) 373–4130.

Gun Room/Riverview Lounge. Lafayette Hotel, 101 Front Street, Marietta, OH 45750. Although its name might be more appropriate in Texas, the Gun Room is decorated in nineteenth-century steamboat and offers up quite a collection of long rifles along with three squares of American cuisine. Those twenty-one or older can enjoy cordials at the Riverview Lounge, which overlooks the Ohio. $$–$$$. (800) 331–9336; www.lafayettehotel.com.

Marietta Brewing Company. 167 Front Street, Marietta, OH 45750. Along with a wide range of fresh brews, this eatery provides a varied menu, ranging from creole chicken to burgers to create-your-own pastas, and more. $$. (740) 373-2739.

House of Wines. SR 60 North, Marietta, OH 45750. Dine in a European-style bistro with wooden tables, fresh flowers, and a patio during the warm months. Specialties include Swiss cheese onion soup, Reuben sandwiches, and cheese boards served with hot mustard. Also available: a large selection of wines, microbrewed beers, and specialty gourmet products. $$-$$$. (740) 373-0996; www.houseofwines.com.

Harmar Tavern. 205 Maple Street, Marietta, OH 45750. Located in the Harmar historic district of Marietta, this casual eatery serves up "Soon to be Famous" fried bologna sandwiches, omelettes and fried egg dishes, and lunch specials. Large breakfasts can be had here on Saturday and Sunday, and there's a beer garden too. $$. (740) 373-8727.

WHERE TO STAY

Lafayette Hotel. 101 Front Street, Marietta, OH 45750. Constructed in the early 1900s, the Lafayette is one of the last riverboat-era hotels standing. Many rooms come with a river view, and the lobby boasts an 11-foot pilot wheel from the steamboat *J. D. Ayres*. Includes seventy-eight rooms, cable, and free airport shuttle service. $$-$$$. (800) 331-9336; www.lafayettehotel.com.

The Buckley House. 332 Front Street, Marietta, OH 45750. Built in 1879 and less than a block from downtown, this bed-and-breakfast faces the Muskingham River. Each of the three rooms has its own bath; a continental breakfast is included. $$. (740) 373-3080.

The Doris Grace House. 833 Third Street, Marietta, OH 45750. Keeping it "all in the family," the present owners, Chester and Susan Martin, have named the bedrooms as a tribute to their respective mothers and include many of the women's personal belongings. Rooms have private baths, double beds, and central air. $. (800) 856-1506; thedorisgracehouse.com.

The House on Harmar Hill. 300 Bellevue Street, Marietta, OH 45750. With three full floors and a panoramic view of the confluence and the city, this Queen Anne Victorian also has a ballroom, grand staircase, and elegantly decorated guest rooms. Children under fourteen by prior arrangement only. $$–$$$. (740) 374-5481.

Twin Doors. 611 Fourth Street, Marietta, OH 45750. This Italianate/Colonial Revival was constructed in 1872. Amenities include private baths, Jacuzzi, gardens, brick porch/patio, and proximity to town. There's a full country breakfast on weekends and extended continental during the week. $$. (888) 762-6922.

BELPRE

Doll collectors in particular will want to visit Belpre, about 12 miles away. From Marietta, take SR 7 south.

WHERE TO SHOP

Lee Middleton Original Dolls. 1301 Washington Boulevard, Belpre, OH 45750. These life-size tiny tots are molded, hand-painted, and assembled in a 50,000-square-foot factory on-site; tours are available. There's even a "newborn" nursery and plenty of new additions to choose from, including "My Own Baby" and others, which are almost as realistic as the genuine article. (800) 233-7479; www.leemiddleton.com.

Lloyd Middleton Dolls Factory Outlet. 1305 Washington Boulevard, Belpre, OH 45750. With detailed outfits and various hairstyles and eye colors, these handcrafted "kids" are unique and classy. You can pick out a doll in your child's image, using molds, body types, hair/eye color, even his or her clothes. You get a certificate with your handpicked offspring's name. (800) 845-1845; www.lloyd middletondoll.com.

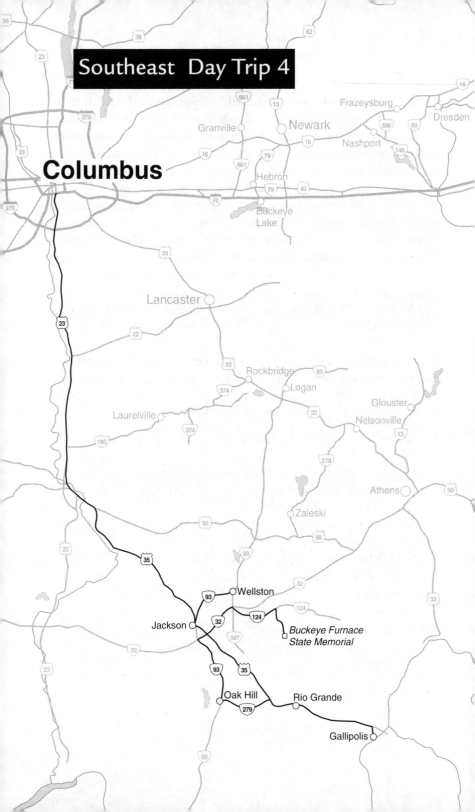

Centuries before palefaces made an appearance, Native Americans used the "licks" on the creek near what is now Jackson for salt. According to legend, they forced Daniel Boone to collect the stuff when they captured him in the late 1700s. When Ohio became a state in 1803, the area was kept as a reserve.

But not for long. By 1815 salt resources had been depleted and settlers began to move in. One was John Wesley Powell, who spent his childhood in Jackson and was tormented because of his parents' abolitionist leanings. He went on to become the first white man to navigate the Grand Canyon.

JACKSON

With lots of greenery, lakes, and historical sites, the Jackson area draws visitors the way its salt used to attract deer. From Columbus, it can be reached by taking SR 23 south to U.S. 35 south and east, a drive of around an hour and a half.

WHERE TO GO

Lillian E. Jones Museum. 75 Broadway, Jackson, OH 45640. This unique house museum is furnished circa 1920s and was the home of Lillian E. Jones, whose family was prominent in the area. Along with changing exhibits and various seasonal events, it also features a genealogy research center. Open Tuesday, Wednesday, and Saturday, May through December. Free. (740) 286–2556; lillianjones. museum.com.

Noah's Ark Animal Farm. 1527 McGiffins Road, Jackson, OH 45640. With more than one hundred animals and birds, train rides, miniature golf, and a petting area, this is a family favorite. You can view cougars, lemurs, llamas, black bears, emus, black swans, and more, although the only "shooting" allowed is with a camera. Open daily. Admission is charged. (800) 282–2167.

Splash Down/Planet Wet. 6173 SR 327, Jackson, OH 45640. Cool off with the kids at six acres of H_2O attractions, which include slides, a "lazy" river, and interactive water playgrounds. You can also relax by the pool, and there's one just for the youngsters. Open daily from Memorial Day until the weather turns cold. Admission is charged. (888) 775–2741; www.splashdownohio.com.

Lake Katharine. From Jackson take U.S. 35 north to CR 59 west. Along with nearby Hammertown Lake (see below), this body of water contains some of the finest fishing in the area as well as picturesque views. Located in a rugged area noted for its excellent foliage and rare plants, Katharine offers scenic hiking trails.

Hammertown Lake. (Also known as Jackson City Reservoir). From Jackson take U.S. 35 south to SR 93 south to Beaver Pike and go west, then turn left on Reservoir Road. Hammertown, a 220-acre, U-shaped reservoir, is a popular recreation locale, especially for picnicking and outdoor sports.

Leo Petroglyph. Township Road 224, Marietta. Mailing address: The Ohio Historical Society, 1982 Velma Avenue, Columbus, OH 43211. Take U.S. 35 north to CR 28 east; turn left on Township Road 224. This is the spot for prehistoric Indian inscriptions, particularly if you think you can figure them out (no one has yet). The thirty-seven primitive drawings include humans, hawks, bear, snakes, and more, and are attributed to the Fort Ancient Indians. Created between A.D. 1000 and 1650, the petro-glyph is protected by a roof and can be viewed from a platform. Hiking and picnicking in this scenic region are also available. Open daily. Free. (800) 686–1535; www.ohiohistory.org.

WHERE TO SHOP

Art & Craft Mall. SR 32 and Burlington Road, Jackson, OH 45640. Local crafters get a chance to strut their stuff in the form of collectible dolls, country and wooden items, jewelry, ceramics, pottery, toys, art, and more. (740) 286-8484.

WHERE TO EAT

Lewis Family Restaurant. Corner of SR 93 and SR 32, Jackson, OH 45640. Specialty of the house is variations of broad-breasted turkey, raised on a nearby farm. Those wishing to feel less connected to their meal might want to opt for charbroiled steaks or a homemade dessert. Buffets are available for Friday dinner (seafood), Saturday dinner, and both lunch and dinner on Sunday. $$. (740) 286-5413.

WHERE TO STAY

The Maplewood. 14701 SR 93, Jackson, OH 45640. Along with a gift shop with handmade crafts and specialty items, this turn-of-the-twentieth-century home is furnished with antiques, reproductions, and more traditional decorations. Four guest rooms have shared baths; a continental breakfast is included. $$. (740) 286-6067.

Jackson Motor Inn. 346 East Broadway, Jackson, OH 45640. Recently remodeled, this accommodation offers single or double beds, microwaves, refrigerators, and access to downtown. $. (740) 286-3258.

Splash Down/Planet Wet Camp Grounds. 6173 SR 327, Jackson, OH 45640. Three lodging options are adjacent to this water park and include comfy log cabins, hookups for RVs, and primitive camping sites for the adventuresome. Cabins come in one- and two-story versions and contain fireplaces, kitchens, and living rooms. Bonus: free fishing year-round. Hookups and campsites, $; cabins, $-$$$. (888) 775-2741.

Lazy Dog Camp Resorts. 1527 McGiffins Road, Jackson, OH 45640. This site has about eighty lots for campers, ten cabins, a pay lake (rate is based on hours fished rather than actual catch), restaurant, camp supply store, swimming pool, and recreation area. Public phones and bathhouse are also available, and kiddies of all ages can keep busy with miniature golf, a playground, and sports activities. $$. (800) 282–2167.

WELLSTON

From Jackson, take SR 93 northeast to the town of Wellston, about 8 miles away.

WHERE TO GO

Buckeye Furnace. 123 Buckeye Park Road, Wellston, OH 45692. This blast from the past, a reconstructed charcoal-fired iron furnace, is typical of those operating in the region more than one hundred years ago. As the second largest producer of iron ore in the nation, Ohio had several such enterprises, many of which created either wealth or bankruptcy. Built in 1852, its fire went out for the last time in 1894. Along with a charging loft used to load materials into the furnace and steam-powered engine compressor, there's a replica company store and office. Open Wednesday through Sunday, Memorial Day weekend through Labor Day. Donations accepted. (800) 860–0144; www.ohiohistory.org.

Lake Alma State Park. Route 1, Box 422, Wellston, OH 45692. This 219-acre state park boasts 4 miles of hiking trails, a paved bicycle path, two beaches, and campgrounds. Originally developed in 1903 as an amusement park by a coal miner, it is now the host to excellent bass fishing. Open daily. Free. (740) 384–4474; www.ohio stateparks.org.

OAK HILL

Backtrack on SR 93 to Jackson, and continue south about 12 miles to Oak Hill.

WHERE TO GO

Welsh-American Heritage Museum. 412 East Main Street, Oak Hill, OH 45656. Located in the Old Welsh Congregational Church, this collection chronicles the life and times of six Welsh families who migrated to the area. They stayed because it reminded them of their native Cilcennin. Along with possible family ties, you'll find heirlooms, books, photographs, and more. Open Tuesday, Thursday, Saturday, and Sunday, May through October. Donations are welcome. (740) 682-7057.

Jackson Lake State Park. 921 Tommy Been Road, Oak Hill, OH 45656. This small but picturesque park offers hunting, fishing, swimming, boating, camping, and picnicking. It was also hot stuff during the mid-1800s, the key production period for iron ore. Remnants can be found in the moss-covered remains of the Jefferson Iron Furnace, which was used to forge the battleship *Monitor* during the Civil War. Open daily. Free. (740) 682-6197; www.ohiostateparks.org.

RIO GRANDE

Rio Grande is located about 12 miles east of Oak Hill. Take SR 279 to U.S. 35 and turn right.

WHERE TO GO

Bob Evans Farm. SR 588, Rio Grande, OH 45674. This 1,100-acre working farm includes a log cabin village, small animal barnyard, farm museum, and craft barn. Visitors can enjoy horseback riding, hayrides, trails, and canoeing, and can hang out with more than forty horses and nearly one hundred head of cattle. The homestead, a large birch farmhouse where Bob and Jewell Evans raised their six kids, is now a corporate museum and historical center. Open daily, Memorial Day through Labor Day. Free. (800) 994-3276; www.bobevans.com.

WHERE TO EAT

Bob Evans Restaurant and General Store. SR 588, Rio Grande, OH 45674. The mother ship of what eventually became a huge restaurant chain, this eatery retains the ambience of an old-time emporium. Along with "down on the farm" home cooking, you can purchase Bob Evans brand products and country kitsch. And you might even encounter the founder or his family, some of who still reside in the area. $$. (740) 245–5324.

GALLIPOLIS

In 1790 the Scioto Company had the Gaul—er, gall—to sell worthless property to middle-class French investors who were lured by its proximity to the Ohio River and potential for commerce. One can only imagine the reaction of doctors, merchants, dancing masters, and minor royalty when they arrived to take possession of a 16-by-20-foot dirt-floor hut complete with neighboring hostile natives, disease, and untamed wilderness. Yet they persevered, and the town retains an aristocratic touch.

Continue on U.S. 35 south to Gallipolis, which is about 10 miles from Rio Grande.

WHERE TO GO

Gallipolis City Park. Second Avenue between Court and State Streets. This six-acre tract in the middle of town was the locale of the original settlement and now boasts a beautifully restored circa 1878 bandstand. How American: It's also the spot for July 4 festivities, war memorials, and a marker denoting various floods. Open daily. Free. No phone.

Our House State Memorial. 432 First Avenue, Gallipolis, OH 45631. Built in 1819, this was formerly a tavern housing travelers and a local gathering spot. Founder Henry Cushing met visitors just off the boat, including Marquis de Lafayette, who visited in 1825. Now restored, the three-story, Federal-style brick structure has been refurbished to reflect the tenor of those times and includes an antique walnut bar in the taproom. Some pieces date back to the original French artisans who settled in 1790. Closed Monday. Admission is charged. (800) 752-2618.

French Art Colony. 530 First Avenue, Gallipolis, OH 45631. The multipurpose arts center curates up to twelve gallery exhibits a year, in a variety of media. Located in a historic Greek Revival home, it also offers arts classes, theater, recitals, and literary workshops. Open Tuesday through Friday, Sunday, and by appointment. Free. (740) 446-3834.

Ariel Theatre. 126 Second Avenue, Gallipolis, OH 45631. Established in 1895, this venue was the pride of the city and saw the likes of Will Rogers, the Ziegfeld Follies, and early "moving pictures" during its heyday. Closed during the early 1960s, it was rescued from disrepair by civic volunteers. Highlights include a luxe crimson drapery, Victorian-style seating, elaborate stenciling, and touches of oak and gold. Excellent acoustics make it a draw for the local symphony as well as regional and traveling performers. Admission may be charged for performances. Call for hours. (740) 446-2787; www.arieltheatre.org.

Fortification Hill. Portsmouth Road/SR 141, Gallipolis, OH 45631. Along with being the location of Mound Hill Cemetery, final resting place of many prominent residents, this historic site bristled with cannons during the Civil War. Today the bluff mostly calls tourists, as it overlooks Gallipolis, the Ohio River Valley, and the hills of West Virginia. Open daily. Free. (740) 466-6882.

WHERE TO SHOP

Aunt Clara's. 4001 SR 141, Gallipolis, OH 45631. Amish arts and crafts can be found here, along with a chance to relax with a cup of coffee and a treat. (704) 446-0205.

French City Mall. 350 Second Avenue, Gallipolis, OH 45631. All manner of antiques, crafts, and collectibles are located on 12,000 square feet of floor space. The diverse selection includes flower arrangements, candles, lawn-goose outfits, hand-painted firescreens, religious artifacts, and old sheet music. Depression glass, mantels, and clothes are but a few more offerings. (740) 446-9020; www.frenchcitymall.com.

WHERE TO STAY

William Ann Motel. 918 Second Avenue, Gallipolis, OH 45631. Knotty pine paneling, refrigerators, and larger rooms are some options in this inexpensive accommodation. Small pets are welcome. $. (740) 446-3373.

Adams County is the kind of place where someone can tell you to turn left at a certain hill and go right at a stand of trees, and you'll locate your destination. The region consists of several small towns and rural areas amid mostly untouched, gently rolling land. Some might call it Amish Lite: Only a few dozen Old Order families can be found in the villages of Unity and Harshaville, which are so minute they fail to appear on a conventional map (they're in the Wheat Ridge area near West Union). So you'll need to watch for buggies and cap the camera, unless permission is obtained.

The locale also offers a bounty of outdoor options, including sacred Indian grounds, preserves, prairies, wildlife refuges, and state forests. Quality shopping, dining, and bed-and-breakfasts can also be found. No bright lights, big city, but a great place to commune with nature and recharge.

PEEBLES

The first town we'll visit is Peebles, about 95 miles from Columbus. Take U.S. 23 south to SR 32 west and you'll run right into this charming village. Many of the roads are winding, so pay careful attention to signs and allow extra driving time.

141

WHERE TO GO

Serpent Mound. 3850 SR 73, Peebles, OH 45660. With an oval embankment at the end that looks like it's about to strike, this effigy is a real rattler. Nearly a quarter-mile long and an average of 3 feet high, it is the largest of its kind in North America. Yet who built it and why remain a mystery, although the prehistoric Adena people constructed nearby conical mounds for burials and implements around 800 B.C.–A.D. 100. A museum contains exhibits relating to the mound and local geology; hours vary. Mound open daily. Admission is charged. (800) 752-2757; www.ohiohistory.org.

Brush Creek State Forest. Route 3, Box 156, Peebles, OH 45660. These 12,000 acres of predominantly hardwood land comprise craggy hillsides, deep hollows, and narrow ridges. Although it's mostly uninhabited, there are 3 miles of hiking trails and 12 miles of bridle trails to explore. Open daily. Free. (740) 372-3194.

Davis Memorial State Nature Preserve. Davis Memorial Road, Peebles, OH 45660. Consisting of diverse plant groups and unusual geological formations, this eighty-eight-acre preserve bisects the boundary of two of Ohio's five landform regions. Two richly forested hiking trails provide for an interesting contrast in flora, fauna, and topography, and there's even a sinkhole. Open daily. Free. (614) 265-6453.

WHERE TO SHOP

Raber's Shoes and Saddlery. 5252 Unity Road, Peebles, OH 45660. This is the place for Red Wing footwear, shoe repair, chaps, and holsters. Accessorize your horse with saddles, bridles, and halters; custom items are also available. No phone.

WHERE TO STAY

Woodland Altars. 33200 SR 41, Peebles, OH 45660. This camp/retreat, run by the Church of the Brethren, offers chalets for individuals and families, along with hiking trails, swimming pools, a lake, and recreational campsites. Lodges are available for large groups only. $–$$$. (937) 588-4411; www.woodlandaltars.org.

SEAMAN

A couple of interesting shopping venues make this town worth a visit. From Peebles, take SR 32 west about 8 miles, then go north on SR 247 for 2 miles to Seaman.

WHERE TO SHOP

Hilltop Designs. 4776 Graces Run Road, Seaman, OH 45679. With a selection that includes dried florals, old-time candy in a barrel, homemade soaps, vintage clothing, hummingbird feeders, grapevine trees, and more, this is the ideal browse. The proprietress, Jo Hall, also offers tours of the area as well as workshops on making an everlasting wreath or topiary. (937) 386–3258.

   Keim Family Market. 2621 Burnt Cabin Road, Seaman, OH 45679. In addition to homemade goods, cheese, crafts, and indoor and outdoor furniture, you'll get lots of information about the Amish community and businesses. Along with free brochures and maps, you can purchase cabins, barns, gazebos, cereals, cookies, pies, and noodles (no yolk). (937) 386–9995.

MANCHESTER

From Seaman, take SR 136 south about 20 miles to Manchester, situated on the Ohio River.

WHERE TO GO

Brush Creek Excursions. 526 Brush Creek Road, Manchester, OH 45144. This canoe "shuttle" runs from upper and lower Ohio Brush Creek to the Serpent Mound to the Ohio River. Excursions vary from two hours to two days and can include camping, hiking, and caving expeditions. Admission is charged. Open Friday through Sunday from Memorial Day to Labor Day. (800) 941–5400; www.brushcreekexcursions.com.

WHERE TO SHOP

Lewis Mountain Herbs. 2345 State Route 247, Manchester, OH 45144. Dozens of herbs and everlasting flowers are cultivated in greenhouses and gardens that are carpeted with flowers in summer. After perusing the excellent selection of plants (including more than sixty varieties of scented geraniums), herbal products, wreaths, arrangements, and books, you can relax in a living gazebo consisting of Ohio apple trees. (800) 714-3727.

WHERE TO EAT

Moyer Vineyards, Winery, and Restaurant. 3859 U.S. 52, Manchester, OH 45144. Constructed in the 1920s as a dance hall that sold bootleg beer, this eatery was a private gambling club during the World War II era, further evolving into a truck stop in the '50s and '60s. Today it's a much classier joint and serves such delectables as fillet of cod with tomato sweet pepper sauce accompanied by fine site-processed—and legal—wines. During the warm months, you can dine on the deck and watch boats and barges float by on the Ohio River. Moyer wines are also for sale. $$-$$$. (937) 549-2957.

WHERE TO STAY

Hickory Ridge Bed and Breakfast. 1418 Germany Hill Road, Manchester, OH 45144. This cozy cabin is located within view of the Ohio River on a 180-acre estate with walking trails. Amenities include luxe linens, heirloom china, and unique furnishings coupled with modern conveniences. Guests are treated to an arrival gift, bedside desserts, and fresh flowers. $$. (800) 686-3563.

WEST UNION

About 2 miles from Manchester, West Union can be reached by driving east on U.S. 52 and north on SR 247.

WHERE TO GO

William Lafferty Memorial Funeral and Carriage Collection. 205 South Cherry Street, West Union, OH 45693. Hearse looking at you: This accumulation includes motorized and horse-drawn vehicles from 1848 to 1967. Highlights are an 1860 "Dead Wagon" used to carry family members to their final resting place, an 1899 Brewster Omnibus for pallbearers and other attendees, and the area's first motorized ambulance, circa 1923. Caskets, mourning clothing, embalming equipment, and more round out this grave display, which is located next to the Ohio's oldest continuously operating funeral business. Open Saturdays; call for appointment. Donations welcome. (937) 544–2121.

Chapparal Prairie State Nature Preserve. Hawk Hill Road, West Union, OH 45693. Home to more than twenty rare or endangered species of plants, this sixty-six-acre habitat mimics prairie areas more commonly found in the Western states. Visitors can explore the ecosystem via a three-quarter-mile loop trail, and there are plenty of wildflowers and butterflies during warm months. Optimal viewing times for plants are late July and early August. Open daily. Free. (937) 544–9750.

Adams Lake State Park. 14633 SR 41, West Union, OH 45693. Located in what's known as Ohio's bluegrass region, this park is noted for its abundance of unique plant and animal species. Colorful prairie flowers, greenery normally found in northern regions, and a variety of birds and mammals can be found here. Along with a forty-seven-acre lake for boating and fishing, hiking and picnicking are available. Because of the area's rare ecology, visitors must stay on established trails. Open daily. Free. Contact: Shawnee State Park, Portsmouth, OH 45663. (740) 858–6652; www.ohiostateparks.org.

WHERE TO SHOP

Miller's Bakery, Bulk Foods, and Furniture. 960 Wheat Ridge Road, West Union, OH 45693. It's three stores in one. Along with tables, chairs, hutches, stools, desks, and more, there is a section for bulk foods. No-sugar food items share shelf space with high-calorie pies, rolls, cakes, cheese, and trail bologna. Wind chimes, cookbooks,

Minnetonka moccasins, and quilts round out the diffuse (to say the least) selections. (937) 544-8524, (937) 544-4520, or (937) 544-8449.

Blake Pharmacy. 206 North Market Street, West Union, OH 45693. This has to be the only place in the known universe where a nickel will still buy a Coke. Decorated with cola memorabilia and with an old-fashioned soda fountain (and prices), you'll also find Hummel figurines, Fenton art glass, Lee Middleton dolls, and more. (937) 544-2451.

Hillside Bird's Nest. 35 Port Road, West Union, OH 45693. Birders can flock to this Amish-owned store. Along with window feeders, thistle sacks, hummingbird supplies, suet, and hooks, there is also a wide selection of pools for feathered friends. (937) 544-9983.

Montana Woodworks. 3645 Wheat Ridge Road, West Union, OH 45693. Although it's pretty far away from its namesake state, this emporium features redwood cedar products, rustic log furniture, tables, chairs, and more. An Amish woodworking shop specializes in carving out home accents. (937) 544-8004.

WHERE TO EAT

Murphin Ridge Inn. 750 Murphin Ridge Road, West Union, OH 45693. Folks come from far and wide to partake of Blue Creek Strip Steak, Cedar Rum Salmon, Parmesan-crusted Catfish, and other regional specialties. Meals are served in an 1828 farmhouse, with many ingredients grown on-site or originating from local suppliers. Dinner reservations recommended. $$-$$$. (877) 687-7446; www.murphinridgeinn.com.

Olde Wayside Inn. 222 Main Street, West Union, OH 45693. Your search for comfort food is over: Home-cooked menu items can include chicken casserole, baked pork chops, meat loaf, whipped potatoes, old-fashioned dressing, candied sweet potatoes, and more. Desserts range from cheesecake and homemade apple dumplings to seasonal pumpkin confections. If you have room left, that is. $$. (937) 544-7103.

WHERE TO STAY

Murphin Ridge Inn. 750 Murphin Ridge Road, West Union, OH 45693. This highly rated lodge is located on 140 acres with a view of Peach Mountain. Rooms are decorated with Shaker reproduction furniture, and there are some luxurious woodland cabins as well. Swimming pool, tennis courts, hiking trails, and other outdoor activities are available, along with an excellent restaurant and a gallery where local artists and crafters strut their stuff. And that's not even mentioning the fabulous breakfasts. $$-$$$. (877) 687-7446; www.murphinridgeinn.com.

Unity Woods. 1095 Marjorie Johnson Road, West Union, OH 45693. Those wanting to dip their toe into the Amish lifestyle might want to check out this 125-acre nature camp. Cottages have baths, fully equipped kitchens, and heat, but no electricity. Along with a well-stocked pond (bass, bluegill, catfish), there are 5 miles of nature trails, observation blinds, and bird-watching. $$. (937) 544-6908.

LYNX

From West Union, take SR 125 East, about 8 miles to the largest privately owned group of nature preserves in Ohio.

Edge of Appalachia Preserve. 19 Abner Hollow Road, Lynx, OH 45650. This 12-mile stretch serves up rocky slopes, colorful meadows, cavernous ravines, and one hundred rare species of plants and animals. The Lynx Prairie section has more than 200 kinds of flora and fauna more commonly found west of the Mississippi, with such monikers as big and little bluestem, side-oats grama, purple coneflower, prairie dock, and rattlesnake master. The area containing Buzzardroost Rock bristles with scenic vistas, overlooking Ohio Brush Creek and the valley below. Should you fall, there are plenty of vultures (the "buzzards" that the rock is named after) soaring overhead, waiting for a handout. Open daily. Free. (937) 544-2880.

Harshaville Covered Bridge. SR 1, Graces Run Road, Harshaville, OH 45693. From West Union, take 247 North to Graces Run Road and turn right (about 4 miles). The last covered bridge still used in Adams County, it was built circa 1855. Confederate General John Morgan and his raiders passed through it during the Civil War. Open daily. Free. (877) 232-6764; www.adamscountytravel.org.

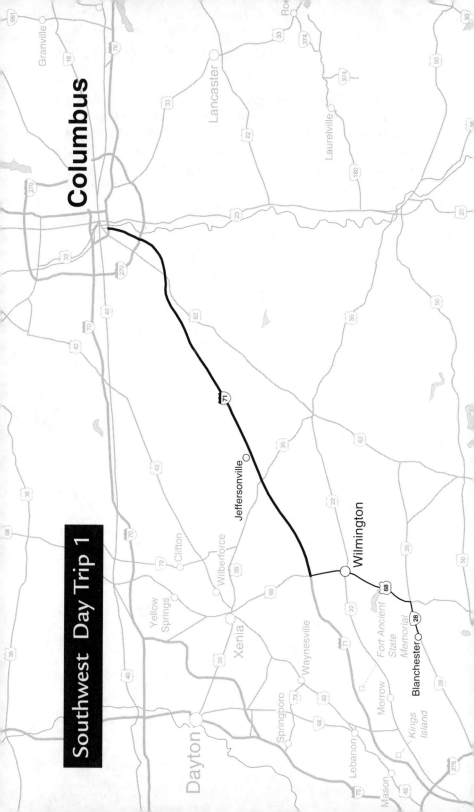

Jeffersonville · Wilmington ·
Blanchester

Clinton County has it all: name brands, antiques, top-of-the-line products, and items of the one-person's-trash-is-another's-treasure kind. The county is named after George Clinton, the fourth vice president of the United States (not the King of Funkadelic, and certainly not Citizen Bill).

JEFFERSONVILLE

Jeffersonville is a shopper's destination; located about forty minutes from Columbus, it's a straight shot south on I-71, off exits 65 and 69.

WHERE TO SHOP

Jeffersonville. 8000 Factory Shops Boulevard, Jeffersonville, OH 43128, off exit 65. Ohio's largest factory-outlet center has more than one hundred stores. Items are discounted up to 70 percent and include mostly first-quality, in-season factory overruns as well as some irregular and damaged merchandise, which is generally marked as such (check your purchases beforehand because returns may involve another day trip!). Shops include apparel for all ages and genders (Talbot's, Tommy Hilfiger, Gap), activewear (Big Dog, Nautica, The Jockey Store), health and beauty (Bath & Body Works, GNC), luggage and accessories (Coach, Samsonite, and Zales), shoes (Easy Spirit, Bass, Nine West), and housewares (Corning, Lenox, Waterford, Noritake). You can even purchase books (Borders, Book

Warehouse), kitchenware (Le Gourmet Chef), sound equipment (Bose), and edibles (Rocky Mountain Chocolate Factory, Harry and David), to mention a few. Although you may save in the long run, expect to spend more time (an average of two hours) and money (about $200) than you would in a regional mall. Don't forget to check the Web site or the office for various discounts and coupons. Open daily, but hours vary. (800) 746-7644; www.primeoutlets.com.

Home Works at Jeffersonville. 1100 McArthur Road, Jeffersonville, OH 43128, off exit 69. This "lite" open-air outlet cluster consists of more than a dozen stores, from Book Warehouse (again) to Carter's children's wear to Casual Male Big & Tall to Dress Barn/Dress Barn Woman to Liz Claiborne/Elizabeth. Legwear and undergarment enthusiasts might also appreciate Reebok/Rockport, Socks Galore, and L'eggs/Hanes/Bali/Playtex. Other shops are planned, and it's neither as large or crowded as the megamall down the road. Free (as long as you don't buy anything). Open daily but hours vary. (740) 426-6991.

WHERE TO STAY

Periodically, several chain hotels offer "shop & stay" deals for consumers, with rooms often priced at well under $100 a night. Following are those located off the malls' exits. Others, which are more of a drive, include Doubletree Guest Suites Cincinnati (6300 East Kemper Road, Sharonville, OH 45241, 513-489-3636) and the Ramada Plaza Hotel & Roberts Convention Center, off I-71 at U.S. 68, 800-654-7036).

- **Amerihost Inn South.** Route 35, exit 65 off 1-71; **Amerihost Inn North.** Route 41, exit 69 off 1-71. Take your choice of lodging at either exit, although the South Amerihost has more fast-food restaurants and heavy-duty shopping than its neighbor to the north. Either way, you get amenities such as a pool and Internet connections, along with a complimentary continental breakfast and a coupon book for Jeffersonville. $$. (740) 948-2104 (South) and (740) 426-6400 (North).
- **Hampton Inn.** Route 35, exit 65 off I-71. With an indoor heated pool, spa, elevator, exercise room, and in-room microwave and refrigerator, this already spiffy but recently renovated property was built in the late 1990s. And it gets better. Along with a

complimentary continental breakfast and Laundromat, you can
have all the rollaway beds and cribs you can handle in the room
for no additional charge. $$. (740) 948-9499.

WILMINGTON

Accolades for the charismatic burg of Wilmington include a listing
in *The 100 Best Small Towns in America* and a designation as a "most
livable" neighborhood by *Cincinnati* magazine. Visitors can enjoy the
Victorian-era downtown with its historic homes, attractions, and, of
course, shopping. Wilmington is another 20 miles from Jefferson-
ville. To get there, take I-71 south to U.S. 68 and continue south
about 5 miles.

WHERE TO GO

Airborne Express Midnight Tours. Airborne Express Park, Wilm-
ington, OH 45177. This huge hub, Clinton County's largest employer,
is mission central for the freight handler. Visitors get a fascinating
glimpse into the wild and wacky world of overnight carriers. Tours
available on a first-come, first-served basis. Call for appointment.
Free. (937) 382-5511; www.airborne.com.

National Weather Service. 1901 South State Road, Wilmington,
OH 45177. Open 24/7, rain or shine, this facility serves up forecasts
for fifty-six counties in Ohio, Kentucky, and Indiana. It's also the
home of the Ohio River Forecast Center, which provides flood guid-
ance for thirteen states. Computer models, satellite, radar, and
weather balloons provide insight into the combination of intuition
and science that makes up weather prediction. Call for tour. Free.
(937) 383-0031.

Clinton County Historical Society. 149 East Locust Street,
Wilmington, OH 45177. Located in an 1885 Greek Revival mansion,
this collection defines eclectic. Highlights include antique clothing,
toys, and dolls; the Wilmington Tablet, an Adena Native American
burial relic; an 1875 steam-powered engine; and paintings and
sculpture by internationally recognized Quaker artist Eli Harvey.
There is memorabilia of original resident General J. West Denver,

who later helped Colorado achieve statehood; Southwestern Indian photography by local native Carl Moon; and last but certainly not least, an 1898 folding bathtub. Open Wednesday through Friday, March through December. Free. (937) 382–4684.

Clinton County Courthouse. 53 East Main Street, Wilmington, OH 45177. Built in 1918, this Second Renaissance Revival structure has been completely spiffed up and restored. Standouts are a colorful 36-foot mural dome, detailed plasterwork, and painted panels depicting agriculture, education, medicine, and industry. Open Monday through Friday. Free. (877) 428–4748; www.clinton countyohio.com.

Murphy Theatre. 50 West Main Street, Wilmington, OH 45177. With a thousand seats in a town of barely five times more than that, this venue was built in 1918 on the big dreams of native Charles Murphy, owner of the Chicago Cubs. Elegantly furnished and recently restored, with a flamboyant, old-fashioned marquee, this theater continues to draw such name acts as Glen Campbell, The Amazing Kreskin, and more. Hours and performance fees vary. Call (877) 274–3848 for schedule.

Cowan Lake State Park. 729 Beechwood Road, Wilmington, OH 45177. Swimming, fishing, sailing, and canoeing are popular pastimes in this peaceful setting. It's particularly picturesque during the warm months when the large, vivid American lotus water lily blooms on the lake. There are also 6 miles of hiking trails and hunting and fishing in season. Open daily. Free. (937) 289–2105; www.ohiostateparks.org.

Cherrybend Pheasant Farms. 2326 Cherrybend Road, Wilmington, OH 45177. Get up close and personal with your food. This 386-acre grain farm has many large ring-necked pheasants that can be hunted from September through April. You can also flip the bird and dine on your catch or let someone else prepare it for you. Trap-shooting is also available. Call for times and rates. (937) 584–4269.

WHERE TO SHOP

Caesar Creek Flea Market. 7763 SR 73, Wilmington, OH 45177. Located on a large outdoor lot and with more than 110,000 square feet of space inside, this bazaar has everything from bizarre home furnishings and military memorabilia to bargain-basement socks and kitchen utensils to museum-quality antiques. Hundreds of vendors are on-site. Open Saturday and Sunday only. (937) 382-1669.

Buffalo Trading Post. 280 West Curry Road, I-71 & SR 68, Wilmington, OH 45177. This 1880s-style emporium peddles cowboy memorabilia, antiques, and collectibles. There's also a full tack shop and historical displays. Don't take any wooden nickels, though. (937) 382-0141.

David Adair Co. 113 North South Street, Wilmington, OH 45177. Covering an entire downtown city block and with two levels, this store has furniture and fixtures for just about every taste and budget. Browsers (the two-legged kind, not the electronic) are welcome. (937) 382-0961.

Grandpa's Pottery. 3558 SR 73, Wilmington, OH 45177. Come watch owner/potter Ray Storer turn raw materials into functional and attractive items. All wheel-thrown pottery and sculpture is created by the Storer family. (937) 382-6442.

Valley View. 2896 Antioch Road, Wilmington, OH 45177. This 150-year-old farmstead is crammed with rugs, clothing, candles, potpourri, dried florals, furniture, pottery, and more. (937) 383-1993.

Beehive Gallery & Browsers Cafe. 156 West Locust Street, Wilmington, OH 45177. Buzz around original works by southern Ohio artists in a late nineteenth-century Victorian-style home. Also featured: custom framing, antiques, collectibles, cards, prints, and a cafe with freshly brewed coffees, teas, cheesecakes, desserts, and other goodies. (937) 383-2700.

Shoppes at the Old Mill. 320 East Sugartree Street, Wilmington, OH 45177. This 100-year-old mill grinds out antiques and collectibles from several periods. Only in a manner of speaking, of course. (937) 655-8181.

Home Again II. 316 East Sugartree, Wilmington, OH 45177. Specialty foods, crafts, toys, Americana, candles, pottery, customized gift baskets, and more can be found in this emporium, which has been around for several years. (937) 383-1899.

WHERE TO EAT

Beaugard's Southern BBQ. 975 South South Street, Wilmington, OH 45177. A favorite as far away as Cincinnati (and possibly farther), this eatery recently moved to bigger quarters and serves barbecued ribs (but of course), brisket, pork, chicken, and more along with sides like macaroni and potato salad and beans. $-$$. (937) 655–8100.

Werner's Pork House. 5356 U.S. Route 68 North, Wilmington, OH 45177. Although you can "pig" out on pork products here as well, this restaurant also offers chicken, shrimp, cod, and other food groups in a casual atmosphere. $$. (937) 382–1111.

Gibson's Goodies. 718 Ohio Avenue, Wilmington, OH 45177. This ice cream parlor not only has thirteen more flavors than that national chain, it makes a banana split that harks back to the good old days of 1907, when the treat was actually invented in Wilmington. $. (937) 383–2373.

68 Family Restaurant. 8295 North U.S. 68, Wilmington, OH 45177. This old-style roadside restaurant offers large portions accompanied by low prices. $-$$. (937) 486–2111.

WHERE TO STAY

The Wilmington Inn. 909 Fife Avenue., Wilmington, OH 45177. Located near Wilmington College, this fifty-two-room hotel features a hospitality room, computer analog system, in-room voice mail, free cable and HBO, nonsmoking rooms, and a courtesy van. Guest rooms offer fine furnishings, comfortable beds, plush carpeting, and color television. Or you can go whole hog with the executive suite, which has a Jacuzzi tub. Continental breakfast included. $. (937) 382–6000; www.wilmingtoninn.com.

Yesterday Again. 3556 U.S. 68, Wilmington, OH 45177. This 1820s farmhouse on a scenic twenty-two-acre spread offers a smoke-free, relaxed atmosphere and privately located rooms and baths. Amenities include a full breakfast, hot and cold beverages and snacks at all times, a wide selection of videotapes, a swimming pool in the summer, and a hot tub year-round. $$. (800) 382–0472; www.yesterdayagain.com.

Cedar Hill B&B. OH 4003 SR 73, Wilmington, OH 45177. This lodging is set amid ten acres of woods and walking trails and has rooms with private entrances and baths, queen-size beds, TVs, refrigerators, great views, and more. Full breakfasts served on weekends, with continental other times. $$. (877) 722–2525, or (937) 383–2528.

The Lark's Nest. 619 Ward Road, Wilmington, OH 45177. Located near Caesar Creek State Park (see Southwest Day Trip 2), this log cabin home on eight acres provides a comfy getaway. All rooms have private baths and entrances. Kitchen is available for meals other than breakfast, which is served daily. $$. (937) 382–4788.

Cowan Lake State Park. 729 Beechwood Road, Wilmington, OH 45177. Two-bedroom cottages include full kitchen, private bathroom with shower, large living room, and a screened porch. The park also maintains more than 230 campsites that are set up for tents and RVs. Showers, flush toilets, laundry facilities, and a private beach/boat launch are nearby, making it such a deal. Campsites, $; cottages, $$$. (937) 289–7139 or 289–2105.

BLANCHESTER

Blanchester, 15 miles southwest of Wilmington, offers plenty of antiquing. Take U.S. 68 south to Midland, then head west on SR 28.

WHERE TO SHOP

Broadway Antique Mall. 102 South Broadway, Blanchester, OH 45107. With more than 10,000 square feet and ninety-five booths, this is the amplest antiques amalgamation around. Collectibles, hard-to-locate items, and furniture are housed in the historic Bindley building. (937) 783–2271.

Arcade Antique Mall. 118 South Broadway, Blanchester, OH 45107. No flea market, this. Quality antiques and collectibles are on display in seventy booths covering 6,000 square feet. Auctions are held the first Saturday of each month. (937) 783–1340.

The Crossings. 139 South Broadway, Blanchester, OH 45107. Antiques and gifts can be found in this small specialty shop. Hours vary, so call before coming. (937) 783–4604.

Main Street Mall. 102 West Main Street, Blanchester, OH 45107. So many booths, so little time. . . . Antiques, collectibles, and variety store with an encyclopedic list of items. (937) 783–5993.

WHERE TO EAT

Ron's Place. 126 South Broadway, Blanchester, OH 45107. With an All-American menu and home-style cooking, this eatery is for the entire family and includes burgers, steaks, fries, sandwiches, and more. $–$$. (937) 783–4929.

Cups & Corks. 412 East Main Street, Blanchester, OH 45107. The place to "see and be seen" during mealtimes in Blanchester. This coffeehouse bistro serves sandwiches, salads, and plated meals, along with several kinds of wine. $–$$. (937) 783–0103.

Lebanon · Waynesville · Springboro

This region offers a bit of everything: history, indoor and outdoor recreation, shopping, and dining. Lebanon alone has more than fifty antiques and specialty shops.

LEBANON

In 1803, the year Ohio achieved statehood, Lebanon resident Jonas Seaman was licensed to operate a "house of public entertainment" (as opposed to one of ill repute). Called the Golden Lamb Inn, the tavern hosted notables of the day, including a dozen American presidents and author Charles Dickens. One of the few communities in Ohio to attract a large number of settlers from the Shaker religious order, Lebanon has also won praise for its simple but architecturally significant downtown, with its nineteenth-century village green and lovingly restored neighborhoods.

A drive of about 75 miles, Lebanon can be reached from Columbus via I-71 south. Go north on SR 123 (exit 32), which will lead into town.

WHERE TO GO

Warren County Historical Museum. 105 South Broadway, Lebanon, OH 45036. Lebanon's Shaker history is aptly churned up in this 1912 building. Drawn to the area's rich farmland, the Shakers formed nearby Union Village, the largest community of its

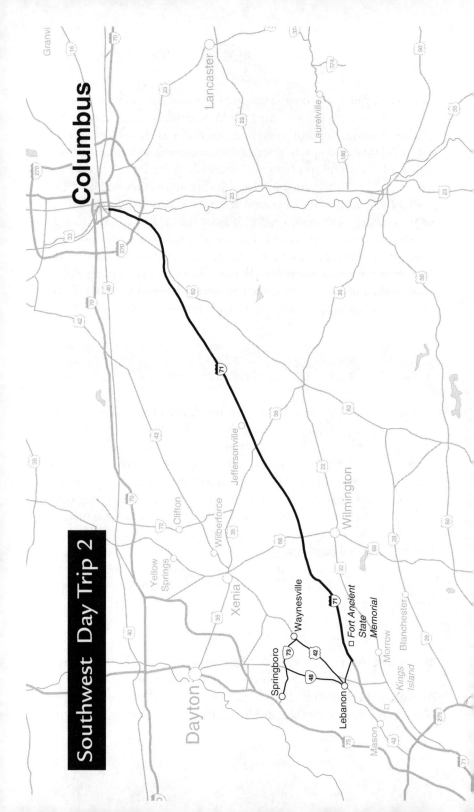

kind in the region. This resulted in a rich legacy of furniture and artifacts, making this museum one of the Midwest's finest collections. Other exhibits focus on prehistoric times, the Victorian age, and genealogy. Open Tuesday through Sunday. Admission is charged. (513) 932–1817; www.wchmuseum.com.

Glendower. 105 Cincinnati Avenue, Lebanon, OH 45036. Built between 1836 and 1840, this Greek Revival crib, the home of Civil War General Durbin Ward, boasts classic cornices and porticoes, columns of the fluted Ionic and unfluted Doric persuasion, and a hipped roof with a captain's walk. Furnished with period Empire- and Victorian-style pieces crafted by original settlers, the thirteen rooms reflect the gracious lifestyle of a bygone era and include a formal drawing room with two fireplaces. Open Wednesday through Sunday. Admission is charged. (513) 982–1817; www.ohio history.org.

Turtle Creek Valley Railway. 198 South Broadway, Lebanon, OH 45036. This one-hour train ride passes through farmland and nearby Turtle Creek, providing panoramic views. Running on track originally laid in 1880, it consists of four enclosed circa 1930 passenger coaches and an open gondola car. There's also a snack bar if you get hungry, and the conductor points out sites of historical interest. Call ahead for schedule. Admission is charged. (513) 933–8022; www.cincinnatirailway.com.

Lebanon Raceway. 655 North Broadway Street, Lebanon, OH 45036. And they're off! The Lebanon Raceway features the excitement of live harness races, which are simulcast with other racetracks and off-track betting parlors. You can also view and make wagers on races for other tracks. It's the "bet" of both worlds. Call for race days. Free (but only if you break even). (513) 932–4936; www.the lebanonraceway.com.

Fort Ancient State Memorial. 6123 SR 350, Oregonia, OH 45054. From Lebanon take SR 123 south, then go east on SR 350, a total of about 5 miles. Two millennia ago, Native Americans utilized deer bones, elk antlers, clamshell hoes, and sticks to build this fortress, carrying nearly forty pounds of soil per basket to create 18,000 feet of earthen walls. Although mostly for defense and social and recreational gatherings, certain areas served as a calendar in conjunction with the sun and moon; no Palm Pilots for these guys. Hiking and interpretive trails, remains of prehistoric mounds, and scenic vistas are other highlights. The recently remodeled museum contains 9,000 square feet of exhibits focusing on 15,000 years of American Indian history in the Ohio Valley. An outdoor re-creation of a prehistoric Indian garden, a resource center, and a shop with Native American offerings round out the excursion. Hours vary according to season. Admission is charged. (800) 283–8904; www.ohiohistory.org.

WHERE TO SHOP

A complete listing of Lebanon's many (more than fifty) and ever-changing specialty and antiques shops can be found on www.lebanonantiques.com. Following is a brief sample.

Hunter's Horn Antiques Center. 35 East Main Street, Lebanon, OH 45036. Arguably the area's largest cluster of dealers, it features antiques from some seventy selected exhibitors. If you can't find it here, it may not be available. Offerings range from jewelry to furniture and cover periods from primitive to Victorian and beyond. (513) 932–5688.

Blue Heron Studio. 28 Cincinnati Avenue, Lebanon, OH 45036. Get "framed" at this gallery, which represents local and regional artists. There's also custom framing, pre-framed pictures, and mirrors (but no smoke). (513) 934–9905.

Oh Suzanna. 16 South Broadway Lebanon, OH 45036. This is the place for quilts and custom bed groupings, including shams, dust skirts, duvets, tapestries, pieced pillows, and needlework. Blankets and china can also be found here. (513) 932–8246.

Exotic Art & Antiques. 34 South Broadway Street, Lebanon, OH 45036. This appropriately monikered assortment ranges from silver jewelry and Native American decorative arts to antique Chinese furniture and porcelain and more. (513) 932–1317; www.lebanon antiques.com/exotic.htm.

The Garden Gate. 36 South Broadway, Lebanon, OH 45036. For the gardener in your life, the selection consists of antiques, collectibles, and gifts and includes books, home decor, ornaments, tools, apparel, and even bath and body-care products. A greenhouse displays seasonal plants and topiaries. (513) 932–8620; www.the gardengate.net.

Dickens Book Shop. 26 South Broadway, Lebanon, OH 45036. A bibliophile's delight, this emporium serves up antique reference tomes as well as first editions and collectibles. Out-of-print searches are also available, and they buy and sell used books. You can also meet Dickens, the resident feline. (513) 932-7001; www.dickens bookshop.com.

Gerhardt Rug Gallery. 6 South Broadway, Lebanon, OH 45036. This place pulls out all the rugs: new and antique Tibetan styles, Persians, afghans, and kilims. There's also an array of painted Mexican furniture. (513) 932-8115.

WHERE TO EAT

Golden Lamb. 27 South Broadway, Lebanon, OH 45036. No baa-d meals here: This restaurant is owned by the same folks who manage Cincinnati's renowned Maisonette. Specialties of the house include roast leg of lamb and turkey with dressing. Much of the food is served using Shaker antiques. Ewe—er, you—can choose from lunch or dinner. $$-$$$. (513) 932-9065.

Village Ice Cream Parlor. 22 South Broadway, Lebanon, OH 45036. Eat dessert first: There's an ice-cream and soda fountain, along with luncheon specials, sandwiches, salad bar, soups, and dinner. $-$$. (513) 932-7918.

WHERE TO STAY

Golden Lamb Inn. 27 South Broadway, Lebanon, OH 45036. Ohio's oldest inn and restaurant has a museum-quality collection of gen-u-ine Shaker antiques, many of which are scattered throughout the property. What began as a two-story log building now has four floors, a lobby, several large public and private dining rooms, and guest rooms with all the modern amenities. A colonial porch and second- and third-floor balconies serve as a reminder of its early American origins. Reservations should be made well in advance, particularly during tourist season. $$-$$$. (513) 932-5065; www.goldenlamb.com.

Shaker Inn. 600 Cincinnati Avenue, U.S. 42, Lebanon, OH 45036. This family-owned, AAA-rated lodging boasts clean rooms in a variety of sizes. There's also an outside swimming pool and suites for families. $. (800) 752-6151.

Hatfield Inn. 2563 Hatfield Road, Lebanon, OH 45036. This nineteenth-century farmhouse is the real McCoy. Completely modernized and located on fifty-five acres, it offers a front porch overlooking two ponds and large shade trees. All rooms have private baths, great views, and use of an outdoor hot tub. Full breakfast included. $$. (513) 932–3193 or (888) 247–9793.

Hardy's Haven. 210 Wright Avenue, Lebanon, OH 45036. Each suite has a private bath, living room, dining room/office, and fully equipped kitchen. You can choose from country, traditional, or Victorian decor, all of which are spiffed up by antiques, lace, and fresh flowers. Breakfast is served in the adjacent March Manor, which was built in 1900. $$-$$$. (513) 932–3266; www.hardysproperties.com.

Burl Manor. 230 South Mechanic Street, Lebanon, OH 45036. Originally built in the 1800s for editor/publisher William Denney, this manse also housed senators, a judge, a dentist, and a jeweler before its present incarnation as a lodge. Along with the usual parlors and dining room, standouts are a center staircase, period wallpapers, and carved fireplaces. There's a swimming pool, lawn croquet, and various "ball" games; rooms have private baths and fireplaces. $$. (513) 934–0400; www.burlmanor.com.

WAYNESVILLE

Waynesville's profusion of curio/relic emporiums earned it the title "Antique Capital of the Midwest" from *USA Today*. Most are located along Main and High Streets. Waynesville is about 10 miles from Lebanon, straight up U.S. 42.

WHERE TO GO

Caesar Creek State Park. 8570 East SR 73, Waynesville, OH 45068. With pristine blue waters, generously abundant woodlands, and plentiful meadows and deep ravines, Caesar Creek is ideal for all types of recreation and has several shelter houses for family reunions and other gatherings. Forty-three miles of hiking trails, 31 miles of horseback riding trails, and a 2,800-acre lake for swimming, boating, and fishing are but some of the highlights. Open daily. Free. (513) 897–3055; www.ohiostateparks.org.

- **Caesar Creek Lake Visitor Center.** 4020 North Clarksville Road, Waynesville, OH 45068. Along with interpretive galleries and a theater, this center provides information regarding water resource management and the Corps of Engineers. Pictures, written material, rocks, and soil samples demonstrate the ecology of the Ohio River Basin, Caesar Creek Lake, and local natural history. Open daily. Free. (513) 897–1050.
- **Caesar Creek Lake Control Tower Tours.** 4020 North Clarksville Road, Waynesville, OH 45068. This tour provides insight into the creation of the dam that formed the lake. More than $2.5 million was saved in flood damages in one year alone. Appointments made by special request. Free. (513) 897–1050.
- **Caesar Creek Pioneer Village.** 3999 Pioneer Village Road, Waynesville, OH 45068. Consisting of nineteen restored log structures, this living museum focuses on Ohio pioneer life from 1793 to 1812. Settlers, militia, frontier explorers, and Native Americans come to life during reenactments, festivals, and other events. Buildings open Monday through Friday; call for schedule of performances. Free. (513) 897–1120; www.caesarscreekvillage.org.

Little Miami State Park. Mailing address: Caesar Creek State Park, 8570 East SR 73, Waynesville, OH 45068. Staging areas and entrances are located at Corwin (directly east of Waynesville, off SR 73), Morrow, and Loveland; call for directions. With nearly 70 miles of paved trails meandering through four counties, this is a hiker's and biker's dream. Cross-country skiing, in-line skating, backpacking, and horseback riding are other options. Rocky and steep cliffs, abundant wildlife such as great blue herons, and huge, ancient sycamores make for a big-time outdoor payoff. The Little Miami River also offers 86 miles of canoeing; smallmouth and rock-bass fishing is plentiful. Bike, skate, and canoe rentals are available at various staging areas. Open daily. Free. (513) 597–3055; www.ohiostateparks.org.

WHERE TO SHOP

Celtic Isles Shop. 260-B High Street, Waynesville, OH 45068. It's the luck o' the Irish, Scottish, Welsh, and English: Here you'll find apparel, bath and body delights, home decor, music, food and kitchen items, and all manner of breakables from across the pond. (513) 897-1566 or (877) 897-1566; www.celticislesshop.com.

The Village Clock Shop. 97 South Main Street, Waynesville, OH 45068. With vintage tickers (including one built in 1798) and such names as Hentschel, Hermle, and Schneider, this store is timeless. They will also clean your clock in the sense that they provide parts and service. (513) 897-0805; www.thevillageclockshop.com.

Waynesville Gallery. 177 South Main Street, Waynesville, OH 45068. Those searching for Amish-crafted Shaker-style furniture will find tables, chairs, living and dining rooms, bedrooms, and office accessories as well as custom-made items. (513) 897-0888.

WHERE TO EAT

Cobblestone Cafe. 10 North Main Street, Waynesville, OH 45068. Chef specials, gourmet sandwiches and desserts, homemade soups, and salads can be found at this attractively decorated eatery. Everything in the dining room is for sale (including the food, of course). $-$$. (513) 897-0021.

Angel of the Garden Tea Room. 71 North Main Street, Waynesville, OH 45068. Five-course Victorian-style lunches and dinners include such caloric delights as orange-cranberry scones; quiche made with tomatoes, cheese, and broccoli; cheddar cheese tartlets; white chocolate peppermint napoleons, and more. Reservations required. $$-$$$. (513) 897-7729; www.angelofthegarden.com.

Der Dutchman Restaurant. 230 North U.S. 42, Waynesville, OH 45068. This Amish-style eatery features panfried chicken, ham, and roast beef, "real" mashed potatoes with gravy, homemade dressing, and much, much more. There's dessert for those who have room: Dutch apple, peanut butter cream, and custard pies, date cake, bread pudding, and angel food cake. And that's not even mentioning lunch. $$. (513) 897-4716, www.dutchcorp.com.

WHERE TO STAY

Sugar Camp Cottages. 711 Collett Road, Waynesville, OH 45068. Located on a working farm, two fully refurbished cottages provide privacy, space, and luxury. A full country breakfast is served. $$. (937) 382-6075.

SPRINGBORO

A different kind of history can be found in the neighboring burg of Springboro. Once a stop on Ohio's Underground Railroad, its basements sheltered runaway slaves on their way to freedom. From U.S. 42 in Waynesville, take SR 73 west about 8 miles.

WHERE TO GO

Springboro Historical Society Museum/Underground Railroad Tour. 110 South Main Street, Springboro, OH 45066. Along with displays of local history, this archive has a room devoted to the Underground Railroad. A major way station from 1820 to 1865, "Springborough" had eighteen safe houses within its city limits, with nine more in the surrounding area. Thirty-four residents were active "conductors." You can get directions for a solo tour, or go with a group by appointment; fee charged for the latter. Museum open Saturday and Sunday; Free. (513) 748-0916.

La Comedia Dinner Theatre. 765 West Central Avenue, Springboro, OH 45066. With seating for more than 600, La Comedia is the nation's fourth largest and the region's only professional dinner theater. Broadway performances and revues are accompanied by a buffet with meats, pastas, and fresh vegetables. Themed dishes are specially created for each show. Call for times and offerings. Admission is charged. (800) 677-9505; www.lacomedia.com.

WHERE TO SHOP

Friesinger's Chocolates. 45 North Pioneer Boulevard, Springboro, OH 45066. Watch your fattening fantasies being formulated. Candies, nuts, Neapolitan coconut bars (the specialty of the house), and other concoctions are created fresh and sold directly to consumers. (513) 743-4377; www.friesingers.com.

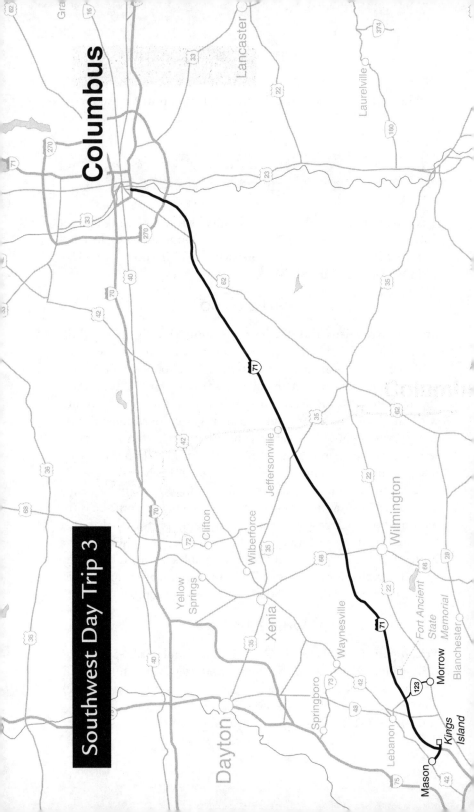

Morrow · Mason

Those looking for thrills, cheap and otherwise, would do well to check out this region. Along with the profusion of heart-thumping and other rides at Kings Island, you can herd cattle, go on a canoe trip, float far above the earth in a balloon or helicopter, or immerse yourself in a watery sanctuary. There's golf as well, although excitement in that realm can be subject to interpretation. Additional shopping, restaurants, and lodging are only about a ten-minute drive to Lebanon (see Southwest Day Trip 2).

MORROW

To get to Morrow from Columbus, take I-71 south to exit 32, then take SR 123 south, a drive of about an hour and twenty minutes.

WHERE TO GO

The Dude Ranch. 3205 Waynesville Road, Morrow, OH 45152. You really are in Ohio, although you might think otherwise during this ninety-minute trail ride and roundup of Texas longhorns. You can try your hand at ropin' and wranglin' or saddle up and meander through heavily wooded trails and meadows. Those who prefer wheels to four legs can opt for a hayride. Campfires, cookouts, and cowboy tales complete the adventure. A variety of combinations is available, as are children's programs. Call for hours and reservations. Admission is charged. (513) 421-3833; www.theduderanch.com.

Little Miami Scenic Trail. Mailing address: Warren County Convention and Visitors Bureau, Lebanon, OH 45036. Call for directions to Morrow staging area. From Morrow, you can pedal, skate, ride horseback, or walk to such attractions as the Valley Vineyards, Fort Ancient, and Lebanon. A 14.2-mile path between Morrow and Corwin leads north through the Ohio River Valley with its spectacular cliffs, rolling hills, lush vegetation, and plentiful wildlife. Stop for lunch at the town of Oregonia, an approximate midpoint. Or you can take the southern Morrow-to-Loveland path (13.5 miles), with its secluded stretches of pristine natural wonders. Open daily. Free. (800) 791–4386; www.ohio4fun.org.

Little Miami Canoe Rental. 219 Mill Street (SR 123), Morrow, OH 45152. They provide the canoe, paddles, life vests, and shuttle (when needed), while you row, row, row down a National Scenic River to Fort Ancient, an old mill, or a covered bridge. Excursions can range from two to eight hours, depending on your destination. Weather permitting, open daily, May through September; weekends in April and October. Admission is charged. (800) 634–4277; www.littlemiamicanoe.com.

WHERE TO SHOP

Harrison Art Studio Santa Gallery. 100 East McKinley Street, South Lebanon, OH 45065. South Lebanon is a few miles west of Morrow on I-71. Located in a 1907 Colonial Revival building that was a town meeting hall, this shop offers mixed media sculptures of Santa and Father Christmas as well as Christmas ornaments. The General Store section peddles candles, quilts, incense, candies, antiques, and more. (513) 494–2244; www.santagallery.com.

WHERE TO EAT

Valley Vineyards Winery. 2276 U.S. 22-3, Morrow, OH 45152. Weekend steak cookouts include a wine tasting, fresh vegetables, homemade desserts, and a tour of the property. Saturday lunch only. Dinner on other days. Call for reservations. $$. (513) 899–2485; www.valley-vineyards.com.

MASON

Mason and Kings Island are only a few miles farther south of Morrow on I-71, off exits 24 and 25.

WHERE TO GO

Paramount King's Island. 6300 King's Island Drive, King's Island, OH 45034. Seven themed areas (including two specifically designed for families), eighty-five thrill rides, and a huge new water park make these 364 acres literally tons of fun that arguably takes two full days to see. Recent innovations include Scooby-Doo and the Haunted Castle. The first interactive family ride in the park's history, this creepfest involves boarding Mini-Mystery Machines, zapping ghosts, and collecting points. Before getting too excited about another new attraction, the 3-D view of Bikini Bottom, teenagers need to realize that it's merely a SpongeBob SquarePants motion-simulator movie. They might get more thrills via the recently opened Delirium, a blue, yellow, and red dervish that rockets passengers nearly 140 feet in the air, spiraling in a 240-degree arc. Riders face outward, with legs dangling free, significantly increasing their chances of losing their lunch. Other highlights include the following:

- **The Kids' Area.** This award-winning section encompasses Nickelodeon Central and Hanna-Barbera Land. Four kids' coasters (more than any in the world), twenty-two rides, and photo opportunities with popular Nickelodeon characters in those hot and uncomfortable costumes make this a major draw.
- **Thrill Rides.** King's Island boasts a dozen "scream machines," including The Beast, purportedly the longest wooden 'coaster in the world; Son of Beast, which claims to be the tallest, fastest, and only looping one of its kind; King Cobra, where you can stand up and be lurched; and Face/Off, a looping, forward and backward, face-to-face inverted number. Drop Zone Stunt Tower, the tallest (315 feet) gyro drop tower in the world, and Congo Falls, a boat ride ending in a five-story waterfall plunge, are other stomach-churners.

• **Boomerang Bay.** A replacement for the Water Works, this new Australian-themed water park is again included in the price of admission. You can actually "surf" on a boogie board via a wave ride, explore lagoons with dramatic waterfalls, and choose from a variety of wild-to-mild water slides. A "tipping tub" dumps gallons of H_2O on willing participants and a four-person raft ride simulates a wild white-water passage.

Nationally known shows, singers, and other personalities and a 10,000-seat outdoor amphitheater round out a pilgrimage to this pop-culture mecca. Open daily, June through August, and weekends in April, May, September, October, and the first weekend in November. Admission is charged. (800) 288–0808; www.pki.com.

The Golf Center at Kings Island. 6042 Fairway Drive, Mason, OH 45040. This twenty-seven-hole Jack Nicklaus–designed course is ideal. Although called the Grizzly, with another eighteen-hole course named the Bruin, it's anything but beastly: This championship course has seen the likes of some of the world's greatest duffers and PGA/LPGA tournaments. It also has a driving range, pro shop, and a competition tennis stadium and courts that host the annual ATP Tennis Championship (www.master-series.com). Open daily. Fee charged. (513) 398–7700; www.thegolfcenter.com.

Alverta Green Museum. 207 West Church Street, Mason, OH 45040. Donated by a longtime resident who is the museum's namesake, this antique-filled home provides a peaceful respite and has historical photographs, documents, and artifacts. It chronicles life in Mason before the 'coaster/water-slide invasion. Open Thursday and Friday; other times by appointment. Free. (513) 398–6750.

The Beach. 2590 Waterpark Avenue, Mason, OH 45040. The Beach consists of thirty-five acres filled with two million gallons of water frolics, 40,000 square feet of sand, and forty-plus rides and attractions. You'll find the Midwest's only water-coaster in the Aztec Adventure, which involves 500 feet of twists, turns, and dips through the mouth of a giant jaguar. Or opt for the Cliff—a five-story freefall that's a real hanger. The Banzai is a triple-drop speedslide while Thunder Beach Wavepool will agitate with 750,000 gallons of crashing, ocean-style waves. Or take the spin cycle down the 470-degree helix Watusi. Floaters might better appreciate the Pearl, with its palm trees, waterfalls, and balmy waves; they can also drift and glide along the Lazy Miami River. Splash Mountain and Jolly Mon' Shores are aimed at the little squirts. Open daily from the end of May through August; some weekends in May and September. Admission is charged. (513) 398-7946; www.thebeachwaterpark.com.

WHERE TO SHOP

Aces and Eights. 2383 Kings Center Court, Mason, OH 45040. This 37,000-square-foot motorcycle emporium was named in honor of an 1876 shootout between Cincinnatian Charlie Henry Rich and his "buddy" Wild Bill Hickok. Go "hog" wild with a selection of Harley-Davidsons, apparel, and gear related to modern-day "outlaws," many of whom are doctors and accountants. (513) 459-1777; www.acesn8sharley.com.

Kings Mill General Store. 5687 Columbia Road, Kings Mills, OH 45034. This specialized shop features all manner of yuletide dolls, ornaments, and nutcrackers for the year-round Christmas enthusiast. (513) 398-1677; www.kingschristmas.com.

WHERE TO EAT

Course View Restaurant. 6042 Fairway Drive, Mason, OH 45040. The menu is American bistro, and there are more than fifty-five items to choose from. Dine with great patio and window views of the greens in the summertime or in front of a cozy fireplace in winter. Lunch and dinner only. $$-$$$. (513) 573-3321; www.thegolfcenter.com.

WHERE TO STAY

Kings Island Resort and Conference Center. 5691 Kings Island Drive, Kings Island, OH 45034. Recently renovated, this 288-room accommodation offers indoor/outdoor swimming pools, exercise and game rooms, as well as shuffleboard, tennis, volleyball, and basketball courts. There's a restaurant on-site, and outdoor barbecues are available. It's across the street from Kings Island; free transportation to the amusement park is provided. $$-$$$. (800) 727-3050; www.kingsislandresort.com.

Ramada Limited. 9665 Mason-Montgomery Road, Mason, OH 45040. Less than 4 miles from Kings Island, this former Country Hearth Inn offers a variety of room types, indoor swimming pool and whirlpool, in-room recliners, and an incredible breakfast of eggs, pancakes, waffles, cappucino, bagels, and more. $$. (513) 336-7911.

CINCINNATI

Had Cincinnati kept its original name of Losantiville, would it be as nifty as it is today? Would this gently rolling metropolis still have a funky downtown with 1920s and '30s architecture, pocket parks, and outdoor sculptures? Would it boast two major league sports teams and impressive venues like the new six-story eye candy Contemporary Arts Center (44 East Sixth Street; 513-721-0390), the Aronoff Center (650 Walnut Street; 513-721-3344) with its multiple performance spaces, and Riverbend Music Center (6295 Kellogg Avenue; 513-232-6220), which draws top-name acts? Or would it be a one-traffic-light hamlet with a Dari Twist and a gas station?

One will never know, thanks to the Society of Cincinnati, a group of Revolutionary War officers after which the city was named in 1790. By the mid-1800s, it was the sixth largest municipality in the nation and particularly popular with German immigrants, who lived in the now historic Over-the-Rhine neighborhood. And, like many places in Ohio, it served as a stopover for the Underground Railroad.

Although Prohibition resulted in the closure of twenty breweries, Cincinnati kept on truckin', adding new businesses and cultural attractions and rehabbing buildings. Visitors can explore Fountain Square in the heart of the city (on Fifth Street, between Walnut and Vine) or get the best views of downtown and the Ohio River from

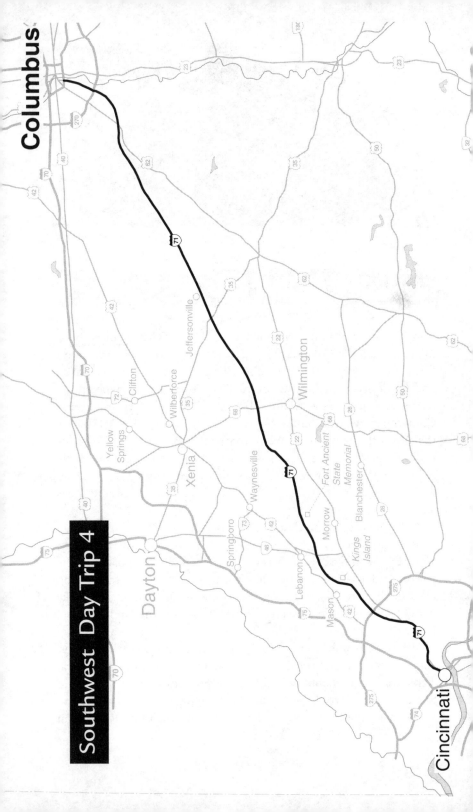

nearby Mt. Adams, a happening place with unique shopping, clubs, and restaurants. Fans of the arts will find plenty at the Cincinnati Opera (the second oldest in the United States), the Cincinnati Pops and the Symphony Orchestra, and the world-famous Playhouse in the Park. Or you can gambol over the state line for gambling at the Argosy Casino and Hotel Lawrenceburg (777 Argosy Parkway, Lawrenceburg, IN 47025; 888-274-6797; www.argosycasinos.com) or the Grand Victoria Casino and Resort (600 Grand Victoria Drive, Rising Sun, IN 47040; 800-473-6311).

From Columbus, Cincinnati is a straight shot down I-71 south, about an hour and a half away. Add more time at rush hour or if there's a Reds game at the spanking new Great American Ball Park or the Bengals are playing at Paul Brown Stadium. Hot dogs, anyone?

WHERE TO GO

Cincinnati Art Museum. 953 Eden Park Drive, Cincinnati, OH 45202. Nearly six millennia of world art is explored here, including

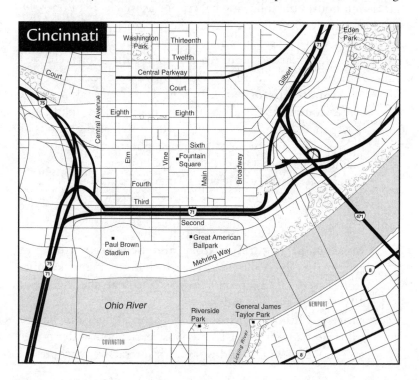

paintings, sculpture, decorative arts, costumes and textiles, drawings, and more. The new Cincinnati Wing, a $10 million renovation of 18,000 square feet of gallery space, makes the museum the first in the nation to have a permanent exhibition detailing its community's art history. Highlighted artists include painter Frank Duveneck, sculptor Hiram Powers, impressionist John H. Twachtman, and others in addition to a display of decorative arts from the Rookwood Pottery Company. Along with works from ancient Egypt, Greece, and Rome, you'll find art from Native Americans, the Near and Far East, and Africa. Displays encompass works by European old masters and American artists up to the 1980s. Standouts include the only collection of ancient Nabataean works outside of Jordan, a Herbert Greer French accumulation of old master prints, and European and American portrait miniatures. Open daily except Monday. Free. (513) 721–5204; www.cincinnatiartmuseum.org.

Cincinnati Museum Center. 1301 Western Avenue, Cincinnati, OH 45203. Located in Union Terminal, a 1933 art deco structure that served as a railway station until the early '70s, this restored combo attraction houses the following collections as well as the Robert D. Lindner Family OMNIMAX Theater, a five-story domed motion-picture screen with acoustics that make for an all-encompassing experience. Hours vary according to attraction. Admission is charged unless otherwise noted. (513) 287–7000; www.cincymuseum.org.

- **Cincinnati Historical Library.** This regional research center contains books, periodicals, manuscripts, maps, and newspapers dating back to the 1750s as well as thousands of nineteenth- and twentieth-century photographs and rare publications. Free. Open daily except Sunday.

- **Cincinnati History Museum.** Time travel, anyone? This re-creation of Old Cincinnati features settlers who tell visitors what it was like back on the frontier. A 90-foot side-wheel steamboat is also on display. Open daily.

- **Museum of Natural History and Science.** Visitors can explore the Ohio Valley landscape, including a Kentucky limestone cavern and a reproduction of Cincinnati's Ice Age from 19,000 years ago. Open daily.

- **Cinergy Children's Museum.** Kids of all ages can have a wilderness adventure in The Woods, learn about water power at The Water Works, and work with interactive machines in

The Energy Zone. Kids' Town and Children Just Like Me provide lessons in making friends locally and globally. Open daily.

Cincinnati Zoo and Botanical Garden. 3400 Vine Street, Cincinnati, OH 45220. With about 600 different animal species and 3,000 types of plants, this is one wild attraction. Not only does it have the most gorilla births of any zoo, but you can also view Komodo dragons, white Bengal tigers, and rare black Sumatran and Indian rhinos. There's a wildlife theater with performing critters and an exotic-cat training program, among other offerings. Camel rides, a renovated birdhouse, and a lush, tropical rain forest round out the exhibits. Open year-round. Admission is charged. (800) 944–4776; www.cincyzoo.org.

Krohn Conservatory/Eden Park. 1501 Eden Park Drive, Cincinnati, OH 45202. This 187-acre green space pretty much lives up to its Biblical namesake. In addition to lakes, statues, and a water tower, two groves of trees honor presidents and war heroes, respectively. Other sites of note include the Melan Arch bridge, a pioneering structure built in 1894; the 30-foot-high Ohio River Monument; and the Seasongood Pavilion, which hosts free summertime concerts. The warm weather also brings out flowering trees and a carpet of more than 50,000 daffodils. Completed in 1933 and one of the country's largest public greenhouses, Krohn Conservatory nurtures exotic tropical, desert, and orchid plants encompassing more than 1,000 species from all over the world. Seasonal highlights include Sherwood Forest (one might expect Robin Hood to leap from the heavily wooded oaks, boxwood, cineraria, primula, and blooming bulbs) and a butterfly show wherein thousands of winged wonders are released in a colorful enclosed garden. Open daily. Free, although donations welcome. (513) 421–5707; www.cinci-parks.org.

Taft Museum of Art. 316 Pike Street, Cincinnati, OH 45202. Built in 1820, this Federal-style structure served as the home of Anna Sinton and Charles Phelps Taft from their marriage in 1873 until their deaths during the Great Depression. Permanent collections include European and American master paintings, such as works by Rembrandt, Hals, Gainsborough, Sargent, and others; Chinese ceramics, mostly porcelains of the Kangxi reign; and European decorative arts, such as French Renaissance Limoges enamels and seventeenth- and eighteenth-century watches. The museum's

$19 million renovation includes expanded educational and exhibition facilities, a performance space, and upgraded gift shop and tea room. Open daily. Free on Wednesday and Sunday; admission charged the rest of the week. (513) 241-0343; www.taftmuseum.org.

National Underground Railroad Freedom Center. 312 Elm Street, Cincinnati, OH 45202. This national clearinghouse and museum is slated for a summer 2004 opening with exhibits, interactive programs, and genealogical research. Stories from the Underground Railroad and other bibliographical/historical data are being collected to add to the body of knowledge. Call for information. (877) 648-4838; www.undergroundrailroad.com.

Harriet Beecher Stowe House. 2950 Gilbert Avenue, Cincinnati, OH 45206. This Cincinnati home of Harriet Beecher Stowe, author of *Uncle Tom's Cabin,* was restored in 1978 and includes a museum, gift shop, and cultural center. Call for hours. Admission may be charged. (513) 632-5120.

Cincinnati Fire Museum. 315 West Court Street, Cincinnati, OH 45202. Along with teaching fire prevention and management techniques, this attraction lights up the area's 200 years of contributions to the field through illustrations, memorabilia, and equipment. Go out in a blaze of glory and slide down the fire pole, "drive" the big red truck, and ring the antique bell. Closed Monday and holidays. Admission is charged. (513) 621-5553 or 621-5571; www.cincinet.com/firemuseum.

Newport Aquarium. One Aquarium Way, Newport, KY 41071. From I-71, take I-471 south to the Newport exit (Route 8) and turn left; it's about five minutes from downtown Cincinnati. Swim with the big fish without getting wet: This million-gallon aquarium has glass floors so you can "walk" on water infested with "bizarre and dangerous creatures" and underwater tunnels for "diving" with the sharks in a coral reef. Larger-than-life murals, special effects, and 11,000 marine animals encompassing 600 species create total immersion. Open daily. Admission is charged. (859) 491-3467; www.newportaquarium.com.

WHERE TO SHOP

Tower Place at the Carew Tower. 28 West Fourth Street, Cincinnati, OH 45202. Three levels have nearly seventy exclusive shops and boutiques that include jewelers, home entertainment, gifts, books, and novelties. Along with a health club, food court, and restaurants, visitors can avail themselves of a downtown view via an observation deck as well as a skywalk to various hotels, the convention center, and stores such as Saks and the "I Love Cincinnati" shop. (513) 241-5888; www.towerplace.com.

The Gilded Age. 1120 Saint Gregory Street, Cincinnati, OH 45202. Those looking for unique gifts will find antiques, framed art, lighting, contemporary silver jewelry, and other home accessories at this Mt. Adams store. (513) 421-6122.

Kilimanjaro African Art. 310 Ludlow Avenue, Cincinnati, OH 45220. Since 1980, the proprietor has been carving and importing African art. Sculptures, masks, music and instruments, clothing, jewelry, and more are among the many authentic offerings bursting at the seams of this store. (513) 221-0700.

Coomers Craft Mall. 455 East Kemper Road, Cincinnati, OH 45246. One of the largest selections of handmade crafts, gifts, and home-decor accessories around, this emporium displays the works of up to 500 crafters in a department store–like setting. (513) 671-5505; www.coomers.com.

Kenwood Towne Center. 7875 Montgomery Road, Cincinnati, OH 45236. With more than 180 stores, this is serious shopping. Along with the usual suspects of Lazarus, Dillard's, Parisian, Banana Republic, and others, many one-of-a-kind boutiques can be found here. (513) 745-9100; www.shopkenwood.com.

WHERE TO EAT

La Normandie Taverne and Chop House. 118 East Sixth Street, Cincinnati, OH 45202. A downtown tradition for almost seventy years, specialties include dry-aged steaks, fresh fish, and rack of lamb. Although it boasts experienced wait staff and original timber and brick walls, you can still throw peanut shells on the floor and enjoy free hors d'oeuvres during weekday happy hours in the bar. $$–$$$. (513) 721-2761; www.lanormandy.com.

Maisonette. 114 East Sixth Street, Cincinnati, OH 45202. The ultimate anti-McDonald's, this French grub has been awarded Mobil's five stars for nearly forty years, more than any other restaurant in America. The opulent decor, sumptuous food, and polished service in a place where everything is prepared with panache make for an unforgettable experience. Reservations required. $$$. (513) 721–2260; www.maisonette.com.

Montgomery Inn Boathouse. 925 Eastern Avenue, Cincinnati, OH 45202. This eatery boasts an irresistible combination: a wonderful view of the river and terrific ribs, among other menu items. Purchase the sauce to make your own at home. $$–$$$. (513) 721–7427; www.montgomeryinn.com.

Roly Poly Rolled Sandwiches. 425 Walnut Street, Cincinnati, OH 45202. This cafe serves more than fifty gourmet rolled tortilla-and-filling combos and hearty homemade soups. Specialties in the former include grilled egg Rolys for breakfast, the monster veggie, basil cashew chicken, smokehouse turkey, pepper steak, and more. $–$$. (513) 721–4499; www.rolypolyusa.com.

Mt. Adams Fish House. 940 Pavilion Street, Cincinnati, OH 45202. Along with fresh sushi and high-quality seafood, this chic restaurant boasts an extensive wine list, daily specials, and carry-out. $$–$$$. (513) 421–3250; www.mtadamsfishhouse.com.

Rookwood Pottery Bistro. 1077 Celestial Street, Cincinnati, OH 45202. Located in the historic Rookwood Pottery building atop Mt. Adams, this casual, upscale eatery features American cooking with a European (mostly French) flair. $$. (513) 721–5456.

WHERE TO STAY

The Cincinnatian. 601 Vine Street, Cincinnati, OH 45202. The region's only Mobil four-star, AAA four-diamond hotel, this accommodation combines elegant tradition with modern amenities. Full-time concierge, evening turndown, in-room safes, newspapers by request, and twenty-four-hour room service are but a few refinements. $$$. (800) 942–9000; www.cincinnatianhotel.com.

Garfield Suites Hotel. 2 Garfield Place, Cincinnati, 45202. It's all suites, all the time, with personalized service, completely equipped full-size kitchens, separate bedrooms, two-line phones, and health club privileges. With a deli, room service, cable TV, and pay-per-view movies, you will neither starve nor suffer from video deprivation. $$-$$$. (513) 421-3355; www.garfieldsuiteshotel.com.

Wallace House Bed & Breakfast. 120 Wallace Avenue, Covington, KY 41014. Located five minutes south of downtown Cincinnati, this 1905 Queen Anne Victorian offers large and luxurious rooms with private baths and queen-size beds. A hearty, home-cooked breakfast, high-speed Internet access, and a centrally located big-screen TV with movies help seal the deal. $$$. (888) 942-8177; www.wallacehousebb.com.

Cincinnati's Weller Haus. 319 Poplar Street, Newport, KY 41073. These two side-by-side Victorian Gothic homes offer uniquely decorated guest rooms with private baths and phones. Breakfast is served by candlelight. $$-$$$. (800) 431-4287; www.wellerhaus.com.

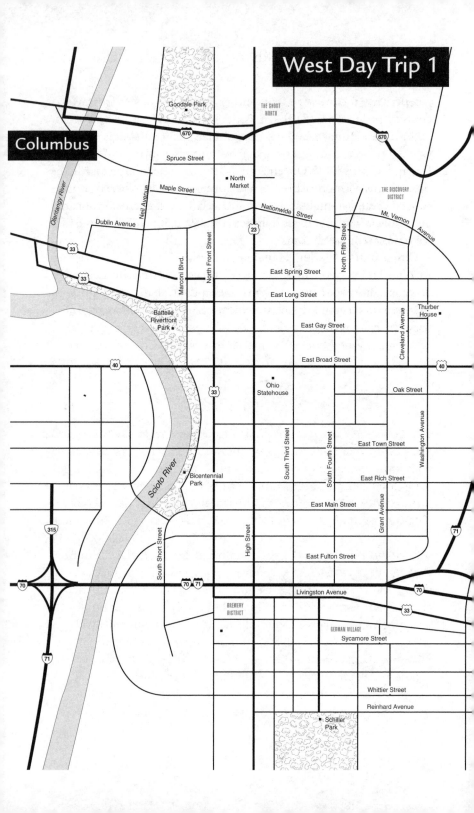

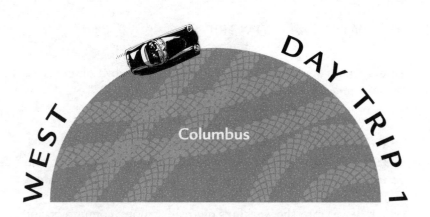

COLUMBUS

For those who'd rather not travel far, there's Columbus. It's listed among *Fodor's* top picks for overlooked/underrated places to visit during the cold months, but Columbus has plenty to offer year-round.

Downtown alone is worthy of serious touring, although the surrounding areas have major sights, too. Along with several unique and varied districts, there's a replica of the *Santa Maria* in Battelle Riverfront Park (614–645–8760) and numerous arts- and science-type draws. And there's lots of sports, ranging from the Columbus Blue Jackets, the city's NHL hockey team, to the Ohio State University's 2002 National Championship football team and its always-popular basketball team. In between are the Columbus Crew (with the first-ever stadium built specifically for a major-league soccer team); the Columbus Clippers minor-league baseball team; the Columbus Marathon, a qualifier for the Boston Marathon; and two—count 'em—race tracks: Beulah Park for Thoroughbred horses (3664 Grant Avenue, Grove City; 614–871–9600; www.beulahpark.com) and Scioto Downs for harness racing (6000 High Street; 614–491–2515; www.sciotodowns.com).

Thanks to Interstates 270, 670, 71, and 70, U.S. 23 and 33, and SR 315 and 161, Columbus is easily navigable. However, should you visit during road construction season (March until November or even December), it's best to ask a local for an alternate route to avoid

185

singing those orange-barrel blues. Could that be why Columbus is a recommended *winter* diversion?

WHERE TO GO

COSI. 333 West Broad Street, Columbus, OH 43215. This learning experience for all ages focuses on everything from *Adventure,* an archaeological dig that offers up ancient puzzles, to *i/o,* which delves into the workings of arcade games, computers, and musical instruments. You'll also explore the mystery of life, the ocean, and space, and you can travel through time in a model town as it develops from 1898 to 1962. There's also a little-kids' area, two traveling exhibition galleries, an outdoor science park, and three theaters, one of which has a seven-story screen and a motion simulator. Open daily. Admission is charged. (888) 819-2674; www.cosi.org.

Columbus Museum of Art. 480 East Broad Street, Columbus, OH 43215. This extensive collection of American and European art from 1850 to 1945 features impressionists, expressionists, cubists, modernists, and "contemporaries" with works by Degas, Monet, Matisse, Picasso, Bellows, Demuth, Hopper, Marin, and O'Keeffe. Highlights include the Russell Page Sculpture Garden, the Ross Photography Center, and an interactive exhibition for children and families, *Eye Spy: Adventures in Art.* The museum also hosts continuous programs of national and international traveling exhibitions. Closed Monday. Admission is charged. (614) 221-6801; www.columbusmuseum.org.

Wexner Center for the Arts. 1871 North High Street, Columbus, OH 43210. A magnet for eclecticism, this venue attracts creative artists and programs from all media. Constructed courtesy of hometown billionaire Leslie Wexner (of The Limited, Bath and Body Works, and other retail conglomerates), its architecture is an amalgamation of contemporary, modern, and classic designs, with local overtones (don't ask). Its unconventional appearance is matched by a layout that can be confusing even to those with a good sense of direction. Still, it's worth the visit if only to see something that has been written up in every architectural magazine around and has been described as "a spaceship that crash landed on the prairies." Open daily. Admission is charged. (614) 292–3535; www.wexarts.org.

Motorcycle Hall of Fame Museum. 13515 Yarmouth Drive, Pickerington, OH 43147. Vroom, vroom . . . in fewer than fifteen years, the Motorcycle Hall of Fame Museum evolved from a favorite of aficionados to a major attraction and caretaker of America's motorcycle heritage, drawing even nonbikers. The twenty-three-acre campus doubles as American Motorcyclist Association headquarters and houses an impressive collection of Harleys, Hendersons, Indians, and Hondas (pre-Acura). The two-story, 26,000-square-foot facility showcases thousands of machines, from early board-trackers and streamliners to competition Superbikes and Motocrossers. Open daily. Admission is charged. (614) 856–2221; www.ama-cycle.org/museum/.

Franklin Park Conservatory and Botanical Garden. 1777 East Broad Street, Columbus, OH 43203. Tired of the weather? Here you can go to a different climate year-round in a series of separate zones that represent four regions of the world. Visit the cool Himalayan mountains or tropical forest. Or hit the desert, then head over to a rain forest. You can also plant yourself in traditional rooms housing palm, bonsai, and orchid collections. Two landscaped courtyards are open during warm weather. Open daily except for Monday (unless it's a holiday Monday). Admission is charged. (800) 214–7275; www.fpconservatory.org.

Columbus Zoo and Aquarium. 9990 Riverside Drive, Powell, OH 43065. Go north on I–270 to the Sawmill Road exit, and go north again. Turn left on Powell Road to Riverside Drive. Talk about animal attraction: Nearly all continents are covered here. There's an African rain forest; a North American section with prairie dogs, migratory birds, and wetlands; and critters from South America, Asia, and Australia. The Manatee Coast is one of three facilities outside Florida to exhibit these endangered critters. The cheetah and lowland gorilla breeding programs and ever-popular ape exhibit have spawned not only offspring, but also imitators (monkey see, monkey do?). The zoo boasts one of the country's largest collections of reptiles, and the director emeritus, "Jungle Jack" Hanna, is a regular on *David Letterman* and other national TV shows. Open daily. Admission is charged. (614) 645–3400; www.colszoo.org.

THE DISTRICTS

One of the neat things about Columbus is that you can explore the following districts 24/7 and not spend a penny if that's your preference or if you're extremely self-disciplined.

German Village. Six blocks south of the State Capitol and south of I–70 (Third and Fourth Street exits). Mailing address: German Village Society, 588 South Third Street, Columbus, OH 43206. This restored nineteenth-century community with renovated homes, quaint shops, and unique pubs and eateries has picture-perfect brick-and-limestone cottages and well-tended sidewalks, gardens, and flower boxes as well as lovely green spaces. Rescued from the wrecking ball in 1960 by the above-mentioned society, it is now on the National Register of Historic Places. But parking's difficult to find: Pay close attention to signage or be prepared for a ticket or tow. (614) 221–8888; www.germanvillage.org.

Brewery District. Just to the west and north of German Village in and around High and Front Streets, this fun and funky area contains happening nightspots, cool restaurants, microbreweries, and wineries. Historically, German residents produced beer and ale here, although Prohibition put a drain on that, resulting in a downward spiral, so to speak. However, many of the warehouses and original buildings have been refurbished to their original beauty, allowing for a taste of history as well.

Arena District. Nationwide Arena, 77 East Nationwide Boulevard, Columbus, OH 43215. Go north up High Street and through downtown, turn left on Nationwide Boulevard, and you'll run into Columbus's newest "star," Nationwide Arena. Home of the Columbus Blue Jackets, this 20,000-seat multipurpose facility hosts concerts and other events. The nifty, parklike area around it has ninety-five acres of sidewalks and paths, an outside giant-screen TV, restaurants, bars, and retail outlets. Cowtown, no more. (614) 677–9000; www.nationwidearena.com.

Short North. Mailing address: 120 West Goodale Street, Columbus, OH 43215. Literally a few blocks north of the Arena District, this popular, revitalized neighborhood hosts gallery hops on the first Saturday of each month. Prints, paintings, ceramics, and more from local to international artists can be found, as well as specially crafted home goods, clothing, and jewelry. There are loads of one-of-a-kind restaurants and plenty of clubs with live music. (614) 228–8050; www.shortnorth.org.

University. Ohio State University, Columbus, OH 43210. Go farther north on High Street and you'll run into 16,000 acres with about 50,000 college students. Along with buildings, libraries, and a strip of campus-related shops, bookstores, and restaurants, you'll find Ohio Stadium, home of the Buckeye football team, and a new Jack Nicklaus museum, which honors the Columbus-born and OSU-grad golfer. (614) 292–6446; www.ohio-state.edu.

WHERE TO SHOP

North Market. 56 Spruce Street, Columbus, OH 43215. This indoor fresh-produce emporium has been around for almost 125 years. Offerings include vegetables, meats, poultry, and baked goods as well as exotic and ethnic foods. You can even dine here; seating provided. (614) 463–9664; www.northmarket.com.

Book Loft. 631 South Third Street, Columbus, OH 43206. This independent bookstore has more than 100,000 hardbacks and paperbacks in thirty-two rooms in a pre–Civil War structure. Best of all, most titles are discounted, some of them quite heavily. There's also a selection of CDs, cards, and posters, and visitors can enjoy their purchases in a peaceful adjoining courtyard. (614) 464–1774; www.bookloft.com.

Polaris Fashion Place. 1500 Polaris Parkway, Columbus, OH 43240. Just what Columbus needs . . . another mall. It got it anyway, and this version includes Saks, Kaufmann's, JCPenney, Lazarus, Sears, and The Great Indoors, plus more than 160 specialty shops and several restaurants. And it's huge, encompassing two levels with more than 1.5 million square feet and four major intersections. You can put on your walking shoes while waiting for the massive traffic to subside. (614) 846–1500; www.polarisfashionplace.com.

Easton Town Center. 160 Easton Town Center, Columbus, OH 43219. This state-of-the-entertainment center is why some cultures regard America as the Evil Empire (at least in the sense of materialism). Almost 150 monuments to consumerism in this nicely laid-out outdoor/indoor mall include AMC Easton 30 Movies,

Gameworks, Virgin Megastore, Cheesecake Factory, Nordstrom, Lazarus, Funny Bone comedy club, and an open-air venue for various performers. (614) 416-7000; www.eastontowncenter.com.

Mall at Tuttle Crossing. 5043 Tuttle Crossing Boulevard, Dublin, OH 43016. Located at I-270 and Tuttle Crossing Boulevard, a little farther from the madding crowd, is this exquisitely decorated 974,000-square-foot shopping arena featuring Lazarus, Nordic Track, Eddie Bauer, Fossil, Talbot's, and more than 120 other stores. Bonus: a children's playscape made up of giant-size breakfast foods perfect for climbing (but not eating). (614) 717-9300; www.shop tuttlecrossing.com.

WHERE TO EAT

The First Wendy's. 257 East Broad Street, Columbus, OH 43215. Named after owner Dave Thomas's daughter, what was destined to become one of the largest and most popular food chains opened at this location on November 15, 1969. To date it's spawned more than 5,000 franchises in thirty-four countries. You know what to expect. $. (614) 464-4656; www.wendys.com.

Mitchell's Steakhouse. 45 North Third Street, Columbus, OH 43215. From one extreme to the other: This cosmopolitan, upscale steak and chop house offers the finest hand-cut, aged, corn-fed USDA prime. Other specialties include lobster tails, fresh bread, and house-made soups, dressings, and sauces. And the decor is as sublime as the food. $$$. (614) 621-2333; www.cameronmitchell.com.

Columbus Brewing Company (CBC). 525 Short Street, Columbus, OH 43215. This menu covers the full gamut: wood-fired pizzas, pasta, steaks, chicken, chops, seafood, salads, and more. No "specials of the house" here; everything is good. The author likes it so much she went there for a recent "decade" birthday. $$-$$$. (614) 464-2739; www.cameronmitchell.com.

Tapatio. 491 North Park Street, Columbus, OH 43215. This Mexican-Caribbean mix results in some delicious combinations and flavors. Menu changes regularly, but the ambience is always friendly and cheerful. $$-$$$. (614) 221-1085.

R. J. Snappers Bar & Gill. 700 North High Street, Columbus, OH 43215. This "seafood with imagination" includes live (but not for long) Maine lobsters, jumbo king crab legs, shrimp, mussels, clams, scallops, and many varieties of fresh fish. Aged steaks, an award-winning pork dish, and chicken are available for nonfin fans. Decorated to resemble a European fishing village, the interior has a mural of Portofino, Italy, plus stone walls and balconies. Upstairs is more sedate dining. $$– $$$. (614) 280–1070.

Elevator Brewery & Draught Haus. 161 North High Street, Columbus, OH 43215. Located in the historic Clock Restaurant and close to many downtown attractions, this eatery is dark wood and stained-glass intensive. Handcrafted microbrews and other beverages complement house-cut steaks, fish, chicken, and pork. There's also a nifty bar area and accompanying munchies like corn brats, chicken wings, and quesadillas. $$. (614) 228–0500; www.elevator brewing.com.

WHERE TO STAY

The Lofts. 55 Nationwide Boulevard, Columbus, OH 43215. This example of nineteenth-century architecture has evolved into a high-falutin' experience. Originally a warehouse, accommodations here include exposed brick walls, beams, and ductwork; New York subway-style tile in the bathroom; and custom designed lighting, furniture, and accessories. They also have high-speed Internet access, personal butler service, and cell doors from the Ohio Penitentiary. Go figure. $$$. (800) 745–6387; www.55lofts.com.

Westin Great Southern. 310 South High Street, Columbus, OH 43215. The only nineteenth-century hotel building still in use, this lodging boasts classy chandeliers, a spectacular stained-glass ceiling, and magnificent marble floors. All rooms have cherry-wood furnishings, luxurious baths, personalized voice mail, and a fitness center. $$$. (614) 228–3800.

50 Lincoln Inn. 50 East Lincoln, Columbus, OH 43215. Situated in the Short North, this recently renovated mid-city retreat boasts eight rooms named after famous artists, each with a queen-size bed, full bath, and cable TV. You can purchase original work, which decorates the common areas, from local artisans, and "exhibits" change regularly. $$$. (888) 299–5051; www.50lincoln.com.

Harrison House. 313 West Fifth Avenue, Columbus, OH 43201. Located in historic Victorian Village, a suburb full of rehabbed

Victorians, this residence is close to downtown, Ohio State, and other local areas of interest. Along with original cut-glass windows, ornate woodwork, lace curtains, and more, four guest rooms include private baths and amenities such as cable and phone. Full breakfast included; those leaving the table hungry do so by choice. $$. (800) 827-4203; www.columbus-bed-breakfast.com.

Worthington Inn. 649 High Street, Worthington, OH 43085. Constructed in 1831 and located in the quaint New England–style community of Worthington, each of the twenty-six rooms is unique and furnished with genuine American antiques. Further pampering takes place in the form of cocktails at sunset, oversize towels and fluffy robes, twice-daily housekeeping, and a full breakfast. $$$. (614) 885-2600; www.worthingtoninn.com.

West Liberty · Zanesfield · Bellefontaine · Lakeview

For diversity, Logan County is tough to beat: Along with skiing and snowboarding in the winter, you can romp at the lake and go horseback riding during the warm months. There are two caverns and two castles, and a few miles east of Bellefontaine is Mount Campbell (actually Campbell Hill, according to the map), a whopping 1,550 feet above sea level. Bellefontaine also lays claim to the first concrete street in America and the shortest road (McKinley Street, just 17 feet long). So many rarities, so little time.

WEST LIBERTY

About an hour northwest of Columbus, the region can be reached a couple of ways. Those wishing to go directly to West Liberty can take I–70 west to SR 68 north. Or you can opt for the more picturesque (i.e., circuitous) route via I–270 to U.S. 33, then north to SR 245 west, which leads directly to attractions such as Ohio Caverns and the Piatt Castles.

WHERE TO GO

Ohio Caverns. 2210 East SR 245, West Liberty, OH 43357. Discovered in the late 1800s by a farmhand, this truly cool (54 degrees, no matter what the outside temperature) underground cave quickly became a tourist draw. Its crystalline stalactite and stalagmite formations, including the humongous 5-foot Crystal King, are ever-evolving,

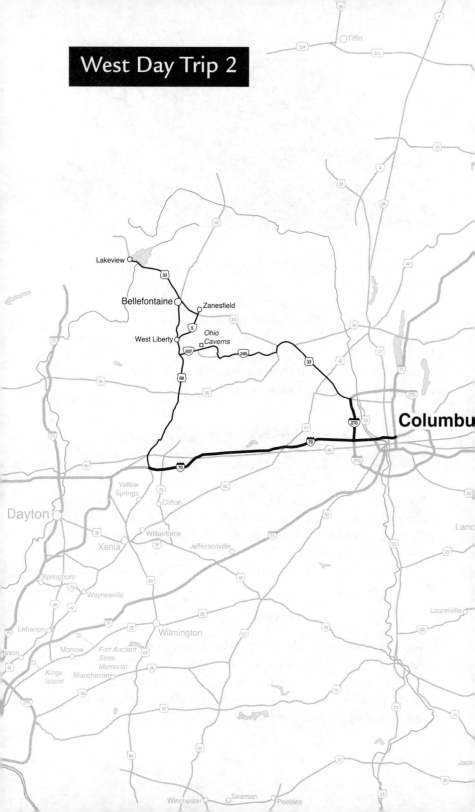

West Day Trip 2

kaleidoscopic, and varied, making each visit a little bit different. Well-lit paved walkways, a gift shop, and shelter house/picnic tables make for a pleasant diversion. Open daily. Admission is charged. (937) 465-4017; www.cavern.com/ohiocaverns.

Piatt Castles. 10051 Township Road 47, West Liberty, OH 43357. Two locally prominent brothers, General Abram Sanders Piatt and Colonel Donn Piatt, decided that their home should truly be their castle(s). In the late 1800s, Abram built Mac-A-Cheek, while Donn constructed Mac-O-Chee. Both were decorated and frescoed by French artist Oliver Frey. "Cheek" has remained in the Piatt family for five generations and sits atop a hill amid awe-inspiring surroundings. "Chee" has extraordinary painted walls and ceilings and unusual architecture. Both are loaded with antiques, Native American artifacts, and relics from the Civil and Mexican Wars, and host various special and seasonal programs. Open March through October, Thanksgiving through New Years; other times by appointment. Admission is charged. (937) 465-2821.

WHERE TO SHOP

Marie's Candies. 311 Zanesfield Road, West Liberty, OH 43357. This sweet success story started in 1956 and has continued to grow, just like consumers' waistlines. More than eighty varieties of chocolates are sold in this historical train depot, and before buying, you get to sample the merchandise. (866) 465-5781; www.mariescandies.com.

Pioneer House/Underground Railroad. 10245 Township Road 47, West Liberty, OH 43357. The historic log home of the Piatt brothers' parents is now a gift shop. Elizabeth Piatt, their mother, sheltered fugitive slaves whenever her husband, a federal circuit court judge, was out of town. He sent a messenger to warn of his return so the slaves could move to the next stop and she could avoid arrest for her "illegal" activities. Today's tamer ambience includes Yankee candles (how appropriate), tinware, quilts, lace linens, antiques, and other Americana. (937) 465-4801.

Global Crafts. 106 Detroit Street, West Liberty, OH 43357. This truly international selection ranges from handcrafted reed baskets to Kenyan carvings to textiles, boxes, jewelry, and soapstone from India. Global Crafts is a nonprofit branch of the Mennonite Central Committee, a relief and development agency. (937) 465-3077.

WHERE TO STAY

Allen House. 206 North Detroit Street, West Liberty, OH 43357. Built in 1867, this comfy, antique-filled home has the distinction of hand-carved woodwork and a ceiling painted by muralist Oliver Frey. Option of private or shared bath. $$. (937) 465–8475; www.countylogan.com/allenhouse.

ZANESFIELD

From West Liberty, take CR 5 north about 8 miles to Zanesfield.

WHERE TO GO

Mad River Mountain Ski Resort. 100 Snow Valley Road, Zanesfield, OH 43360. With an elevation of 1,460 feet, this place has lots of altitude. There are more than twenty trails for skiing or snowboarding. A major snowmaking system covers 125 acres in case Mother Nature decides not to cooperate. Trails range from gentle slopes for children and beginners ("Placid Trail," "Big Easy") to "most difficult" and "experts only" with shiver-making names like "The Chute" and "Peril." Those who prefer sled riding can take advantage of the tubing park. Lessons, a beginner's area, accessory shop, and cafe round out the offerings. Open daily, December through March. Admission is charged. (800) 231–7669; www.skimadriver.com.

 Marmon Valley Farm. 5807 CR 153, Zanesfield, OH 43360. With 480 acres of fields, woods, hills, and streams, these riding stables offer English and Western options on more than one hundred horses and ponies. It also hosts summer camps, barn dances, sledding, and sleigh-riding activities as well as church retreats. Hours vary. Call for reservations and fee information. (937) 593–8000; www.marmonvalley.com.

WHERE TO SHOP

Country Patchwork. 4815 Bellefontaine Street, Zanesfield, OH 43360. Along with pottery, collectible china, and antique boxes, quilts, and other home accessories, this emporium also sells gently used clothing. (937) 592–1769.

The Court House Square. 2799 Sandusky Street, Zanesfield, OH 43360. Heritage lace, Yesteryear pottery, and Taronga West candles are but a few of the items for purchase. Crystal, ceramics, pottery, various handcrafts, lawn art, and dry and silk flowers can also be obtained. (800) 592-6415; www.court-house-square.com.

The Village Basketry. 3077 Main Street, Zanesfield, OH 43360. This well-trodden emporium contains handmade oak-bottom baskets, among other things. (937) 592-2449.

WHERE TO STAY

Myeerah's Inn. Sandusky Street, Zanesfield, OH 43360. Formerly a stagecoach stop and goods store in the early 1800s, this large two-story brick structure now boasts three guest rooms furnished with Ohio antiques. Fresh flowers, mints, and a hearty French country breakfast are other niceties. Bonus: The proprietor's husband is the county coroner. $$. (937) 593-3746.

BELLEFONTAINE

Just 5 miles from Zanesfield, Bellefontaine can be reached by going west on U.S. 33.

WHERE TO GO

Zane Shawnee Caverns. 7092 SR 540, Bellefontaine, OH 43311. This a"maze"ing conglomeration of chambers and corridors consists of three levels of varied formations of stalactites and stalagmites. Ohio's only "cave pearls," created from dripping mineral-laden water, can be found here. The caverns also have the somewhat creepy distinction of being a hibernation center for bats. Located in Southwind Park and owned and operated by the Shawnee Nation, the site also features a Native American museum. Open daily. Admission is charged. (937) 592-9592; www.zaneshawneecaverns.org.

Orr Mansion/Logan County Historical Museum. 521 East Columbus Avenue, Bellefontaine, OH 43311. In 1908 a local lumber baron built this neoclassical mansion, which also serves as the county museum and archives. Highlights include two-story columns, a third-floor porch, and oak woodwork, with vintage furniture, clothing, musical instruments, and more scattered throughout. Local railroad items, an antique toy collection, and military artifacts share space with a one-room school and general store. Open Wednesday and Friday through Sunday, May through October; Friday and Saturday, November through April. Admission is charged. (937) 593-7557.

WHERE TO SHOP

Garden of Glass. 1229 South Main Street, Bellefontaine, OH 43311. Don't throw stones in here. Original stained-glass artwork includes window inserts, boxes, lamps, and other designs. (937) 599-2223.

WHERE TO EAT

The Belle Deli. 210 West Columbus, Bellefontaine, OH 43311. Choose from several fresh-cut meats and cheeses and design your own sandwich with chips and a pickle. Premade salads are also available, as are a variety of soups and desserts. $. (937) 262-7600.

WHERE TO STAY

Whitmore House. 3985 SR 47, Bellefontaine, OH 43311. This century-old Victorian home sits amid four acres of lawns and gardens. Three bedrooms and a restaurant are provided; a full breakfast can be purchased. $. (937) 592-4290.

Mountain Top Inn. 308 North Main Street, Bellefontaine, OH 43311. This friendly, family-owned motel has fifty rooms with all the usual suspects: A/C, cable, microwave, refrigerator, laundry, and outdoor pool. $-$$. (937) 593-9622.

Woodland Hotel. 1134 North Main Street, Bellefontaine, OH 43311. This recently built one-hundred-room accommodation has such extras as indoor pool and hot tub, complimentary continental breakfast, on-site restaurant and bar, and fitness center. Mention that you're going to Mad River Mountain to get a special rate. $-$$. (937) 593-8515.

LAKEVIEW

From Bellefontaine, Lakeview is a straight shot northwest on U.S. 33, less than 15 miles.

WHERE TO GO

Indian Lake. 12774 SR 235 North, Lakeview, OH 43331. A fancy resort at the turn of the last century, Indian Lake was once labeled the Midwest's Million Dollar Playground. Now a public park and the state's second largest artificially made body of water, its 5,800 acres of H_2O are ideal for boating, fishing, and picnicking. A nature center offers up historical displays, a wildlife room, aquarium, and hands-on area. Two beaches, campgounds, 7 miles of easy walking trails, and a paved bike path add to the big puddle's appeal. Open daily. Free. (937) 843-2717; www.ohiostateparks.org.

WHERE TO EAT

Brothers Bar & Grill. 11977 SR 235, Lakeview, OH 43331. This unassuming eatery specializes in burgers, fried fish sandwiches, chicken gizzards, and bar food, and hosts live local entertainment. $. (937) 843-3449.

   Cranberry Resort. 9667 SR 368, Huntsville, OH 43324. It sounds like a hotel but is actually a restaurant/club. Along with appetizers, a huge selection of sandwiches, salads, pies, and a kids' menu, there's a full lineup of local entertainment. Beer 'n' ribs are a feature on Thursday. Patrons can arrive by land or by boat and just pull up at the dock. $. (937) 842-4947; www.cranberry-resort.com.

WHERE TO STAY

Indian Lake State Park Campground. 12774 SR 235 North, Lakeview, OH 43331. Three hundred seventy sites for tents and RVs and seventy-three nonelectric hookups can be found at this first-come, first served area. Showers, flush toilets, laundry facilities, miniature golf course, and bike rental are included. Or you can rent a tepee, camper cabin, or tent. $. (937) 843-2717; www.ohiostateparks.org.

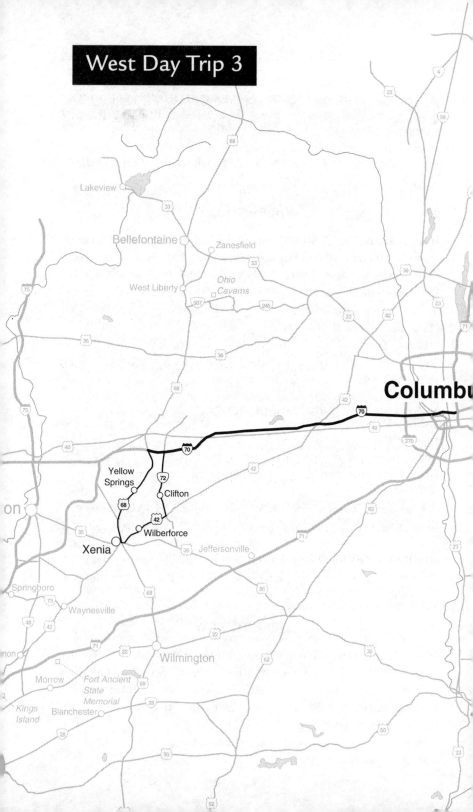

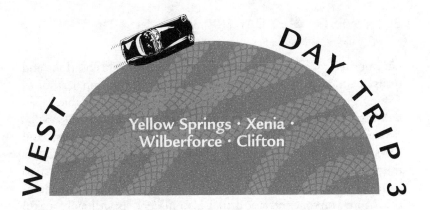

Yellow Springs · Xenia · Wilberforce · Clifton

Those looking for a change of pace would do well to visit this area. Along with what some might call hippie-dippy Yellow Springs, there's an old mill stream, Rails-to-Trails hiking and biking, plus an African-American history museum.

YELLOW SPRINGS

Although it's only about an hour from Columbus, Yellow Springs could be in an alternate universe. A hotbed of radicalism during the Vietnam era, the home of Antioch College (795 Livermore Street, Yellow Springs, OH 45387, 937-769-1000; www.antioch-college.edu) retains its patina of cutting-edge unconventionality through its shops, artistic life, and political interest groups, whose flyers and brochures seem to proliferate from every bulletin board and telephone pole. This is the place to go if you want to revisit the '60s—sort of.

To get to Yellow Springs, take I-70 west, and go south on U.S. 68, a total of about 60 miles.

WHERE TO GO

John Bryan State Park/Clifton Gorge State Nature Preserve. 3790 SR 370, Yellow Springs, OH 45387. This spectacular example of your geological forces at work encompasses Clifton Gorge, a designated national natural landmark with distinctive rock formations, massive trees, and varied, lacy stands of wildflowers. The park itself has hundreds of oaks and maples, as well as various shrubs, flora, and birds, making it a scenic event no matter what the season. Camping, fishing, boating, hiking, rock climbing, and more are available. Open daily. Free. (937) 767–1274 or 964–8794; www.ohiostateparks.org.

Glen Helen Nature Preserve. 405 Corry Street, Yellow Springs, OH 45387. With 1,000 acres of thickets, forests, meadows, and rivers, this is the point from which Yellow Springs' namesake waters, once believed to be a cure-all, originate. There's also an ecology institute, outdoor education center, raptor center, and trailside museum, as well as beautiful walking and hiking terrain, making it a favorite of nature lovers and inquiring minds of all ages. Open daily. Donations welcome. (937) 767–7375; www.glenhelen.org.

Young's Jersey Dairy. 6880 Springfield-Xenia Road, Yellow Springs, OH 45387. Along with indulging in arguably the best milk shakes and ice cream around, visitors can pet and visit farm animals, play eighteen holes of miniature golf, and hone their putting and batting skills. Depending on the time of year, you can watch cows being milked, wander through a cornfield maze, take a hayride, or participate in holiday-themed events. Altogether an udderly mooving experience. Open daily. Admission may be charged. (937) 325–0629; www.youngsdairy.com.

Little Miami Scenic Trail. Yellow Springs station: on the bike path between Xenia Avenue and Dayton Street. Mailing address: Rails-to-Trails Conservancy, Ohio Field Office, 65 East Wilson Bridge Road, Suite 203, Worthington, OH 43085. The Yellow Springs to Xenia route runs about 10 miles over scenic natural surroundings, ending on Third Street in Xenia. Many of the paths originated from unused tracks and are part of the national Rails-to-Trails program. Expect to encounter all ages and levels of fitness on the trail itself, from senior citizen hikers and moms with new babies to serious cyclists who zip by at amazing speeds. Constructed from railroad buildings and refurbished, both the Yellow Springs and Xenia stations provide restrooms, concessions, and displays, and serve as a stopover. Open daily. Free. (937) 370–7445.

WHERE TO SHOP

Yellow Springs has an abundance of specialized and eclectic stores, many of which have been around for well over twenty years. You can spend an hour or a day, and prices are generally reasonable. The shops feature compelling and unusual items from a regional colony of artists who, like shopkeepers and other locals, have found permanent refuge in the alternative lifestyle.

Angelic Devas. 245½ Xenia Avenue, Yellow Springs, OH 45387. Seekers of environmental spiritualism will be enlightened by books, classes, gifts, and more. (937) 767-7273.

Bonadies Glass Studio. 220 Xenia Avenue, Yellow Springs, OH 45387. This emporium specializes in custom stained-glass windows, lamps, and other art, along with restoration of existing items. One of the best facilities of its kind. (937) 767-7021.

Brunings Clock Shop. 257 Xenia Avenue, Yellow Springs, OH 45387. Brands range from Bulova to Sligh. The company buys merchandise in bulk, passing along discounts to customers. Casual, contemporary, colonial, and conservative can be found under one roof, meeting all your timely needs. (937) 767-1055.

Dark Star Books. 237 Xenia Avenue, Yellow Springs, OH 45387. With more than 40,000 used fiction and nonfiction tomes in all categories, you'll never run out of reading material. Comic books, gaming and trading cards, and even bumper stickers are also tendered. (937) 767-9400; www.darkstarbookstore.com.

Earth Rose. 221 Xenia Avenue, Yellow Springs, OH 45387. Who needs mall-wear when you can choose from among Birkenstock shoes, Indian print and handwoven clothing, tapestries, and imported gifts? No phone.

Epic Bookshop. 118 Dayton Street, Yellow Springs, OH 45387. Bone up on self-development, Buddhism, and Yoga; selections include memoirs and children's books. Leather journals, incense, statues, prayer flags, toys, yoga mats, meditation cushions, and goddess jewelry can also be purchased. (937) 767-7997; www.epicbookshop.com.

No Common Scents. 220 Xenia Avenue, Yellow Springs, OH 45387. But lots of nice smells, including 175 essential and aromatherapy oils. This shop has more than 250 herbs and spices, including twenty-five spice blends. In addition to twenty varieties of teas, there are five green teas and nearly two dozen special and potpourri combinations. (800) 686-0012; www.nocommonscents.com.

Julia Ettas Trunk. 100 Dayton Street, Yellow Springs, OH 45387. Unique women's apparel covers all ages, sizes, and styles. Some items are pricey; others are deeply discounted. (937) 767-2823.

Ohio Silver. 245 Xenia Avenue, Yellow Springs, OH 45387. The name aptly describes this huge selection of earrings, rings, bracelets, and other accessories. Some gold and items in other media can be found. There's also an in-store cat to visit while contemplating purr-chases. (937) 767-8261.

Organic Grocery. 230 Keiths Alley, Yellow Springs, OH 45387. No weekly specials or piped-in music, just healthy, natural, and often hard-to-find foodstuffs that are good for you (taste may be another story, however). (937) 767-7215.

Yellow Springs Pottery. 222 Xenia Avenue, Yellow Springs, OH 45387. Selections originate from a consortium of potters (as opposed to a pot cooperative, which is illegal, even in this town). Works of art are colorful, functional, and make for distinctive and useful gifts. (937) 767-1666.

WHERE TO EAT

Golden Jersey Inn. 6880 Springfield-Xenia Road, Yellow Springs, OH 45387. Specialties of the fresh and varied menu range from omelettes to baked potato soup to a variety of sandwiches. Dinner serves up bacon-wrapped pork chops, meat loaf and mashed pota-toes, barbecued pork ribs, char-grilled ham steak, and more. $-$$$. (937) 324-2050; www.youngsdairy.com.

Winds Cafe. 215 Xenia Avenue, Yellow Springs, OH 45387. This gourmet eatery features seasonal items and flavorful combinations. Regular menu changes ensure that each visit is a different dining experience. Special dinners and beer and wine tastings are also offered. $$-$$$. (937) 767-1144 ; www.windscafe.com.

Sunrise Cafe. 259 Xenia Avenue, Yellow Springs, OH 45387. Three squares, Yellow Springs–style, include a portabello and spinach omelette with fontina cheese; pasta with handcrafted sauce; tabouli; thai peanut tofu; and moon plate (rice, beans, vegetables, and salad), to mention a few. $-$$. (937) 767-7211; www.sunrisecafe.com.

WHERE TO STAY

Springs Motel. 3601 U.S. 68, Yellow Springs, OH 45387. Constructed in the 1950s, this clean but no-frills lodge has twelve rooms and has been recently refurbished with such essentials as new showerheads and data ports. $. (937) 767–8700.

Hearthstone Inn & Suites. 10 South Main Street, Cedarville, OH 45314. From Yellow Springs, take SR 343 East to SR 72 South; it's about ten minutes away. Everything new is old again: this recently established country inn features twenty guest rooms that combine traditional furnishings with all the amenities. The lobby boasts high ceilings, stone fireplaces, and comfy sofas while outside is a wooded park with baseball, tennis, jogging, and picnic facilities. $$–$$$. (877) 644–6466; www.hearthstone-inn.com.

XENIA

Xenia and nearby Fairborn are known for Wright Patterson Air Force Base and tornadoes. Although Wright-Pat is located in Dayton (see West Day Trip 4), many of its personnel reside in Greene County. So when aliens are mentioned, it may be in the context of little green men and not green cards. Plucky Xenia suffered through two major twisters in 1974 and again in 2000. Although fatalities, injuries, and major property damage resulted, the town continues to offer cultural and recreational opportunities. From Yellow Springs, continue on south U.S. 68 about 10 miles to Xenia.

WHERE TO GO

Greene County Historical Society. 74 West Church Street, Xenia, OH 45385. Relive the story of Greene County through permanent and special displays, which include a 1799 log house and an 1876 Victorian dwelling. Along with a general store and railroad memorabilia, the collection encompasses farm equipment, china, books, toys, and furniture. Hours vary; closed Monday. Admission may be charged. (937) 372–4606.

Blue Jacket. 520 South Stringtown Road, Xenia, OH 45385. Or *How a Guy Named Marmaduke Van Swearingen Became a Shawnee War Chief.* This outdoor drama, played out on what was originally the tribe's sacred ground, depicts the Revolutionary War–era struggle of Native Americans, frontier settlers, and escaping slaves. Horses, cannons, flaming arrows, and more add excitement and authenticity. Dinner and backstage tours available. June through September only. Admission is charged. (877) 465-2583 or (937) 376-4318; www.bluejacketdrama.com.

WHERE TO STAY

Alpha House. 758 Alpha Road, Alpha, OH 45434. Alpha is in Beavercreek, just a few minutes west of Xenia on U.S. 35. Guests get the run of a two-story brick Federal-style home built in 1843. Formerly a general store and post office, the inside has been refurbished and is full of antiques, along with having a piano and record player. Some rooms come with private baths; a full breakfast is included. $$. (800) 337-2852; www.alphahousebandb.com.

WILBERFORCE

Wilberforce is just a few miles northwest of Xenia on U.S. 42.

WHERE TO GO

National Afro-American Museum and Cultural Center. 1350 Brush Row Road, Wilberforce, OH 45384. Located next to Central State University, this 50,000-square-foot center includes a museum and galleries. Focus is on research and education; the permanent exhibit explores African-American history from the end of World War II to the Voting Rights Act of 1964. Recorded narratives, gospel tunes, and artifacts such as jewelry, clothes, sports equipment, and consumer products breathe life into a '50s-era barbershop, beauty salon, and church interior. Changing exhibitions encompass art, music, inventors, and other aspects of black heritage. Closed Monday. Admission is charged. (800) 752-2603; www.ohiohistory.org.

CLIFTON

More history can be found in nearby Clifton. Take U.S. 42 east to SR 72. Drive north about 4 miles to Clifton.

WHERE TO GO

Historic Clifton Mill. 75 Water Street, Clifton, OH 45316. Built in 1802 and one of the largest working gristmills remaining in the United States, this well-preserved attraction gets down to the real nitty-gritty with a detailed tour. Other points of interest include a Christmas light display, a Santa Claus collection (3,000 Santas, from 1850 to the present), and a restaurant. Open daily. Admission may be charged. (937) 767-5501; www.cliftonmill.com.

WHERE TO EAT

Millrace Restaurant. Clifton Mill, 75 Water Street, Clifton, OH 45316. Home-cooked breakfast and lunch includes pancakes and corn bread made right in the mill. Breads, pies, and cookies are also baked fresh daily. Menu encompasses hearty country eggs and pork product combos, sandwiches, salads, soups, and desserts. $$. (937) 767-5501.

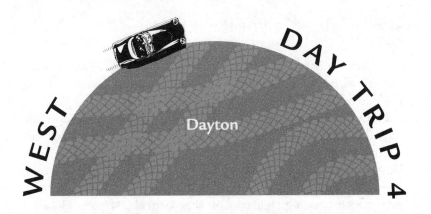

Dayton

DAYTON

In addition to being the birthplace of aviation, Dayton has spawned inventions such as the automatic car self-starter, the heart-lung machine, the cash register, and the room air-conditioner. Along with the Wright Brothers, Dayton innovators include the late humorist Erma Bombeck, actor Martin Sheen, baseball star Mike Schmidt, and well-known wordsmith John Jakes.

Thanks in part to the one-hundreth anniversary of flight, which expanded many existing historical attractions, Dayton has undergone a renaissance of late. Added to the truly nifty culture magnets such as the Victoria Theatre (138 North Main Street, Dayton 45402; 937-228-3630; www.victoriatheatre.com), a fully renovated, exquisite Italian marble– and brass-laden venue built in 1866, is the Schuster Performing Arts Center (1 West Second Street; 937-228-7591; www.schustercenter.org). Home of the Dayton Opera, Dayton Philharmonic, and Broadway Series, the latest jewel in the Gem City boasts a towering glassed-in Wintergarden, which features art-deco accents and palm trees. Also reminiscent of '30s elegance is its 2,300-seat Mead Theatre, whose domed ceiling re-creates the fiber-optic star-scape of December 16, 1903, the evening of Wilber and Orville's first powered flight.

Another new sparkler is Fifth Third Field (220 North Patterson; 937-228-2287; www.daytondragons.com). Playground of the single-A baseball team, the Dragons, this 7,200-seat stadium is modeled after such American classics as Wrigley Field and has enjoyed major success, with sold-out games and several promising players making the leap to the major leagues.

From Columbus, take I-70 west and go straight; you'll run right into the outskirts (to get downtown, take I-75 south). Dayton's about 100 miles away, an easy ride of about an hour and a half. Unless, of course, it's summertime and the highway gods have chosen a section of the interstate for construction, something that occurs with amazing regularity on this particular stretch. Then it's anyone's guess.

WHERE TO GO

United States Air Force Museum. 1100 Spaatz Street, Wright-Patterson Air Force Base, OH 45433. This is on the way to Dayton, so get off I-70 at exit 44A and take I-675 south to exit 15, Colonel Glenn Highway. Follow Colonel Glenn Highway to Harshman Road/Wright Brothers Parkway and turn right. Turn right again at Springfield Pike; the museum is on the right. The oldest and largest military aviation museum in the world houses more than 300 aircraft and missiles. Highlights include Wright Brothers memorabilia, World War II artifacts, the *Apollo 15* capsule, and diaries and medals from the early 1900s to the present. Galleries focus on the Air Force's early years, the Korean War, modern and space flight, and more. The addition of a third hangar includes aircraft from Desert Storm and other recent conflicts; there's a flight simulator as well. Experimental and presidential aircraft—including the Air Force One that flew JFK's body from Dallas back to Washington D.C.—and rotating special displays as well as a six-story IMAX theater make this a high-flying experience and the best deal in town. Open daily. Museum is free; admission is charged for IMAX. (937) 255-3286; www.wpafb.af.mil/museum.

National Aviation Hall of Fame. Located at the Air Force Museum, 1100 Spaatz Street, Wright-Patterson Air Force Base, OH 45433. This new attraction features interactive exhibits emphasizing scientific and historical contributions of air and space pioneers. An induction ceremony is held each year to recognize outstanding aviators in the United States; honorees range from such legends as the Wright Brothers, Amelia Earhart, Chuck Yeager, and John Glenn to lesser-known names like Marion E. Carl, the first Marine helicopter pilot, and Albert Lee Ueltschi, founder of FlightSafety International and other organizations. Admission may be charged. Call for hours. (937) 256-0944; www.nationalaviation.org.

Wright B Flyer. 10550 Springboro Pike, Miamisburg, OH 45342. From I-70, take I-675 south to Springboro Pike and go south. Want to experience the "Wright" stuff? Take a spin on this replica of the world's first mass-produced airplane (circa 1910) designed by Orville and Wilbur Wright. (Not to worry, previous flight problems such as those encountered at Kitty Hawk have been corrected.) Built by a group of aviation aficionados and run by volunteers, this "B" is housed in a hangar at the Wright Brothers Airport. Open Tuesday, Thursday, and Saturday. Museum is free, but flights do cost. (937) 885-2327; www.wright-bflyer.org.

Dayton Aviation Heritage National Historical Park. Various locations. On October 16, 1992, Congress established this national park to honor Wilbur and Orville Wright and Paul Laurence Dunbar, who also happened to be childhood friends. Visit the park's Web site at www.nps.gov/daav. The following sites are included:

- **The Wright Cycle Company.** 22 South Williams Street, Dayton, OH 45407. This shop, operated by the Wright Brothers from 1895 to 1897, has been completely restored and contains period bicycles and machinery. A just-opened interpretive center features a Wright-Dunbar timeline, a collage on inventions and technology, a reproduction of Hale's Grocery, and Dunbar memorabilia, among many other things. Open daily from Memorial Day to Labor Day, Wednesday through Sunday the rest of year. Admission is charged. (937) 225-7705.

- **Dunbar House State Memorial.** 219 North Paul Laurence Dunbar Street. Mailing address: P.O. Box 1872, Dayton, OH 45401. The Paul Laurence Dunbar home in Dayton has been restored to appear as it did when he lived there, including rooms furnished with his own possessions. In addition to the library and a Native American artifact collection, a standout is a bicycle given to Dunbar by the Wright Brothers. The site also hosts frequent programs on Dunbar, his legacy, and African-American history. Open daily. Admission is charged. (937) 224-7061.

- **Carillon Historical Park.** 2001 South Patterson Boulevard, Dayton, OH 45409. Sixty-five wooded acres of buildings, attractions, and exhibitions include the 1905 *Wright Flyer III*, the world's first craft capable of controlled (this being a key word here) flight. Several automobiles manufactured in Dayton such as the Stoddard and the Maxwell, vintage bicycles, a 1930 print shop, and a ninety-seven-year-old schoolhouse can also be found. Bonus: Deeds Carillon, Ohio's largest bell tower, a real chimer. Closed Monday. Admission is charged. (937) 293–2841.
- **Huffman Prairie Flying Field, Wright Memorial and Interpretive Center.** To access the field, take Route 444, Wright-Patterson Air Force Base, OH 45433. Accessed through Gate 12A. The interpretive center is also off 444. After their first successful powered flight in 1903, the Wright Brothers erected a hangar for their plane on the Huffman Prairie outside of Dayton; a replica stands there today. They used this farmland to perfect their flying skills in 1904 and 1905, and as the site of the Wright Company School of Aviation/Wright Exhibition Company from 1910 to 1916. The newly opened interpretive center features additional information, books, and friendly rangers who will fill you in with the "Wright" lore. Open daily during daylight hours. Free. (937) 257–5535, ext. 254.

Woodland Cemetery and Arboretum. 118 Woodland Avenue, Dayton, OH 45409. This is a sort of A-list of the Dayton dead. Along with the Wright Brothers and their parents and sister, Paul Laurence Dunbar, his mother, and Erma Bombeck are buried here. Along with ornate headstones and a Tiffany stained-glass window in the stone chapel, there are more than 200 species of trees on these heavily wooded grounds. Open daily. Free. (937) 228–3221.

Sunwatch Prehistoric Indian Village. 2301 West River Road, Dayton, OH 45418. This re-creation provides insight into the Fort Ancient Native American tribe that settled along the banks of the Great Miami River more than 800 years ago. Along with a reconstructed village, you'll find what has been described as an elaborate wooden counterpart to England's Stonehenge. Posts placed in the center of the village provided a complex system of charting time and seasons and were used to schedule planting and harvesting. Closed Monday. Admission is charged. (937) 268–8199, www.sunwatch.org.

Boonshoft Museum of Discovery. 2600 DeWeese Parkway, Dayton, OH 45414. A learning experience for kids of all ages: Hands-on activities consist of water tables, a two-and-a-half-story climbing tower and slide, and a zoo featuring live animals. A state-of-the-art digital planetarium features a variety of shows and special effects matinees. Environmental exhibits and science programming are also emphasized; there's an early childhood area as well. Open daily. Admission is charged. (937) 275–7431; www.boonshoftmuseum.org.

Dayton Art Institute. 456 Belmonte Park North, Dayton, OH 45405. The permanent collection of this historic Italian Renaissance building includes works by Claude Monet, Edgar Degas, and Andy Warhol, as well as various media in American, European, and Asian galleries. Special exhibits focus on Africa, regional artists, and exploring the human body in art as well as photography, painting, and glass sculpture. EXPERIENCENTER, an interactive showcase, is geared toward children. Open daily. Free, but admission may be charged for special exhibits. (800) 296–4426; www.daytonartinstitute.org.

Riverscape Metropark. East Monument, between Jefferson Street and St. Clair, Dayton, OH 45402. Located downtown, this popular gathering spot features a multicolored fountain, which shoots colored streams of water hundreds of feet into the air. "Invention stations" provide insight into the workings of such great minds as Charles Kettering and the Wright Brothers and everyday minutiae like Dayton-originated ice-cube trays, pop-top cans, cash registers, and more. Several "walks" highlight local luminaries and history. Hydro-bikes, pedal boats, roller blades, and regular bicycles are also available for rental, and a sidewalk Interactive Fountain provides "blasts" of H_2O for all ages. Open daily. Free. (937) 274–0126; www.riverscape.org.

Citizen's Motorcar Company: America's Packard Museum. 420 South Ludlow Street, Dayton, OH 45402. This fully restored 1930s Packard dealership re-creates the glamour of the era through an art-deco showroom and more than twenty completely refurbished automobiles. Artifacts from the Packard Motorcar Company can also be found. This favorite of old-car buffs and preservationists has won several awards. Open daily. Admission is charged. (937) 226–1917.

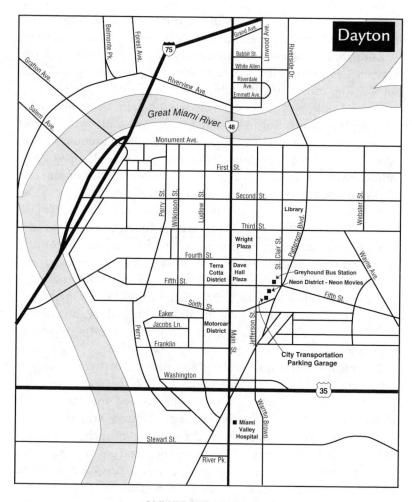

WHERE TO SHOP

Pilots and Poets Gift Shop. 12 East Third Street, Dayton, OH 45402. Where else would you find a Wright Flyer ballcap, one of the largest selections of model airplanes around, and a Paul Laurence Dunbar T-shirt among many other mementos? (937) 222-7811; www.pilotsandpoets.com.

    Feathers. 440 East Fifth Street, Dayton, OH 45402. Located in the Oregon District, here you'll find vintage clothing, art-deco items, and 1950s "modern" memorabilia. (937) 228-2940.

Rutledge Gallery. Kettering Tower Lobby, 40 North Main Street, Dayton, OH 45423. Along with contemporary art, sculpture, paintings, and drawings, this enterprise hosts work from both local and international artists. Framing services are also available. (937) 226-7335; www.rutledge-art.com.

Dayton Mall. 2700 Miamisburg-Centerville Road, Dayton, OH 45459. One of the region's first megamalls, this conglomeration boasts 160 stores, including anchors Lazarus, JCPenney, Elder-Beerman, and Sears. (937) 433-9833.

Town and Country Shopping Center. Corner of Stroop Road and Far Hills Avenue, Kettering, OH 45429. From I-675, take exit 10 and go west; turn left on Stroop Road. Favorite hunting grounds of local shoppers include dozens of classy stores such as Stein Mart, Books & Co., the Secret Ingredient, and Sally's. (937) 293-7516; www.daytontownandcountry.com.

The Mall at Fairfield Commons. 2727 Fairfield Commons, Beavercreek, OH 45431. From I-675, go south on North Fairfield Road. This new addition to the area's mall-stellation includes 150 shops. Selections range from anchors like Parisian, Sears, Lazarus, Elder-Beerman, and JC Penney to specialty shops, including Northern Reflections, Bath & Body Works, and The Museum Store. (937) 427-4300.

WHERE TO EAT

Blue Moon Cafe. 524 East Fifth Street, Dayton, OH 45402. This Oregon District restaurant offers nouvelle cuisine with a twist, including such delicacies as wild mushroom ravioli, smoked fish Napoleon, and artichoke fritters. They also make a great martini. $$-$$$. (937) 586-4250.

The Trolley Stop. 530 East Fifth Street, Dayton, OH 45402. Eclecticism abounds in the atmosphere, food, staff, clientele, and music. Enjoy vegetarian entrees, homemade soups, and sandwiches while sitting in the New Orleans–style courtyard in the Oregon District. $-$$. (937) 461-1101.

Stockyards Inn. 1065 Springfield Street, Dayton, OH 45409. This is a great place for your basic steaks, ribs, prime rib, and fresh seafood. $$-$$$. (937) 254-3576.

The Pine Club. 1926 Brown Street, Dayton, OH 45409. This is the town's most popular steak house, so expect to wait. But the locals keep coming back, and with good reason. $$-$$$. (937) 228-7463.

Citilites. Schuster Center, Dayton, OH 45420. This newly opened eatery features such comfort foods as grilled cheese with tomato bisque and meat loaf as well as more exotic fare like eggplant lasagna and a house sushi plate. With cinnamon ice cream, whipped cream, and touches of chocolate and root beer, the black cow float is a lot more appetizing than the name implies. $$. (937) 222-0623.

Jay's Seafood Restaurant. 225 East Sixth Street, Dayton, OH 45402. Located in an 1852 gristmill and the site of the historic Pony House Saloon, the most excitement that occurs now is the arrival of fresh fish, flown in daily. Entrees can be served gussied up with sauces, baked, char-grilled, or blackened. Poultry and steak are also available. $$-$$$, (937) 222-2892; www.jays.com.

WHERE TO STAY

Crowne Plaza Hotel. 33 East Fifth Street, Dayton, OH 45402. Get connected to the Dayton Convention Center and many of the sites via a walkway to this 280-plus-room hotel which features such amenities as an airport shuttle, fitness center, and pool. Free parking's also available—almost unheard-of in a downtown city— and room rates can be very reasonable if you ask about specials. $$. (937) 224-0800.

Candlewick Bed and Breakfast. 4991 Bath Road, Dayton, OH 45424. Run by a retired engineer and his teacher wife, this Dutch Colonial home sits on five rolling acres. Breakfast includes fresh fruits and juices, pastries, and a main dish. Specialty of the house is the Danish Puff, which has an almond-flavored custard topping with a powered-sugar glaze and nuts. $$. (937) 233-9297.

Yesterday Bed & Breakfast. 39 South Main Street, Dayton, OH 45458. Located in the historic Centerville area, this 1882 home is filled with antiques and unique furnishings and boasts a wrap-around porch and courtyard. Each of the three rooms is decorated with a particular theme; each has a private bath. $$. (800) 225-0485.

Regional Information

DAY TRIP 1

Sandusky/Erie County Visitors & Convention Bureau
4424 Milan Road, Suite A
Sandusky, OH 44870
(800) 255-3743
www.buckeyenorth.com

Cedar Point
Cedar Point Causeway at Perimeter Road
Sandusky, OH 44870
(800) 237-8386
www.cedarpoint.com

DAY TRIP 2

Sandusky/Erie County Visitors & Convention Bureau
4424 Milan Road, Suite A
Sandusky, OH 44870
(800) 255-3743
www.buckeyenorth.com

Ottawa County Visitors Bureau
109 Madison Street
Port Clinton, OH 43452
(800) 441-1271
www.lake-erie.com

Kelleys Island Chamber of Commerce
General Delivery
Kelleys Island, OH 43438
(419) 746-2360
www.kelleysisland.com

Port Clinton Chamber of Commerce
304 Madison Street, Suite C
Port Clinton, OH 43452
(419) 734-5503
www.portclintonchamber.com

Put-in-Bay Chamber of Commerce
P.O. Box 250
Put-in-Bay, OH 43456
(419) 285-2832
www.put-in-bay.com

The Peninsula Chamber of Commerce
210 West Main Street
Marblehead, OH 43440
(419) 798-9777
www.marbleheadpeninsula.com

The Lakeside Association
236 Walnut Street
Lakeside, OH 43440
(419) 798-4461
www.lakesideohio.com

DAY TRIP 3

Milan, Ohio, Web site
www.milanohio.com

Seneca County Convention and Visitors Bureau
114 South Washington Street
Tiffin, OH 44883
(888) 736-3221
www.senecacounty.com

Bellevue Area Tourism and Visitors Bureau
P.O. Box 63
Bellevue, OH 44811
(800) 562-6978
www.bellevuetourism.org

Sandusky County Convention and Visitors Bureau
712 North Street
Fremont, OH 43420
(800) 255-8070
www.sanduskycounty.org

NORTHEAST

DAY TRIP 1

Malabar Farm State Park
4050 Bromfield Road
Lucas, OH 44843
(419) 892–2784
www.ohiostateparks.org

Mansfield/Richland County Convention and Visitors Bureau
124 North Main Street
Mansfield, OH 44902
(800) 642–8282
www.mansfieldtourism.org

DAY TRIP 2

Holmes County Chamber of Commerce and Tourism Bureau
35 North Monroe Street
Millersburg, OH 44654
(330) 674–3975
www.visitamishcountry.com
If possible, use Web site for information; written material may be difficult to obtain.

DAY TRIP 3

Canton/Stark County Convention and Visitors Bureau
222 Market Avenue North
Canton, OH 44702
(800) 533–4302
www.visitcantonohio.com

Zoar Village State Memorial
198 Main Street, P.O. Box 404
Zoar, OH 44697
(800) 262–6195
www.ohiohistory.org

Tuscarawas County Convention and Visitors Bureau
125 McDonald Drive SW
New Philadelphia, OH 44663
(800) 527–3387
neohiotravel.com

DAY TRIP 4

Akron/Summit Convention and Visitors Bureau
77 East Mill Street
Akron, OH 44308
(800) 245-4254
www.visitakron-summit.org

DAY TRIP 5

Hale Farm & Village
2686 Oak Hill Road
Bath, OH 44210
(877) 425-3327
www.whco.org/halefarm

Peninsula Area Chamber of Commerce
1619 West Mill Street
Peninsula, OH 44264
(330) 657-2788
www.explorepeninsula.com

DAY TRIP 6

Convention and Visitors Bureau of Greater Cleveland
3100 Terminal Tower
50 Public Square
Cleveland, OH 44113-2290
(800) 321-1001
www.travelcleveland.com

EAST

DAY TRIP 1

Granville Information
141 East Broadway, P.O. Box 514
Granville, OH 43023
(740) 587-0707
www.granville.oh.us

Licking County Convention and Visitors Bureau
50 West Locust Street
Newark, OH 43055
(800) 589-8224
www.lccvb.com

Buckeye Lake Tourism Bureau
5192 Walnut Road
Buckeye Lake, OH 43008
(740) 928-7100

DAY TRIP 2

Longaberger Main Office
1500 East Main Street
Newark, OH 43055
(740) 322-5000
www.longaberger.com

Dresden Village Association
P.O. Box 704
Dresden, OH 43821
(800) 315-1809
www.dresden-ohio.com

DAY TRIP 3

Wheeling Convention and Visitors Bureau
1401 Main Street
Heritage Square
Wheeling, WV 26003
(800) 828-3097
www.wheelingcvb.com

SOUTHEAST

DAY TRIP 1

Hocking Hills Tourism Association
13178 SR 664 S
Logan, OH 43148
(800) 462-5464
www.1800hocking.com

DAY TRIP 2

Athens County Convention and Visitors Bureau
667 East State Street
Athens, OH 45701
(800) 878-9767
www.athensohio.com

DAY TRIP 3

Marietta/Washington County Convention and Visitors Bureau
316 Third Street
Marietta, OH 45750
(800) 288-2577
www.mariettaohio.org

DAY TRIP 4

Jackson Area Chamber of Commerce
200 Broadway
Jackson, OH 45640
(740) 286-2722
www.jacksonohio.org

jacweb (Web site only) www.jacksoncountyohio.org

Gallia County Convention and Visitors Bureau
61 Court Street
Gallipolis, OH 45631
(800) 765-6482
www.visitgallia.com

SOUTH

DAY TRIP 1

Adams County Travel and Visitors Bureau
6809 U.S. Route 52
West Union, OH 45693
(877) 232-6764
www.adamscountytravel.org

SOUTHWEST

DAY TRIP 1

Prime Outlets Jeffersonville
8000 Factory Shops Boulevard
Jeffersonville, OH 43128
(800) 746-7644
www.primeoutlets.com

Clinton County Convention and Visitors Bureau
131 North South Street
Wilmington, OH 45177
(877) 428-4748
www.clintoncountyohio.com

DAY TRIP 2

Warren County Convention and Visitors Bureau
313 East Warren Street
Lebanon, OH 45036
(800) 433-1072
www.ohio4fun.org

Waynesville Area Chamber of Commerce
P.O. Box 281
Waynesville, OH 45068
(513) 897-8855
www.waynesvilleohio.com

Springboro Chamber of Commerce
325 South Main Street
Springboro, OH 45066
(937) 748-0074
www.springboroohio.org

DAY TRIP 3

Paramount's Kings Island
6300 Kings Island Drive
Kings Island, OH 45034
(800) 288-0808
www.pki.com

Warren County Convention and Visitors Bureau
313 East Warren Street
Lebanon, OH 45036
(800) 433-1072
www.ohio4fun.org

Cincinnati Visitors Bureau
300 West Sixth Street
Cincinnati, OH 45202
(800) 543-2613
www.cincyusa.com

DAY TRIP 4

Cincinnati Visitors Bureau
300 West Sixth Street
Cincinnati, OH 45202
(800) 543-2613
www.cincyusa.com

WEST

DAY TRIP 1

Greater Columbus Convention and Visitors Bureau
90 North High Street
Columbus, OH 43215
(800) 345-4386
www.experiencecolumbus.com

DAY TRIP 2

Logan County Convention and Visitors Bureau
100 South Main Street
Bellefontaine, OH 43311
(888) 564-2626
www.logancountyohio.com

DAY TRIP 3

Yellow Springs Chamber of Commerce
101 Dayton Street
Yellow Springs, OH 45387
(937) 767-2686
www.yellowspringsohio.org

Greene County Convention and Visitors Bureau
1221 Meadowbridge Drive, Suite A
Beavercreek, OH 45434
(800) 733-9109
www.greenecountyohio.org

DAY TRIP 4

Dayton/Montgomery County Convention and Visitors Bureau
1 Chamber Plaza
Suite A
Dayton, OH 45402
(800) 221-8235
www.daytoncvb.com

Destination Dayton Web site
www.dayton.com

Festivals and Celebrations

Ohio seems to have cornered the market on festivals, especially those concerning food. Subjects of adulation range from popcorn to tomatoes to pumpkins, with melons, walleye, and bratwurst thrown in for good measure. Some may not be in day-trip locales discussed in this book, but they might be worth the detour, particularly if you like to chow down on a particular item.

Among this cornucopia you'll also find festivals that celebrate different cultures, the arts, even autos. For more information and to obtain a list, contact the Ohio Department of Development, Division of Travel and Tourism, 77 South High Street, Columbus, OH 43216; (800) 282-5393; www.ohiotourism.com. Additionally, local convention and visitors bureaus and chambers of commerce publish detailed information on area festivals, and there's a resource dedicated to all festivals, all the time: The Ohio Festivals and Events Association, 2055 Cherokee Drive, London, OH 43140; (419) 668-5231; www.ofea.org. Call for admission prices, dates, and times.

JANUARY

African Culture Fest, Cincinnati Museum Center, Cincinnati. African drummers and dancers, storytellers, and cuisine make for a fun wintertime diversion. (800) 733-2077.

FEBRUARY

Snow Trails Ski Carnival, Mansfield. Shiver your timbers. Events include a bikini race, shovel cup event, slope style competition, team cross-skiing, and more. (800) 644-6754.

MARCH

Maple Syrup Festival, Indian Lake State Park, Lakeview. Take a wagon ride through the sugar bush and stop off at a production shack to watch park staff boil the sap. You get to sample the results. (937) 843-2717.

Great Midwest Quilt Show and Sale, Lebanon, Warren County Fairgrounds. Quilters from all over the United States display their hand-crafted wares. Antique quilts are featured as well. (513) 932-1817 or (513) 932-8246.

APRIL

Geauga County Maple Festival, Chardon. A rite of spring, this festival celebrates the production of maple syrup, a leading agricultural money-maker. There are two—count 'em, two—parades, maple syrup judging and auction, queen pageant, photo contest, sap run, bathtub races, and more. (440) 286-3007; www.maplefestival.com.

MAY

Wild Turkey Festival, McArthur. Just in time for spring gobbler season, this gathering features car and quilt shows, crafts, rides, games, and food. A queen is crowned, but she's no turkey. (740) 596-4945.

Moonshine Festival, New Straitsville. A working moonshine still display, local history museum, moonshine burgers, and moonshine pie are but a few highlights. Other temptations include carnival rides and games, free entertainment, food, souvenirs, talent show, fiddle and banjo contest, and car/truck display. (740) 394-2838.

Annual Dulcimer Days, Roscoe Village, Coshocton. National dulcimer performers and crafters in addition to the Mid-Eastern Regional Dulcimer Championships are featured here. (800) 877-1830.

Port Clinton Walleye Festival, Perry Street, Port Clinton. Along with enjoying the fruits of the "Walleye Capital of the World," you can stroll down a midway filled with rides, games, arts and crafts, and vendors of both the food and non-edible kind. (419) 732-2684; www.walleyefestival.com.

Feast of the Flowering Moon, Downtown & Yoctangee Park, Chillicothe. Despite its almost Zen-sounding name, this gathering features a mountain-man encampment, a Native American Powwow and juried craft shows along with many commercial exhibits. (800) 413-4118; www.visithistory.com.

JUNE

Columbus Arts Festival, downtown Columbus. Hundreds of fine artists and craftspeople are selected from a large pool of talented individuals. Add music, arts activities for all ages, food from the city's most popular restaurants, and special exhibitions and you have one of the top arts festivals in the United States. (614) 224-2606.

International Washboard Festival, Logan. "Clean up" with washboard-based live music and wandering minstrels, along with street vendors and Hocking Hills cuisine (nonroadkill category). This colorful and entertaining festival highlights the historic downtown, culminating in a free tour of the Columbus Washboard Company, the only manufacturer of guess-whats in the United States (800) 343-7967; www.columbuswashboard.com.

Lancaster Old Car Club Spring Festival, Fairfield County Fairgrounds, Lancaster. Antiques, classics, and hot rods share space with a flea market featuring more than 300 vendors. Old auto parts, steam and stationary engines, antique tractors, and more can be found here. (740) 654-9434.

Hockhocking Folk Festival, Robbins Crossing, Nelsonville. Along with headline entertainment, there are local and regional musicians, arts and crafts, and food. You can even bring your instruments and participate in jam sessions. (740) 753-1924; www.hock hockingfolkfest.org.

Coshocton Hot Air Balloon Festival, Coshocton. Fly high for two days, weather permitting. There are also rides, arts and crafts displays, merchandise, food and beverage stands, and live entertainment. (740) 622-5411 or (800) 589-2430.

Strawberry Festival, London. Formerly known as the Marigold Festival, this event recently switched its focus. Events include two parades; the crowning of a queen; a 5K race; car, motorcycle, and antique tractor shows; live entertainment; a strawberry recipe bake-off; and other diversions. (740) 852-1582 or (614) 879-5726; www.londonstraw berryfestival.com.

JULY

Berea Grindstone Festival, Cuyahoga County Fairgrounds. Those sticking their noses to this one will find a parade, a Miss Berea Grindstone scholarship pageant, pizza challenge, pancake breakfast, rides, midway, car show, games, contests, and more. It's around the Fourth of July, so there are fireworks, too. (440) 816-0606.

Lancaster Festival, Lancaster. More than seventy-five events consist of classical and popular music, jazz, dance, and art exhibits by international artists and musicians. Highlights include Splendor in the Brass, Candlelight Chamber Music Concert, Farm Fare Day, the Young People's Concert, and evening fireworks. (740) 687-4808.

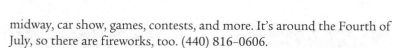

AUGUST

Ohio State Fair, Ohio State Fairgrounds, Columbus. This granddaddy of all fairs features agriculture and horticulture, livestock, and youth activities, as well as culinary and craft offerings. Along with learning how to milk a cow, get the most out of your admission by cruising the midway with more than seventy rides, by seeing big-name entertainers as well as a variety of shows for children and adults, and by taking the world's longest portable sky ride, to mention but a few options. Foodstuffs range from sausage sandwiches to elephant ears to french fries to funnel cakes. (614) 644-3247.

Dublin Irish Festival, Dublin. Recognized as one of the best of its kind in the United States, this fast-growing event features vendors, Irish entertainers and dancers, international and local bands, as well as cultural and children's activities. (877) 674-7336; www.dublinirishfestival.org.

Sweet Corn Festival, Millersport. This "ear-resistible" happening is hot buttered sweet corn heaven with more than eighty food and game concessions. There's also a parade, free entertainment stages, and several contests. (740) 246-6217; www.sweetcornfest.com.

Bucyrus Bratwurst Festival, Bucyrus. Perfected by local butchers whose families emigrated from Germany, bratwurst from Bucyrus has a unique flavor and is roasted over an open fire. Parades, continuous entertainment, crafts and art shows, rides, games, beer gardens, and friendly folks make for a spicy diversion. (419) 562-2728.

Obetz Zucchinifest, Lancaster Park, Obetz. Finally, a festival celebrating a healthy vegetable! Along with the usual arts and crafts and games, there's a pageant (zucchini queen for a day?) as well as zucchini burgers, fudge, bread, and other products. (614) 497-2518.

Twin Days, Twinsburg. This somewhat redundant experience focuses on socializing, celebration, and fun, and draws multiple submissions in the form of twins, triplets, and so on from around the world. (330) 425-3652; www.twindays.org.

Renaissance Festival, Harveysburg (runs through October). Step back into sixteenth-century Elizabethan England. Thirty acres encompass more than 150 costumed performers and one hundred daily shows. Surely they joust, as well as offer crafts, feasts, and theater-in-the-ground (as in encounters of the muddy kind). (513) 897-7000; www.renfestival.com.

Milan Melon Festival, Town Square, Milan. This well-rounded experience includes an elaborate car display, a tractor pull, muskmelon ice cream, and watermelon sherbet as well as plenty of the fresh stuff. (419) 499-2766 or 668-5231.

SEPTEMBER

Oktoberfest, German Village, Columbus. Voted a top event by the American Bus Association, this venerable and popular gathering boasts authentic German music, dancing, food, and crafts, even though it is held in September. (614) 224-4300.

Wellston Coal Festival, Wellston. Strip away modern-day cares with coal-miner Olympics, a coal dust sundae-eating contest, coal-mine memorabilia, coal crafts, and rides, as well as exhibits and live performers. The final immersion: a tour of a working coal mine. (740) 384-6669.

Mantua Potato Festival, Buchert Park. This rural farming community celebrates its moneymaking spuds with live entertainment, food, rides, and games. Along with the crowning of a festival queen and her court, there's a 15K Potato Stomp and 1-mile fun run. (330) 274-0770.

Geneva Area Grape Jamboree (JAM-boree, get it?), Geneva. Have a "grape" time sampling grapes, freshly squeezed grape juice, wine, and other products. You can even stomp them for free when not partaking of the art show, craft fair, grape culinary contest, concession booths, farmer's market, antiques, ethnic foods, amusement rides, street dancing, and much more. (440) 466-5262; www.grapejamboree.com.

Reynoldsburg Tomato Festival, Civic Park, Reynoldsburg. OK, so maybe free tomato juice sounds rather bland, but there are fried green tomatoes, an agricultural exhibit, a Grand Champion Tomato Contest, and a talent show. Attack of the killer tomatoes, anyone? (614) 866-2861; www.reynoldsburgtomatofestival.org.

Marion Popcorn Festival, downtown Marion. Explosive excitement includes popcorn sculpture and a trip to the Wyandot Popcorn Museum at Heritage Hall. There's free entertainment; arts, crafts, and food; a 5K run, and a Popcorn 100 bike tour. (740) 387-3378; www.popcornfestival.com.

Ohio Swiss Festival, Sugarcreek. Holey cow! Attractions in this Alpine setting include Swiss music, costumes, and tons of cheese from eleven manufacturing facilities. There's also Steinstossen (stone throwing), Schwingfest (Swiss wrestling), and polka dancing as well as a children's parade. (888) 609-7592.

OCTOBER

Circleville Pumpkin Show, Circleville. Ohio's oldest festival has two daily parades and a world's largest pumpkin contest as well as food-stuffs such as pumpkin fudge (which tastes much better than it sounds). Squash, gourds, fruits, and vegetables are also welcome. (740) 474-7000 or 474-8973; www.pumpkinshow.com.

Ohio Gourd Show, Mt. Gilead. Fruit or vegetable? This question may never be answered, but you can learn about gourds and gourd craft in five buildings. Demonstrations on cleaning, carving, wood burning, painting, and more are also offered. (419) 965-4661.

NOVEMBER

Buckeye Book Fair, Wooster. More than seventy authors from in and around the state autograph their tomes at a discount. And it's just in time for the holiday season. (330) 262-3244.

DECEMBER

Dalton Holidays Festival, Dalton. Along with handcrafted treasures, this Christmas-themed gathering features entertainment, a country-style breakfast, Mrs. Claus's pantry, a fireman's ham dinner, and Christmas Parade. The entire village participates with lights and other seasonal displays. (330) 828-2444.

Winterfair, Ohio State Fairgrounds, Columbus. All manner of unique arts, crafts, jewelry, and more can be found here, making it the ideal shopping opportunity for the hard-to-satisfy giver and receiver. (800) 582-7294.

Sandra Gurvis (www.sgurvis.com) is the author of nine books and hundreds of magazine articles. Her titles include *Careers for Nonconformists* (Marlowe, 2000), which was a selection of the Quality Paperback Book Club; *The Well-Traveled Dog* (TFH, 2001); *America's Strangest Museums* (Carol/Citadel, 1998; 1996); *30 Great Cities to Start Out In* (Arco/Macmillan, 1997); and *Way Stations to Heaven* (Arco/Macmillan, 1996); among others. A novel about campus uprisings in a small Ohio town, *The Pipe Dreamers* (www.thepipedreamers.com), was published by Olmstead Press in 2001. A nonfiction title about the Vietnam protests, *Where Have All the Flower Children Gone?*, is forthcoming from University Press of Mississippi. She lives in Columbus, Ohio, and is working on a second novel.